A Japanese company in crisis

Japanese white-collar workers have been characterised by their intense loyalty and life-long commitment to their companies. This book is based on very extensive ethnographic research inside a Japanese insurance company during the period when it was going through a major crisis which ended in the company's bankruptcy and collapse. It examines the attitudes of Japanese employees towards their work, their company and related issues at a time when the established order and established attitudes were under threat. The wide range and detail of the reporting of workers' attitudes, often in their own words, sustained over a considerable time-scale, makes this study a particularly valuable resource.

Fiona Graham was the first Western woman to study at Keio University, Tokyo. Upon graduation, she worked at a traditional Japanese company in the life insurance industry. She completed her doctorate in Social Anthropology at the University of Oxford and has worked since then writing and directing anthropological documentaries. She is the author of *Inside the Japanese Company*, also published by RoutledgeCurzon.

RoutledgeCurzon Contemporary Japan Series

1 **A Japanese company in crisis**
Ideology, strategy, and narrative
Fiona Graham

A Japanese company in crisis

Ideology, strategy and narrative

Fiona Graham

RoutledgeCurzon
Taylor & Francis Group
LONDON AND NEW YORK

First published 2005 by RoutledgeCurzon
2 Park Square, Milton Park, Abingdon, Oxon, OX14 4RN

Simultaneously published in the USA and Canada
by RoutledgeCurzon
29 West 35th Street, New York, NY 10001

RoutledgeCurzon is an imprint of the Taylor & Francis Group

Typeset in Times by Taylor & Francis Books Ltd
Printed and bound in Great Britain by Antony Rowe,
Chippenham, Wiltshire

British Library Cataloguing in Publication Data
A catalogue record for this book is available from the British Library

Library of Congress Cataloging in Publication Data
A catalog record for this title has been requested

ISBN 0–415–34685–1

Contents

1 Introduction

In 1999 I received a grant from the Japan Foundation to make a documentary film on C-Life, a major life insurance company at which I had worked for two years as a fresh graduate more than ten years previously. I mentioned the project to NHK – the Japan Broadcasting Association – who agreed to show the programme. By making a documentary film on C-Life I was able to spend a further three-to-six-month period inside the company, during which time I conducted a series of in-depth interviews with a wide range of employees.

Why the intense interest in C-Life? C-Life was, at the time, a major white-collar, very traditional company, which was ailing badly as the Japanese economic downturn continued. It was to go spectacularly bankrupt in October 2000. This book follows the demise of C-Life from the point of view of the employees working inside the company.

C-Life was one of the eight major life insurance companies in Japan and an investment power-house in the days of Japan's economic 'bubble' in the late 1980s. At this time, the life insurance industry was one of the most prestigious in which to work. Life insurance companies had begun to invest in overseas securities for the first time and the future looked bright for the largest life insurance industry in the world. But in 1999, hit hard by the near-ten-year recession that followed the stock market crash of 1990, C-Life had a crumbling asset base, diminishing returns, and new insurance policy sales were dwindling. It was teetering on the brink of failure, with some observers believing it might be the first major insurance company to go under in the post-war period – an assessment that, as events turned out, was proved absolutely correct. Looking at the lives of C-Life's employees during its last days, surrounded by conflicting information, uncertain values and insecurity, provides a fascinating case study of life in a traditional white-collar Japanese company in distress. But it also sheds light onto how individuals and groups strategise in different ways to maintain or improve their position.

Objectives of this work

The literature on Japan has looked extensively at companies, both from the point of view of management techniques and social organisation. But there have been few works that have looked at the company in times of economic downturn. Thus the view of the Japanese company in the literature is rather static. Japan has been experiencing economic downturn now for over ten years. By 2001 the benchmark Nikkei stock index had fallen to 1985 levels, effectively wiping out fifteen years of growth. Bankruptcies have been common and stories of restructuring and unemployment are splashed over the headlines of newspapers.

But we have little idea of what is happening inside these companies. How have Japanese employees handled the economic downturn? How do they feel about the state of the economy? How do they feel about living with the constant threat of restructuring? Has this changed their famous loyalty to their companies? Does anyone believe in life-time employment anymore?

In my previous book *Inside the Japanese Company*, I presented a detailed ethnography of C-Life. My focus there was on what it was like to work at the company, from the point of view of the individual employees. One distinctive feature of that work, compared to other ethnographies of Japan, was the fact that it was based on employees of different ages within one department of the company, seen during three separate stages of fieldwork, conducted over a fifteen-year period during which time the company was going through great changes, both economic and social. In this book, by contrast, the focus is on the final stages of C-Life's demise and how the employees have coped with it. It is a study of strategies, particularly the strategy of each individual faced with changing and uncertain circumstances.

In particular, I look at a group of employees, all of the same age and all of whom started out in C-Life during the same year – 1985. I look at where this generation – of fifty people – has got to, by choosing seven typical patterns of reaction and career models from among these people and describing them in detail. By doing so, we get a real, in-depth picture of what these employees' lives are like, how their careers progressed and how they are managing in the economic downturn. We get a sense of the current situation in Japan and a sense of direction; where these employees – the important middle-management generation – are headed and what the future in the Japanese company is likely to look like.

I look at the employees and the company – not in isolation as a self-enclosed entity, but against the economic background and restructuring taking place in Japan today. It is against this atmosphere of great change that we must look at the employee to get a true view and to gain a real sense of the era. Above all, the company must be seen in the context of the economy if we are to make sense of the thinking and life-view of the Japanese employee. I look at how employees in C-Life react to the economic downturn in different ways, and especially at how they strategise to improve their lot as the fortunes of their company wax and wane and, eventually, as the company collapses altogether.

Plan of the book

I begin, in the first chapter, with a brief discussion of economic strategising, with reference particularly to the work of Pierre Bourdieu. This serves to introduce the focus of the book and the primary theme of the fieldwork chapters. In chapter 2 I set out the context for this study by describing briefly the rise and fall of the Japanese economy prior to the collapse of C-Life and look at the state of the life insurance industry in particular.

These chapters set the scene for the fieldwork chapters which follow and which focus on the employees themselves; through their voices we gain a vivid picture of life at the company as it starts to go under. Throughout, I quote extensively from the employees themselves. As a result, the atmosphere of the company at the time is easy to appreciate. The first three fieldwork chapters explore what the employees experienced during this period and what their views of the current situation were.

Chapter 3 looks at the current situation with regard to the economy and C-Life, as viewed by the employees. We see that they are quite realistic about the situation, although they take little action about it. Their plight is illustrated not only by quotations from interviews with them but also by several short case studies, featuring the stories of particular employees. These bring home the real human cost of C-Life's downfall.

Chapter 4 looks in detail at the effects of the restructuring itself. I describe the increasingly radical steps taken by C-Life's management as it attempted to stave off the company's collapse, culminating in the dismissal of 800 employees. The effects of these policies on the employees is examined and discussed. At the same time, I consider the issue of responsibility for the company's situation, an important question for the employees at the time, and how they envisage the future for C-Life.

In chapter 5, I build on the issues discussed in the previous two chapters. Why is it that the management of C-Life – and of many Japanese companies in general – has found it so hard to adapt to the changing economic circumstances? Here, I examine the employees' views on these important issues. I look at their attitudes towards Japanese management itself and what they think the future has in store.

Having discussed the employees' situation in depth, I then turn to an examination of how they are coping with changing circumstances. In chapter 6, I present case studies of eight employees, all '*doki*', or members of the same year-group, at C-Life. These individuals represent several different typical responses to the changing times at C-Life: some escaped from the company as quickly as possible, whilst others condemned such actions and remained with the company to the last. There was a whole spectrum of possibilities in between. These case studies show the range of individual reaction among employees in Japan today, and demonstrate both the range of individuality and the degree to which employees have changed from the days when 'life-time employment' was regarded as normal.

The case studies also illustrate how different individuals use different techniques to advance their own interests, an issue I discuss in more depth in chapter 7, where I take up the themes introduced in my discussion of Bourdieu in chapter 1 and reflect on the fieldwork, using it to illustrate my theoretical conclusions. I discuss the different ways in which individuals and groups strategise to pursue their own agendas. In particular, I focus on the ways that ideology is used in these strategies; the first part of the chapter is devoted to a study of the nature and role of ideology, with a focus on its different levels and the relations between them, The points I make here are reflected in chapter 8, where I describe the process of filming at C-Life. Everybody involved in the filming was actively pursuing their own agendas and using the filming as a tool to do so.

In chapter 9, I reflect on the methodology of this study and some of the themes to have emerged from it: the role of narrative in company life and in an ethnography of that life, myth and ideology. The chapter includes a brief look at the way that the '*nihonjiron*' literature had mythical qualities within Japan.

I conclude, in chapter 10, with an account of the final collapse of C-Life. I also present the responses to this event of some of the employees described earlier in the book.

Economic strategising

First, then, I introduce the subject of strategising and consciousness. This establishes the primary theoretical focus of this work: not only *how* people manipulate ideology, but *why* they do it. My discussion centres in particular on the work of Pierre Bourdieu.

Bourdieu and economic strategising

I have found Bourdieu's ideas to be particularly useful in understanding the means and purposes of strategising. Bourdieu attempts to escape the 'economism' – as he calls it – of Marxism, which reduces the social field entirely to economics. He also breaks with the objectivism of Marxism, which ignores symbolic struggles within the social world (Harker, Mahar and Wilkes 1990) and concentrates solely on the economic realm. Bourdieu's novel approach is also helpful in collapsing the individual/structure dichotomy without falling into the mire of either structuralism or post-structuralism. He does this by re-focusing attention on individual action and strategy. Rather than opposing objective structures and subjective representations, Bourdieu argues that it is necessary to understand both 'the genesis of social structures and … the agents who live within these structures'. So we need both to look at 'the company' and also to look at the individual employees inside the company to see the range of individuality, the range of individual choice and thinking, and the ways in which the individual interacts with the company. The individual conforms to the company on one level, but on another, s/he acts to advance his or her own strategies, to promote individual goals and to achieve satisfaction of individual needs.

Bourdieu's crucial point is that the scarce goods for which people compete include all kinds of categories, not just the merely economic, as Marxist theorists believe: they are any social and symbolic goods that are valued in a particular society. Thus, as we shall see, in the Japanese company status is the primary symbolic good – even more important than economic goods. Corresponding to the variety of goods being played for, there is therefore a variety of different games occurring at any one time, and any individual may be playing in more than one of them at the same time.

The social realm is divided into 'fields', which are separate domains of forces and tensions. Each field is the arena for a game, the playing of which determines what happens to the field. All the fields taken together make up 'social space'. Although distinct, the different fields touch each other, since the same players may be active in different fields or transfer capital between them. Capital is whatever is played for in the different fields. It may be material goods, or other things that are valued such as prestige. The value of any cultural notion is not its meaningfulness or its usefulness but the social distinction embedded in such meaning or use, that is, the effects of the cultural products on the social positions of the producers. This works in reverse also: the rebel derives his or her cultural capital from a refutation of the dominant ideology. Capital, in short, is all the goods that are sought after in a particular social formation. It is convertible, since a player may sacrifice capital in one game to gain a different kind in another. However, such strategising may not happen consciously. Moreover, symbolic capital is not always recognised as a convertible source of power. The process of conversion may be 'masked' by agents' 'structuring' of the world. Agents construct their social world, then they act to reproduce their positions and to gain position in the social world. For Bourdieu, ideology often functions to hide the calculations that lie behind the strategising which forms much of social life. For example, the economics of gift-giving is disguised by reconceptualising it within the ideals of honour, generosity, reciprocity and so on. So the company's agenda – to survive as a company and to be profitable – may be hidden behind a mask of Japanese values.

Central to this is the concept of habitus. By using the concept of habitus – internalised schemes which, having been constituted in the course of collective history, are acquired in the course of individual history – Bourdieu attempts to unite the individual/social structure divide. While he speaks of different kinds of strategies by which players seek to improve their standing in various fields, or even move between them, he claims that their ability to do this is limited by 'habitus', which, for Bourdieu, is an essentially unconscious structure. This concept means, in essence, that we act habitually, without thinking consciously about much of what we do. Partly as a result of this, habitus is very hard to change: Bourdieu thinks of it as constructed during childhood, as the individual learns the rules and structures of its society. Habitus therefore has a dominating role for the rest of the individual's life, being largely unchanged by later experience.

Bourdieu's ideas incorporate both the individual and a larger theory of domination in the social field. As a method, Bourdieu's ideas are neither symbolic nor material; they are about the relationship between the two spheres. His contribution has therefore been a synthesis of the economic and the symbolic orders. Symbolic power is a form of power with material force. His theory, therefore, unites both the individual and social structure by looking at how individuals behave in the context of society. He has also united the economic/cultural spheres by looking at how people behave in the context of the economic world and the economic goods that they strategise to obtain.

The relevance for this book is that I use these theories in order to look at the ways in which the individuals in C-Life acted in relation to the overall demands of the organisation of the company, and I look at the economic and symbolic goods that they desired and how they strategised in order to obtain these. I also look at how all of this changed as the economy changed and the company faltered. In relation to Bourdieu's notion of habitus, I look at how conscious the individuals in C-Life were of the social rules and how conscious they were of the fact that both they themselves and the individuals around them were engaged in a strategic struggle to improve their economic and symbolic positions.

Other views

Other schools which are of relevance to this argument include transactionalism, or action/practice theory (associated with Barth, Bailey, Paine and the Manchester School: Cohen, Comaroff, etc.), which is also an attempt to look at how individuals behave in the context of the overall society. It looks at people as centres of action, capable of making individual decisions, competing with each other to create meaning and achieve their goals. Individuals actively strategise to create their futures. Individual agency, in this view, comes first – is privileged above social structure – and gives rise to socio-cultural processes which are in use for a certain time and participated in by a certain number of people for variable amounts of time. Barth (1959, 1966) argues that we need to look at society as a whole, or social structures, in terms of how individuals use them in strategising. Thus, social structures remain in place because of the decisions made by different individuals seeking to further their own personal ends. As a result, they are not fixed but change as the strategies of individuals change, or as new individuals with new strategies come on the scene. At the same time, individuals are influenced in their decisions by the structures that they or others have set up; there is therefore a reciprocal relationship of influence between individuals and social structure. The main point, however, is that individuals ultimately are free to ignore the directional factors and follow their strategies. Bailey (1971) takes a similar approach. For him, social structures function as the 'rules of the game' in which individuals are engaged. In forming their strategies, individuals are influenced by these rules, and in so doing partly determine the subsequent rules.

An important alternative view stresses not competition between individuals as they strategise, but their co-operation. Frankenberg (1966: 238) suggests that 'those who live in a community have overriding economic interests which are the same or complementary.... Their common interest in things gives them a common interest in each other'. To put it another way, it is not just individuals that strategise – individuals join hands in strategising as a group. This is connected to the role of group ideology. Thus, a recognition that strategising also exists upon different levels, as an activity of groups as well as individuals, is an important part of this book. I hope that it will be clear in the fieldwork that there were many individuals in C-Life who were involved in different ways in strategising towards their own greater economic and symbolic good.

Having established the theoretical context of the present work, I turn now to the economic context. In the next chapter I outline the varying fortunes of the Japanese economy, and the life insurance industry, before and during my periods of fieldwork.

2 Economic background

In this chapter, I present the background to the situation of C-Life that I explore in the rest of the book. I begin with a very brief account of the general situation in Japan during and after the 'bubble', before moving on to a more detailed look at the crisis facing the insurance industry in particular. None of this material is intended to be exhaustive or definitive; in particular, I do not seek to give an account of the structure or nature of the insurance industry. Rather, I aim to describe those factors that affected C-Life in particular. The purpose is simply to provide the backdrop of economic change against which the drama of C-Life was played out, and to set out the context for the fieldwork chapters which follow.

The Japanese economy

During the 1950s and 1960s, Japan truly achieved a miracle. The country grew at a faster pace than any economy to date so far. In the 1955–1973 high-growth era, GDP per worker quadrupled. Once the economy was rebuilt Japan began to challenge developed countries in one industry after another. This was brought about by a combination of factors: the 'catch-up effect', very high rates of investment and a concentration on trade. This served to create a positive effect throughout the economy, with investment leading to higher GDP per worker, which in turn led to higher standards of living and higher savings, which then led to higher investment rates.

The bubble

Japan's incredible growth continued, albeit at a slower pace after the oil shock of 1973, right into the 1980s. But as Japan conquered one export market after another, her trade balance, particularly with the USA, increasingly became a point of controversy. In September 1985 the Plaza Accord – an international agreement to drive down the value of the US dollar – was agreed in an attempt to provide a remedy to Japan's extreme trade surpluses with the USA and, to a lesser extent, with Germany. However, the strategy worked more than was originally intended. The dollar fell sharply while the yen appreciated, damaging the export-dependent economy of Japan under which companies rely on selling their goods cheaply in terms of overseas currencies. With the higher yen, Japan began to suffer.

As a remedy, the Japanese government tried to boost the economy by loosening monetary policy. The USA also urged Japan to follow this strategy. Consequently, after the agreement of the Louvre Accord, the Bank of Japan lowered the discount rate to its lowest level since World War II: 2.5 per cent. Flooding the economy with cash through lower interest rates had more than the desired effect. It led to the easy credit that began the bubble. The central bank's move sparked a speculative boom that careered spectacularly out of control. Most of the money went in two directions: into the stock market and into the property market. New investments were financed using land and stocks as collateral rather than secured based on projections of future earnings. This resulted in both land and stock prices going through the roof. These fed on each other and culminated in the creation of a financial bubble where the stock market followed land prices in a seemingly endless upward spiral. The Tokyo stock market went up and up, reaching ludicrous levels. At its height it was worth more than 40 per cent of the total capitalisation of the world's stock markets.

Where the Japanese manufacturing industry had been at the centre of attention in the high growth period, during the 1980s finance came to the fore. Banks and financial institutions expanded rapidly, increasing their international profile. Because of the super-easy credit as the bubble inflated, banks had access to money with which they financed overseas loans, property purchases and the expansion of Japanese firms abroad. Japanese corporations began to acquire assets overseas at a rapid pace.

While the bubble economy lasted, Japan seemed to defy accepted economic theory. Some even suggested that Japan had become a different type of economy, one that contradicted economists' general expectation that non-Western nations would be forced to adopt Western practices as they matured. In the USA some analysts talked of a 'Japanese economic system' that had gone 'beyond capitalism' (in Katz 1998: 9).

The bubble bursts

The end of the bubble was triggered by the central bank, which finally realised that the bubble economy had got out of control. They doubled interest rates between 1989 and 1990 to end the easy credit and thus burst the bubble. Once again, the results were more dramatic than intended. The era in which credit had been almost free changed overnight into one in which credit was exceedingly difficult to obtain. Banks were overwhelmed by their own problems in trying to deal with a mass of bad debts accumulated as businesses went bankrupt after the crash. These problems made them reluctant to lend further, especially on the basis of property, the prices of which had not ceased to fall. Tight credit exacerbated the problems of struggling companies, and they began to go bankrupt at record rates.

The stock market crash

The so-called 'economic miracle' came abruptly to an end with the Tokyo stock market crash of 1990. From its high on 31 December 1989, the benchmark Nikkei index had dropped almost 50 per cent by October 1990. It went on to fall further over the next ten years, dropping into the 12,000s in 1999, a 70 per cent decline from its peak. Together with the crash in stock prices, the price of the land supporting the borrowed credit also tumbled. Banks began to fail, on account of their massive bad loans, for the first time in the post-war period. The decline in bank shares in turn brought down stock prices further. Japanese companies are mostly tied together in a complicated system of cross share-holding. The approximately 60 per cent of shares held in cross share-holding arrangements, and which were never traded, aggravated fluctuations in an illiquid market. With the bursting of the bubble many companies decided to start unwinding these cross share-holdings, exacerbating the negative spiral.

Adding to the problem, Japan began to deregulate in the 1980s. Among other changes, duties were lowered on imported goods and retail laws were liberalised, encouraging increased competition and a more severe domestic operating environment for companies.

The Japanese response

Most Japanese seemed to think that the bubble economy was a temporary phenomenon and that once it had been corrected life would continue as normal. They were thus surprised and unprepared for the grinding ten-year economic downturn that followed. Their response was largely passive as they waited in the hope that the economy would somehow naturally rebound. 'Instead of responding to adversity, meeting the challenge, and moving on, senior managers in Japan's financial institutions are more like frightened rabbits caught at night in a car's headlights' (Wood 1992: 12). The Japanese seem to be waiting for a recovery that is not likely to come – according to analysts – until they take the initiative in restructuring. At several points during the last ten years it has seemed that Japan might recover, notably in 1995–1996. However, Japan's productivity is at present well below the 4 per cent per annum it averaged from 1975 to 1990 and the stock market is still only half its level at the height of the bubble. The nation has slowly come to terms with the fact that the prolonged recession will not fix itself; that structural reform and a restructuring of Japan's ailing industries and debt-laden banks is necessary.

If the typical Japanese response to the country's economic woes has been one of uncertainty, then the life insurance industry has certainly been no exception. Except where otherwise stated, all information in this section is drawn directly from Reuters wire service and from internal C-Life documents.

The crisis in the life insurance industry

The Japanese life insurance industry is the largest in the world - twice as large as that of the USA, the next biggest. In 1999 Japanese life insurers held 190 trillion yen in assets and about 95 per cent of Japanese households have life insurance policies. Premium income is 40 per cent of the world's total. Japanese life insurance companies wield enormous financial power in terms of the sheer amount of money they have available to invest. This was especially so during the 1980s, the first decade in which they made substantial investments in overseas stocks and bonds.

In the 1990s, however, the industry was suffering from the collapse of the bubble and the subsequent recession. Life insurers are currently battling falling premium income and low investment returns. This has resulted in a 'negative spread', a gap between the money they receive in premiums and what they pay out to policy-holders. A report by Andrew Smithers of economic consultancy Smithers and Co. Ltd stated that, for the industry as a whole, total returns for the fiscal year ending March 1998 were 2.2 per cent, against required returns of 3.3 per cent – a significant shortfall. In additional, insurers are struggling with a mountain of bad loans, and dwindling numbers of new policies. All eight of the biggest life insurers showed a decline in income from insurance premiums for the fiscal year ending March 1999. C-Life fell the most, by 23 per cent. Combined bad loans for the industry were as much as 1.11 trillion yen (approximately US$9.4 billion) according to financial statements for the year ending March 1999. In June 1999, Moody's Investors Service downgraded a number of life insurance companies following concerns over bad loans and investment losses. The ranking of C-Life was lowered from B3 to Caa1, raising concerns among the media that the company might be facing bankruptcy.

The 1980s

During the 1980s Japanese life insurance companies became major players in world markets. This was the first decade in which Japanese law enabled them to make substantial investments in overseas securities. At the end of September 1998 the 'big eight' held a combined 75 trillion yen worth of securities. Because of their sheer size, their investment strategies have been watched closely as they have the ability to move markets.

Investment overseas in the 1980s was a new area for life insurers. Traditionally, the investments made by life insurers have been conservative and domestic-oriented because of the long-term nature of their business. There was little need for them to invest overseas during Japan's high-growth period. In decades of high growth there had been little risk of losses; but companies ventured into riskier investments during the 1980s. First, they branched out into overseas bonds, then into the stock markets. More than half of the enormous capital outflows from Japan during this period was caused by the life insurance companies starting to invest in overseas assets. Overseas investment made increasingly high returns possible, which allowed the insurers to bring out an array of new non-life-insurance-related investment products for clients which offered high guaranteed returns.

But despite the high returns, overseas investment was a much more risky game than domestic investment, and the insurers had little experience of these kinds of investments. In particular, they had little knowledge of currency risk and hedging techniques. 'At no time in history has a country ever had to assume such foreign-exchange risks with such a large body of assets from which it hoped to derive its future prosperity' (Wood 1992: 88). Even those insurance companies that recorded good investment performance ended up making huge losses on foreign exchange when the yen moved against them. The financial health of these companies now is directly related to the risks they took on their investments during the 1980s.

The seeds of the crisis

Investing in overseas assets had allowed the life insurers to bring out an array of new investment products, some of which had nothing to do with life insurance at all. Time has proved this to be an unwise move. One of the most popular policies in the 1980s was a common annuity-type policy that pays out a guaranteed rate of interest when it matures. These so-called single-premium endowment policies guaranteed returns usually of around 5 per cent, though sometimes as high as 6 per cent, and were wildly popular. They were savings instruments that earned high interest partly because some of the funds were invested overseas where they could take advantage of high interest rates. They earned investors far higher interest rates than were obtainable elsewhere in Japan, where interest rates were in the 3 per cent range. Their popularity meant that a huge outflow of funds poured from the banks into the life insurance companies.

For some companies, these endowment policies constituted half of all new products. This situation did not last long, as the finance ministry eventually intervened and encouraged the life insurers to cease offering these products. But the damage was already done. Most of the life insurers were now locked into providing 5 per cent gains on these products for years to come, even after the bubble burst and interest rates had fallen below 1 per cent. The trouble that ensued from having provided these products was compounded by the fact that Japanese law prevented, and still prevents, insurance companies from lowering yields on existing insurance policies. But even if the law were changed, providing immediate help for the negative spread situation, and possibly preventing further company failures, the downside is that the public would probably be scared away from taking out new policies with the life insurance companies.

The pyramid scheme

How have insurance companies managed to pay out guaranteed returns on such policies well into the 1990s even after interest rates have fallen to near zero? Life insurers have filled in the negative spread by tapping into unrealised profits on their share-holdings, which are about 15 per cent of their total assets. Life insurers are mutually owned companies. This means that they are owned by their policy-holders and thus have no shareholders to report to. Disclosure regulations are less strict for such companies than for public companies: they have no requirement to disclose the average cost of their stock portfolios or their capital gains. They hold all their investments pooled together in a common account. Shares bought for 100 yen decades ago are lumped in together with shares bought when the Nikkei had soared to 36,000 at its peak.

This has made it possible for life insurers to ride out some of the losses of recent years because of the accumulated gains they hold from past decades. Japanese insurers carry their assets on their books at book value (the value at which they were bought). This means that, until the 1990s, the insurers had huge unrealised share gains. Because funds were pooled in a common account, companies are able, when necessary, to pay out higher interest than is available at the current interest rates. This has allowed insurers to offer higher returns than the general market during slow growth years, and to build their profits back up by paying out less in years of high growth. Thus, they subsidise present policy-holders with the gains won from investments made decades ago, with gains that rightly belong to long-term policy-holders. This adds up to a kind of pyramid scheme, where insurers take in new money to subsidise high pay-outs for older policies. Like all such pyramid schemes it is able to continue as long as new money comes in, and as long as there is no crisis in confidence.

Closely intertwined with the fate of the stock market

Japanese life insurers hold more Japanese shares than any other institutions, even the banks. At the end of the 1990 fiscal year they held 13 per cent of the Tokyo stock market, although this has now decreased to around 9 per cent. Because of the enormous size of their investments, any net losses would throw the entire market in confusion. But because of the lack of disclosure, it is impossible to tell exactly what is happening inside the life insurance companies. They do not disclose the average book value of their stock portfolios, so it is impossible to tell at what point life insurers would be left with no capital gains on their portfolios. The oft-quoted claim is that if the Nikkei dropped to 12,000, as it almost did at one stage in 1999, there would be no capital gains at all. However, more pessimistic analysts calculate that capital gains could be wiped out with the Nikkei at 15,000. In any event, when the Nikkei fell below 15,000 and kept on falling, the first life insurers began to fail.

The recession

In April 1997 Nissan Mutual Life was the first Japanese life insurer to collapse since World War II. The news sent shock waves through the industry. It won the attention of the media, which until then had focused mainly on the problems of the banking industry. Articles appeared questioning the safety of the other companies and asking whether public funds would be used to bail out the insurance companies, as they had for the banks. The general public, 95 per cent of whom hold some form of insurance policy, were left wondering how much the policy-holders would retain from their policies. This sparked a furious public debate over whose responsibility it was to pay the policy-holders. Eventually the 1.2 million policy-holders of Nissan Mutual were left with a 50 per cent cut in the amount of interest they were expecting.

The damage to the industry was severe. In the April/June quarter following the failure, 45.3 trillion yen worth of policies were cancelled. This represented more than twice the value of policies cancelled in the same period a year earlier. Cancellations of group policies by companies also rose. Japanese companies invest in group insurance policies so they can make payouts to families if something goes wrong and an employee dies. These policy cancellations rose twenty-six-fold. Individual life insurance policy cancellations rose by 21 per cent. The following year, GE Capital Corp. agreed to buy the sales operations of ailing second-tier insurer Toho Mutual. But in June 1999 the century-old company collapsed under the weight of thousands of unprofitable policies. The company, which was ordered to stop operating after Toho's auditor refused to sign off on the company's financial statements, failed with a 200 billion yen capital deficit. Later, losses were found to have mounted to more than 300 billion yen.

The government's response: the FSA

The FSA (Financial Supervisory Agency), which took over the Finance Ministry's functions of inspection and surveillance in July 1998, is increasingly concerned with the state of the insurance industry. This is especially so since the banking crisis has been settled by a massive pay-out in public funds to shore up weaker banks. The FSA introduced solvency margin ratios – similar to the capital adequacy ratios for banks – for the first time in June 1998 in response to calls for greater disclosure in the life insurance industry. Stricter standards were introduced in April 1999. The standards were brought in as an important gauge of the health of a life insurance company and as a sign that action might be needed. They are intended to indicate the ability of the insurer to deal with unforeseen risks. The solvency margin ratio should be above 200. The FSA has said it will use the ratios to assess whether they need to implement 'prompt corrective action'. Such action includes drastic restructuring or closure. However, it is questionable how tough the FSA will be. Analysts I spoke to said that they suspect the FSA is putting considerable pressure on companies to come up with their own options, including finding foreign partners.

Public funds

For most of the decade, the government successfully avoided taking the same kind of action over the life insurance companies as it had with the banks. In the banking sector, the government injected 7,450 billion yen of public funds into fifteen banks and made provision for a 25,000 billion yen safety net to provide protection for depositors in case of a bank failure. But until recently it looked unlikely that the government would do the same for the 190,000 billion yen insurance sector. This lack of initiative has caused intense debate among the policy-holding public. According to ING Barings analyst David Threadgold, the likelihood of failure in the banking industry necessitates prompt action by the government because of the spectre of a mass panic that a bank failure could cause and the ensuing crisis as account-holders withdraw funds. For the insurance industry, company failures may have grave long-term consequences, but because of the penalties involved in cancelling contracts there is not the immediate threat of a mass panic.

The Ministry of Finance continued to insist as late as 1999 that no public funds would be used, even while it seemed obvious that with the size of the shortfalls public money would eventually be needed. Instead, the largest life insurers were 'encouraged' to set up their own industry fund in 1998. This has been the general pattern of the government – to pressurise stronger industry players to help clean up the failed institutions in their industry. Naturally, the insurance companies balked at doing this, at least initially.

The investor protection fund

Under government pressure the Policy-holders Protection Corp. was set up in December 1998 after the failure of Nissan Mutual. It was established as a corporation licensed by the Ministry of Finance with compulsory participation by all the insurance companies and oversees the transfer of policies of failed companies. Its purpose was to provide a safety net in case of an insurance company collapse. Policies of failed insurers that are not absorbed by healthy companies are transferred to the fund. However, the upper limit it set of 400 billion yen was only adequate to handle the collapse of a small company. It was never large enough to handle collapses on the scale of Toho Mutual, which went bankrupt shortly after the fund was set up. The collapse of Toho Mutual was large enough to take half of the money in the fund in one go, leaving little left over for further collapses. Naturally, the companies who contributed to the fund were unhappy about this turn of events. Pressured by the government into setting up the fund at the outset, they felt they were left alone to fund Toho's collapse. An additional problem is that the fund would not become fully funded for ten years anyway. The protection scheme provides for loans from the Bank of Japan in case it is short of funds but policy-holders in another failure could still be left short.

Finally, in December 1999 an agreement was made for public funds to be diverted into the insurance industry. On 17 December the Japanese life insurance industry accepted a Ministry of Finance proposal to pay an extra 100 billion yen to the industry fund. The Ministry of Finance presented a bill to the ruling Liberal Democratic Party suggesting that the Policy-holder Protection Fund be raised to 1 trillion yen, 400 billion yen of which would come from public funds. The International Insurance Council (IIC), which represents US insurers overseas, opposed the decision. IIC President Kevin Cronin said in a statement: 'We believe this proposal disproportionately impacts US insurers, lacks transparency, ignores due process, and actually penalizes well-run companies'.

The current situation

The investment environment remained severe as I conducted my fieldwork in 1999 and 2000. Bond yields continued to fall, and the rise in the yen caused huge losses on foreign bond portfolios. Stock prices were still half of bubble-era levels. Property prices continued to fall for the seventh straight year.

Life insurance companies are still deeply affected by property prices. Some of their investments are in the form of direct loans for property; others are for loans that are secured in this way. They are still dealing with a mountain of bad loans on their books – much of these secured by property – from companies that have also been hit hard in the recession and are unable to repay.

According to some analysts, the insurance industry as a whole still has liabilities in excess of assets. Although they have made efforts to restructure through staff cuts and by writing off bad loans, they continue to suffer from the negative spread between the returns they receive on their investments and the returns they must pay to their policy-holders. It has become increasingly difficult to continue to pay out guaranteed returns to policy-holders in an era of interest rate deregulation. Life insurers are struggling with lower and lower rates of new policy-holders joining up, and, at the same time, with large numbers of existing policy-holders cancelling. From April 1999 insurers lowered guaranteed yields on new individual life insurance policies from 2.5 per cent to 1.5 per cent; but as this is applicable only to policies taken out after that date it is unlikely to do much to relieve the pressure. The negative spread is the most serious of the problems, as it cannot be corrected overnight. Even on new policies the gap is large. And it becomes larger when one takes into account that a higher average yield must be paid after older policies still remaining from when interest rates were even higher are factored in.

It is difficult for the insurance companies to restructure themselves: their assets are not very easily disposed of. A large percentage of assets are in domestic loans, the bulk of which are backed by property. Around 6 per cent are invested directly in property. Moreover, policy-holders can cancel their policies relatively easily – although, given steep cancellation penalties, it is unlikely that large numbers will do so en masse.

Deregulation

Now the insurers are being hit by industry deregulation as well. They have to compete with banks and other financial institutions that are making inroads on the life insurance market. Banks were able to regain ground and offer a range of new products as interest rates were deregulated. Pension fund management, for example, used to be the prerogative of the life insurers and trust banks. Deregulation will allow other entrants into the industry. Most of the life insurance companies are ill equipped to compete in an unregulated environment, especially against foreign insurers who are now making inroads into the Japanese market. Pressure to open up the insurance industry is felt from the USA in particular. A 1996 insurance pact was agreed, opening up the 'third sector' niche markets for cancer and other speciality insurance to domestic competition in 2001. This sector is currently dominated by foreign companies. Newcomers such as Orix Life Insurance Co., a subsidiary of computer maker Orix, or Sony Life Insurance Co., the subsidiary of Sony Corp., are making inroads into the traditional terrain of the large life insurers.

Some industry analysts suggest the industry will be forced to regroup into large players that can offer a comprehensive range of products, and niche players that can survive in a deregulated climate, with those that fall between disappearing or being forced to merge.

Consolidation and competition

The increasingly severe conditions in the industry have brought about a string of mergers and acquisitions, including the following:

25 April 1997
Nissan Mutual Life Insurance Co. Existing policy contracts taken over by Aoba Life Insurance Co.
9 February 1999
Manufacturer's Life Insurance Co., Canada's largest life insurer, announced it would pay $700 million for the business of Daihyaku Mutual Life Insurance Co.
5 June 1999
Toho Mutual Life Insurance Co. – which sold most of its operations to a unit of GE Capital Corp. – sold its remaining businesses.
17 September 1999

Aoba Life Insurance, set up to take over the business of Nissan Mutual Life Insurance Co., is sold to France's Artemis SA for 25 billion yen. This was the first Japanese life insurance takeover by a foreign investor.

Meanwhile, sleeker, more efficient foreign insurers have been able to accumulate good results while operating in Japan without the dead weight of an accumulation of bad loans. Foreign companies are pouring into Japan with a new style of management and more modern selling methods. Prudential Life Insurance of America sells insurance through 'life planners' who tailor life insurance products to fit their clients. Other companies such as France's Axa Life Insurance Co. have competed favourably with the majors by holding down personnel costs through the use of mail order and telephone services.

Possible options for Japanese insurers

Japanese insurers will need to change their business methods radically in order to survive. A variety of possible strategies exists, including some of the following. First, they could choose to specialise, occupying niche markets left untouched by the larger companies. Telephone sales, or specialising in niche areas of insurance such as medical add-ons, are growth areas. Orix Life has been successful at this approach. Alternatively, they may decide to form alliances with each other. Larger players, unable to devote themselves to a specialised area, may have no option but to tie up with other insurers or financial institutions – or foreign firms – that can provide them with a desperately needed capital injection and asset management expertise in the longer term. The deal made between GE Capital Corp. and Toho Mutual Life Insurance Co. or that between Canada's Manulife Financial and Daihyaku Mutual Life Insurance Co. are likely to become a model for future deals. They were made in such a way that the incoming foreign partner is shielded from the accumulated problems on the Japanese partners' balance sheet. The tie-ups give foreign insurers a presence in Japan and Japanese companies better asset management technology. Other tie-ups, such as that between Asahi Life subsidiary Asahi Life Investment Management Co. and Metropolitan Life Insurance (MetLife), are focused on sharing money management.

Japanese insurers are also merging. Taiyo and Daido, two medium-sized insurers, tied up in 1999. The merged group will become the fifth largest in the industry. A similar solution may be absorption by keiretsu companies. The business group to which a life insurance company belongs may subsume it into a holding company structure. However, the largest players may be able to remain solo.

Finally, demutualising as mutual companies and issuing shares would allow companies access to fresh capital. In 1998, Mitsui Life became the first company to do so and other companies are now following suit.

The stock market

The one thing that saved the insurance industry through 1999, as I conducted my research, was the unexpected performance of the Nikkei, which gained around 30 per cent over the year. But this is only a temporary stop-gap. Because of the huge amounts of Japanese shares held by the life insurers, the companies are intertwined with the fate of the stock market. If they turn net sellers to reap the profits of a rising market, the value of their remaining assets goes down.

Life insurers are increasingly reliant on dividend income from their domestic stock investments and must sell stocks that are not performing. But this, in turn, has increasingly meant an acceleration in the pace of the unwinding of cross share-holdings. In the Japanese system of cross share-holding, groups of companies hold each others' shares in long-term business arrangements. These arrangements were originally intended to cement relationships between the companies, but they also make it impossible for other companies, including foreign companies, to stage hostile takeover bids. But as companies unravel, these cross share-holding arrangements, and the sheer volume of money they involve, pull the stock market down in their wake in a negative spiral. Results for the fiscal first half of 1999 which ended 30 September showed little sign of improvement for the industry.

The media's response

Meanwhile, the media have hammered life insurance companies. Large black headlines proclaiming 'Dangerous Life Insurers' or the 'The Danger of Insurance Payment Cuts is Approaching!' loom large in newspapers. The first paragraph of Shukan Toyo Keizai's 26 June 1999 edition read:

> The Life Insurance Industry is now in the position of that well-known luxury liner: the Titanic. What was once the richest industry in Japan is in danger of sinking, weighed down by bad loans, its investment performance irreparably damaged by the super low interest policy pursued by the Bank of Japan. Meanwhile, the Policy-holders Protection Corp fund – the industry safety net – is still too weak to hold up. It is by no means sure that all of the policyholders will be able to make it to the life boats.

Such media reports have fuelled the sense of alarm among consumers and hastened the number of policy cancellations.

I now turn to C-Life itself, which, as I conducted my fieldwork in 1999 and 2000, was in the most precarious position of all the major life insurers.

C-Life

C-Life, founded in 1904 by Ikunoshin Kadono, is a mutual insurance company; the first in Japan with an Anglo-American structure. Somewhat ironically, the name given to the new company means 'eternal' in Japanese.

When I returned to the company in 1999, C-Life – traditionally the smallest of the so-called 'big eight' – had fallen out of the top eight into around fourteenth position. Total life insurance in force in the company was 54 trillion yen. The 1999 annual report says of the company: 'The C-Mutual Life Insurance Company has grown into one of the leading life insurers in Japan. This steady progress is rooted in our alertness to emerging trends, the skills of our financial professionals and the confidence of policy-holders'. The facts say otherwise. C-Life was generally recognised by analysts to be the weakest of the majors at this stage.

As previously noted, all eight of the biggest life insurers showed a decline in income from insurance premiums for the fiscal year ending March 1999. C-Life fell the most, by 23 per cent. Its results were dismal. Premium income fell 23.2 per cent, investment income dropped 23.1 per cent and premiums were down 42.1 per cent. Ordinary profit fell 7.6 per cent and dividends lost 33 per cent. Total assets fell 13.3 per cent. For the first half of the fiscal year 1999 ending 30 September, the situation had not improved. For the first six months of the business year the company earned 244.6 billion yen in premium income, down 18.6 per cent from a year earlier. New individual insurance policies were down 0.6 per cent. The balance of individual insurance policy contracts had fallen 9.2 per cent from the level of the previous year. Analysts and the media grew increasingly sceptical about how long the company could last. According to ING Barings analyst David Threadgold: 'C-Life is dead. Unfortunately, they are the only ones that are not aware of the situation'.

C-Life implemented a restructuring plan in 1995 called the Challenge 100 Plan, to end on the company's hundredth anniversary in 2004. The company also tied up with US insurer Unum Corporation and its subsidiary Unum Japan to sell disability coverage alongside C-Life's insurance plans. Ties with other insurers – in the UK, Switzerland, the USA and Hong Kong – are mainly to aid Japanese clients setting up operations abroad.

One bright spot was the pension fund business. Pension assets under management saw good investment returns, largely because of the rising stock market. Investment gains are important for life insurers because they are linked to a particular type of group annuity that life insurers are depending on in the competition with asset managers in foreign companies. C-Life had the second-highest return of the largest insurers.

The company was still weighed down by over 100 billion yen in bad loans at the end of March 1999. The financial stabilisation laws require insurers to separate loans into four classes: sound loans, doubtful loans, highly risky loans and irrecoverable loans. Bad loans comprise the last three categories. C-Life's ratio of loans for which reserves had been put aside is just 55 per cent, compared to 100 per cent for industry leader

Nippon Life. As noted, the media have waged a virtual war against life insurers since interest in banks died down after the government bailout of 1999. C-Life was a particular target as the most precarious major insurer.

C-Life's management did introduce a series of measures in an attempt to stave off the company's demise and these steps formed the backdrop to my fieldwork at the company.

Restructuring

In 1999, the company decided to concentrate mainly on managing individual and medical insurance, with peripheral businesses sold off. Restructuring efforts were focused on outsourcing, spinning off non-core business sectors – including group insurance and systems development. However, under increasingly intense pressure to restructure and against the media onslaught, C-Life announced in September 1999 that it would slash 800 jobs – 30 per cent of its workforce – under a three-year restructuring plan. The company decided on 30 November, halfway through my fieldwork, to hasten this plan by bringing it forward to a deadline in early 2000. Basically, one in every three people in head office was asked to leave, throwing the company into turmoil. At the time, this news was still not public. Company employees I interviewed expected that policy cancellations would increase dramatically once the news was out.

Neither this nor any other of management's attempts to save the company were succeeding either in staving off bankruptcy or improving the company's image. On 18 June 1999, Moody's rated C-Life and concluded:

> A certain degree of financial support may be expected from Tokai Banks and Asahi Bank (C-Life's long-term business partners), but the company will nevertheless continue to face a difficult business environment and will be challenged by the impact of deregulation. C-Life's investment assets are moderately exposed to high risk segments including non-marketable securities. After realizing some hidden gains on securities, its capitalization has become extremely weak and may not be sufficient to cover its exposures to non-performing assets. C-Life's financial flexibility is very limited....
>
> The outlook for C-Life is negative. Moody's believes that the current adverse operating environment for Japanese life insurers will continue to pressure C-Life's earnings and capital formation. As deregulation occurs over the next several years, C-Life's ability to weather the transformation of the financial system and the insurance industry may depend largely on its ability to raise new capital.

In this chapter, we have seen the situation that faces the people we will meet in chapters 3 to 6, knowledge that is essential for understanding their concerns. It is to those chapters that we now turn. First, chapter 3 looks at employee reactions to the situation described in this chapter.

3 The current situation

C-Life – and Japanese management – has been going through a period of great change, from the height of the bubble to ten years of recession. In this chapter and those that follow, I focus on the changes that have come upon C-Life, and its responses to those changes, particularly the restructuring plan. My aim in this chapter is not to describe the economic situation in detail. Rather, it is to discover what the situation was for the individual employee. I therefore focus on employees' own views of the situation, and on the way that the restructuring has affected them.

In the wake of Japan's economic woes, there has been much comment or analysis published by financial experts on the causes or likely consequences of the economic downturn. There has been relatively little work showing what ordinary people, such as company employees, think about it and how they view their prospects. This chapter aims to do something to redress this imbalance. Throughout it, and the two chapters which follow, I quote the employees themselves to illustrate or reinforce my comments. These quotations are all taken from the extensive interviews I conducted during the last phase of my fieldwork, as I was filming the company, between January and October 2000. Around sixty hours of interviews were recorded on film and transcribed. I also occasionally cite business analysts whom I interviewed at the same time.

The present situation

I was interested to know how the employees of C-Life were interpreting the changes that they had seen in the period since 1985, when I had first entered the company as an employee. Would they have rejected Japanese management altogether? Would they be looking forward to a new period of 'American-style' management, or would they be fearful of the prospect? I begin by examining their attitudes towards the economy in general.

The economy

The C-Life employees I interviewed seemed to have clear ideas about the Japanese economy and where and how it had gone wrong. They were conscious that the Japanese economy had been very protected by the bureaucracy, and that this is no longer sustainable in the present period of increased international competition. But it had achieved remarkable results in the post-war period.

H: I think that Japanese started from zero after World War II. But the economy was strong and whatever anyone did they made money, and the confidence that tomorrow will be better than today continued until the 1990s. Money flowed into C-Life at a rate of more than 20 per cent until 1984. You could have been asleep and it still came in. That was how the world was.

There is a consciousness that a major reason for Japan's success was the fact that the economy was highly protected, and that the USA has been instrumental in forcing Japan's financial markets open.

W: Companies until now had *keiretsu* and groups; without any real competition they were just able to grow anyway. Growth was at 5 or 6 per cent. Companies didn't have to do anything. There was no pressure from overseas (*gaiatsu*), and inside Japan was governed by countless rules, so there was no need to worry about competition from abroad.

There is also recognition that C-Life – as a major company – had been in a protected position compared to smaller companies, which operated in a much more competitive world.

C: Before, we had a large company, small company dual structure in Japan, so the larger companies, whether they were banks or manufacturing, were very stable. And Japan was very advanced in technology development so I think that they had the earnings capacity. Amidst an environment where they had a large leeway to experiment, they were doing all kinds of things. Because it was a period of expansion.

However, the employees look back on the good things about Japanese management and reminisce about its merits, although they accept at the same time that it is now inevitably about to change dramatically, as it no longer suits the present era.

H: If they can't let go of the co-operative body (this is H's word to describe the Japanese company as a co-operation of people all working together), then it must be because there's merit in it. There were merits in the system – there were. Because Japanese companies were co-operative bodies the Japanese economy grew until the 1990s and in that period of growth the corporation was exactly suited to the expansion of the economy. So they were able to come this far always using the same pattern. But that was the success model for the past, and since the 1990s the paradigm has changed, and they should have changed what's inside their heads as well (*atama o kirikaenakute wa ikenakatta no ni*). They just continued with the same attitudes as in the past until they were on the verge of bankruptcy. So it's not anything surprising.

They are also conscious of competition and what the company needs to do in order to compete in the future. There are now sharp divides between those employees who have skills – and therefore the ability to change jobs – and those who do not. This has implications for the future of the company as well as that of individual employees. In the competition between companies, employees are conscious that companies which do not hire and foster specialists are losing out to companies which do.

W: Once specialists like that arrive, consumers go to the ones that give them a better deal. And so a general awareness arose of the need for specialists. So our company is now trying to specialise the workforce and split into different areas. For instance, in the pension business, if you don't pay good wages you won't get a good workforce. So the age where you can use generalists is now over. That is because of the increased competition from abroad and the larger numbers of specialists that they have. Generalists were good in the age where there was no competition. When you have to compete against the whole world, specialists win. Companies have to build a new system that can compete.

On a general level, employees all recognise the need for the change from generalists to specialists. But on a personal level, many are terrified of changes that would render their own generalist skills useless.

Some employees are outspoken about the lack of 'real' management in the easy post-war era. Many are openly disillusioned and critical of Japanese management and the way in which C-Life has been run until now. Unsurprisingly, this is especially true of some of the employees who were forced out of the company during the restructuring moves.

H: You didn't need real management in the post-war period. Everyone was just basking in the sun of the company, they didn't have to try and the company got bigger anyway. There was plenty of work and everyone was happy. What you needed instead of management were cosy clubs of buddies (*nakayoshi kurabu*), people who didn't speak out against the 'village' of the company, people who were happy just to get along all together.

There is also a strong consciousness that Japan will have to move to a more efficient form of organisation if companies are to survive. The 'socialist' type of Japanese management will no longer suffice. There seems to be considerable awareness that other countries have also struggled with different versions of bureaucratic involvement in the economy, and 'Japanese management' is, to some employees, merely one type of possible management style.

W: I think the question of efficiency in companies comes down to whether they are socialist-type organisations or not. That is the same as for the market as a whole. Having too many rules disrupts efficiency. Both Japan and Europe have struggled with that kind of inefficiency. America is a more efficient system; if you brought that kind of a system over here a huge amount of capital would flow in and we would get an efficient system.

H: Japan was a world where there was little competition and a socialist kind of system. Now in the twenty-first century Japan is on the verge of having to change to a real market system.

C: There was a time that America's efficiency was quite bad and Japan's overall economic strength was quite powerful. But now America has done a lot of restructuring and regained business efficiency.

'Efficiency' has become a key word. And it is interesting to note that it is invariably coupled with market systems. Employees have realised that the Japanese system as they knew it – whether they personally liked it or not – was not a true market system.

W: There is a lot of awareness of the corporate guidance problem lately. In bureaucracy-ridden companies it is not a question of ability. You just need the right permission to be able to do business. So companies were no longer operating in a free market system at all.

The bureaucracy's extensive involvement in Japanese business – extolled during the 1980s – is now severely criticised.

H: Japan is basically not a very democratic economy. Finance is strictly controlled by the Ministry of Finance – it is a socialist economy.

A foreign analyst remarked:

> Governments are spectacularly bad at deciding what are good and profitable things for capital to do because their concerns are different. Their concerns are usually with being re-elected. And being elected and allocating capital in the most efficient ways are, in my opinion, incompatible. The best thing the government can do is get out of the

way. They can create the framework. Obviously, you need rules. You need a structure, you need fair trade commissions, whatever, I am preaching capitalism here tooth and claw! But once government decides either directly or in Japan's case, through bureaucracy, how capital is going to be allocated, then I think ultimately that becomes extremely difficult because I think governments are spectacularly bad at picking winners. I think that any individual is spectacularly bad at picking winners. The beauty of an open market system is that nobody has to pick the winners. The winners just appear by lots and lots of people failing and a few people succeeding. You don't have to pick Bill Gates. You just have to allow him to have a shot.

What we have seen so far in this chapter suggests that C-Life employees are now starting to share this kind of viewpoint. They are quite realistic about the Japanese economy and management structures. They appreciate some of the reasons why the economy did so well before and has now experienced a sharp downturn, and they are aware of the different courses management techniques could take in the future. I now deal with their views on the bubble period and its aftermath.

The bubble and after

The C-Life employees generally remembered the bubble with a degree of incredulity, as of a memory that they could not quite believe happened. The following quotes give an idea of how euphoric the age was, especially for those working in the life insurance industry. They were the most popular companies for employment among new recruits, and were lauded continually by the mass media.

P: It was really fun back then in the bubble. It was so much fun that you couldn't help wondering if it was OK for it to be this much fun. It was a really wonderful age.

S: It was a really good period then economically. Everything seemed like it was floating. Stock prices were zooming. The life insurance companies were called 'The Lifers' in capital letters because they were fat with money and all-powerful. Life insurance companies were no longer just selling life insurance but were making money from the investment of that money.

C: The economic climate in Japan was one of high growth for almost all of the period until the bursting of the bubble in 1991. So I experienced both the good times and the bad. In periods of high growth there isn't enough money and then when the bubble came … as for stocks? Every day there was a difference of around 200 billion yen. Every day! …

Stocks spiralled up and up by the day. Company-held stocks increased by the tune of around 200 billion per day.

S: In the bubble period, everything was glittering. And every second man had an opinion about what a salesman should be like … that there should be lots of sales people in the company … or they should be flamboyant in what they do.

K: Various newspapers like the Asahi newspaper put out huge articles saying 'The Amazing Life Insurers!' (*Za Seiho*) flattering the life insurers but now they are trying to beat them down. Because there were these huge articles saying 'Magnificent Life Insurers!' we got a lot of confidence. Life insurers – and employees – as a whole got increased confidence. It would have been OK if people had actually had the strength (*chikara*) or ability together with increased confidence, but a lot of people who didn't have ability got increased confidence as well.

C: At the time of the bubble every Japanese life insurer bought large buildings on Fifth Avenue in New York. 'Japan as Number One' appeared; the country was afloat in euphoria. Even if it wasn't number one it certainly was challenging America on the production front and it had a strong competitive position in world terms. C-Life's international strategy? The high-growth period had led straight into the bubble. Of course, there had been the oil shock and a few glitches along the way but not any really large recessions – until the bubble collapsed. So rather than concentrating on increasing management efficiency, the concentration was on expanding a dream. That was the same both for individuals and for departments.

P: It was really good. It was a period of growth and abundance. At the end of the period there was a time when we had already reached the limits of our growth but it was a very abundant time. If we tried really hard (*gambaru*) we got as many good things in return as the effort that we put in. It was that kind of period.

C: Of course, with the increasing numbers of employees, management was looking at how to most efficiently organise the company and use the manpower, and at personnel management issues and organisational issues, but there was no such thinking like the 'mergers and acquisitions' type thinking that there is now, it was still an age of pure expansion.

We can see that employees at C-Life were caught up in a period of euphoria where investment was expanding so fast that there was no time to sit back and assess the situation properly. The age had the air of unreality, but, caught up inside it, there was no incentive to try and swim against the tide, even if people had wanted to. The employees talk of the bubble as a 'dream'. The company was no longer chasing realistic expansion, only a dream.

The employees also speak of an enormous lift in pride in Japan. This was especially so for the insurance industry. I saw this first-hand when I worked in C-Life's international department myself during the build-up to the peak of the bubble. I was constantly congratulated for having got into the most popular industry for my generation of graduates. Inside the company, I was assisting in managing and making investment recommendations for a portfolio of 2 billion yen. The analysts from the foreign securities companies would come to us regularly to give us their recommendations and try to get our business. These were highly experienced professionals in the financial world who would turn up at C-Life hungry for the enormous business potential in the hands of my 28-year-old colleague and me – just 23 – in a primitive and tiny investment department with not a computer in sight. I remember one of the employees saying at the time that if he had asked them to kiss his feet they would probably have done so. The pride was also caught up in the feeling that Japan was now top of the world and beating the 'West' – mainly the USA – which, since World War II, has invariably been the mirror in which Japan sees itself reflected. The foreign analysts scrambling for our business were one proof of this in practice for the C-Life employees. Many Japanese very much wanted to believe in a superior Japanese form of management.

C: Internationalisation was really going forward rapidly before the bubble. Foreign exchange was really liberalised. And it was possible to invest in overseas assets much more freely than before. We could deal in futures too. We had to really study a lot to acquire new knowledge to handle all of this and to raise specialists. There was a sense of danger in that whole period, I think, in terms of responding to globalisation. And we had to learn management skills to deal with that response. The company set up the international department as part of that response. And they made offices in London and New York and sent people over there to manage them. It was partly a bid to increase investment opportunities and partly to raise people. We hired people from outside of C-Life and we got them to increase their specialist knowledge.

The atmosphere portrayed here is of a company expanding at top speed into the blue without the expertise or past knowledge of what they were doing. They were faced with a new environment, and they had seemingly limitless amounts of money to put into it.

At some time during this, however, the situation began to get unrealistic, something that C-Life employees outside Japan in the overseas offices could see. But for those wallowing in the excitement of the age in Japan, there was no time to reflect on the situation. C-Life, like all the life insurers, was focused on increasing its investments as fast as possible.

P: Unfortunately, right in the middle of the bubble I went to America. When I came back from time to time, I did think that everyone was very 'bubbly' – unsteady (*fua fua*). I thought that. Although it was supposed to be a high-yen recession (*endaka fucho*). When I came back everyone was wearing really nice clothes and spending a lot of money going out drinking in really good places, and saying, 'Have you been here? Have you been there?' – boasting about where they had been. I wondered what was happening. I would get orders from head office, saying, we have this much money behind this plan, so it will be OK to go ahead, and I would think, 'When did things suddenly get this much better?'

Anecdotes of these heady times are endless. One that I like in particular is the story told to me by an analyst in a foreign company which had been involved in securing a major building in New York for one of the Japanese insurers. The Japanese company significantly upped the price that they paid for the building, simply in order to ensure that they could say they were buying the most expensive building in the world at that time.

Apart from the general sense of euphoria, the C-Life employees stressed the importance of domestic competition as a standard of comparison. With each company comparing itself to the others, the reality of the standards was somehow left behind while all the companies slid into dangerous ground together. Watching the other companies led to a sense of security, of the 'we are all in this together' nature.

T: If you were an incredibly switched on business man and a top gun kind of person, I think that you might have changed to safer forms of investment or put stricter conditions on the loans that you were dispersing. But in life insurance companies, there was severe (domestic) competition to get dividend income (*haito rimawari*); to raise the amount of dividends that could be paid out on policies. So they had to make the investment returns better and better. In order to win on that front, they had to invest in stocks, and to invest in places where they could expect large capital gains. There was a lot of competition and you had to compete in that severe competition year after year. So you went on investing in those risky years. And to get out of that spiral would have taken an incredible amount of bravery. There was a very strong consciousness of being in a horizontal line of comparison (*yoko narabi ishiki*). I think that it would have been better if we had got out of that but it wasn't something that you could just think about doing and immediately do. I think that now that we have experienced that once, things will change dramatically.

Once the situation turned sour and the insurers began to rack up large foreign exchange losses, turning their investment profits to nil, they were at a loss what to do.

T: As to why the company didn't change but went on and on toward a bad direction, I think that I had a certain responsibility as one person inside that situation. However, Japan had never had the experience of bad loans increasing rapidly like they did. So they had to face a first-time situation; that combined with the fact that there was a phenomenon of too much money around.

Inevitably, the bubble burst.

T: The bubble burst in 1990 or 1991. Land prices came down; stock prices came down; and everyone thought that it was going to be a temporary thing. New regulations (*soryo kisei*) came in saying don't lend on the basis of real estate. That kind of instruction came from the bureaucrats (*o-yakusho*). That created a hole of demand and the jusenos (finance companies) were rapidly filling in that hole by making loans to fulfil that demand, which everyone thought was really strange at the time.

It took a long time for awareness of how serious the situation was to filter through the country, the industry and C-Life too.

T: But everyone thought that stock prices would recover again before long. I think that everyone thought that. Nobody thought that it would slide into a ten-year recession. It has already been ten years. We had no idea that that would happen. So the company didn't really make any response at all to the situation ... You could still get quite a lot of insurance and money was still flowing into the company. As long as the money was flowing in you had to invest that money somewhere. And as long as you are investing you have to spend a lot of effort into that. So even though a few bad loans appeared they didn't put extra people onto that area at all. They should have done that and the situation might have ended a little bit differently. But even if someone had said that at the time, I really doubt whether it would have been accepted (*toota*) in the company. If you had said something like that at the time, people would have thought that you were a pretty strange character (*kawarimono*). I think that was roughly the same for all financial institutions – not just for us – and it was the common factor pulling everyone down.

The main reason for this was the fact that all of the companies were in the same boat. Moreover, they took a passive stance, expecting the stock market to recover eventually of its own accord. However, people reacted differently from the way they did when the Japanese banks faced similar difficulties; this was because of the peculiarities of the life insurance industry. As one foreign analyst said:

> I would say that people started to get concerned in the '93, '94 period. It didn't take very long for concerns over the banking system to begin to raise issues about whether other financial companies which would face many of the same problems because they were doing many of the same things, and the external environment was common to all of them, in that there was a real estate bubble that burst, and real estate prices collapsed, and you had a stock market bubble that burst and stock market prices that collapsed … Those factors were equally applicable to life insurance companies as they were to banks. The advantage you have in life insurance companies is that you don't have to own up to it. They are mostly mutual, none of them are quoted so they are under no shareholder pressure for disclosure so many of the forces that came to bear on the banks and brought them under pressure to at least discuss the state of their balance sheets were not present for the life insurance companies, and the authorities, particularly the Ministry of Finance, were not interested in discussing the issue, presumably because they didn't have any solution to it.

One employee comments:

T: In 1990 I was in the loan department. And at that time, I was in a section that was doing some of the accounting for the company. So I could see which were the bad loans and which loans money was no longer coming in on. So from that time I could see that things were getting worse and worse. I could see that actually myself in my heart (*mi ni shimite wakattandesu*). I thought this was a really bad situation (*mazui*). I kept on thinking, 'Has this one gone bad as well? And this one too?' From that time onward I had an inkling that we were in a dangerous position (*ususu yabai na to omotta*), and I thought it was going to get really bad. That was the situation already in 1990.

As there was no direct information from the company for a long time about the bad loan situation, the C-Life employees began to realise that the situation was serious. The employees in the loan recovery sections could see that something was wrong with the state of C-Life's loans, as the above comments suggest, and those in the investment sections realised that the losses on C-Life's securities were growing. This kind of information filtered out from those departments through the company by word of mouth. No single employee had all the information. The bad loans, moreover, were not the only problem. Insurance sales began to dip seriously as the recession following the bubble gathered force.

H: The company got really involved in international investment, and they did it on a large scale, but after the bubble it shrank quite a bit. We bought a lot of real estate and expanded our investments in London,

New York and Paris; it was very international. We made large losses domestically; we made large losses internationally; but overall the financial strength of the company dwindled and our overseas activities had to shrink.

According to the employees, not even top management had a grip on the situation.

T: At the time that the bubble burst, there were a lot of disquieting, alarming things happening, and they came out clearly in the figures. I think that the bosses really had the situation on their minds as well. But I think they were far too optimistic about the situation then.

After the bubble burst, Japanese insurers withdrew en masse from international investment. From large-scale forces in international investment they transformed again into what they had been before – domestic companies involved in the sale of life insurance. The international department shrank dramatically, and was eventually disbanded altogether.

S: When the bubble burst, the life insurance companies reverted to being companies that were in the business of selling life insurance … If I knew where the glitter had gone from that period we wouldn't be facing the battle we are facing now!

H: When the time comes to shrink the company, the first cuts they make are to the overseas department; that's the same for banks as well. Now the only banks that are heavily involved in overseas business are those that have a lot of capital. At the time of the bubble, even regional Japanese banks or smaller banks were doing big business in New York, but everyone withdrew. So the only ones left are large-scale companies. So the ones without the financial strength to maintain an international presence came back to domestic business.

In practice, how did the bursting of the bubble affect the everyday lives of the C-Life employees?

Q: Even though it's a recession, it's still usual to see people in a country like Japan walking around looking really well dressed.
P: Well, I think that's because everyone's still wearing the coats that they wore in the bubble. I bought my coat in America in the bubble and I'm still wearing it!
V: Well, mine too – I bought mine a long time ago in Japan.
P: It's that kind of case. At that time, everyone was buying really good quality ones. Mine's 15 per cent cashmere. So there are lots of people still wearing the same clothes. Although I no longer have my Gucci bag,

because it got damaged! But I think the situation is like this now. I didn't think things had gone too far at the time, but I did think, 'This is incredible. The world has really got heaps better'. You couldn't help but think that, if you went back to '87, 8, 9, '90, '91.

V: When the bubble actually burst, I was in England. I went in March of 1990, when the English economy was getting worse and worse, and in March of 1992 I came back to Japan and thought that the Japanese economy was really good. At that time, in England, black clothes were very popular. But now in Japan people are wearing more and more black, and I think it's the same kind of atmosphere. When I first went to England, there were heaps of broken BT public phones. And I wondered if there any public phones that actually worked, because you never saw a broken phone in Japan. But now, about one in every three or four public NTT phones are broken in Japan. I don't have a mobile phone, so I notice things like that. And I think Japan has become closer to the way England was then. When a recession comes, all countries become alike, and violence increases as well.

The bubble, then, together with its aftermath, was an extraordinary period in the lives of these employees. To illustrate this, I here present two case studies. K and C both worked for C-Life throughout the bubble period and during the harsh times that followed.

K: a career through the bubble

When you lend money it's very easy; you do it on the basis of a simple examination. But when you have to get the money back, it is extremely hard (*shindoi*) work. The trend in the world is like that at the moment, and it is really bad news. The person who has the money is the winner – it's like that. They say that they have no money so they can't pay it back. The current trend is that that has become a norm.

I am actually out in the field now (collecting loans – he works for a lending company, a subsidiary of C-Life), so I can feel that this is the case, through my own perceptions (*jikkan*). For example, my schedule today will be like this. I go to work and it is not the loan guarantee company that I do today, it's the capital lease company. There is an audit next week, so I have a meeting about what we are going to do about the settling of accounts at the end of March, the ending of this fiscal year. We have to look at what the situation is with the bad debts, and how we are going to clean them up. I have to be on the receiving end of a series of harsh questions. There is another meeting to decide how we are going to answer those questions today at 11:00. Well, I can't tell you what the content will be, but it's clear from what is happening in the world now. We will be considering how best to accelerate getting the bad loans off our book. We're doing it faster than we'd scheduled to, but the present mood in the world is to tell us to do it faster and faster. So the point will be how much ahead of schedule we'll be told to do it. There's really a lot of pressure on us. For example, if we were a bank – they had a capital injection of public funds; and they used that to clean up the bad loans quickly. But we don't have that benefit. We have to do it with the money that we already have. We are doing it according to plan, but because the banks are doing it so fast, and everyone is calling for a fast recovery of the Japanese economy, the trend is to pressure us to do it faster. So that is the current topic, and it is extremely hard (*shindoi*).

Over the last fourteen years what has happened? The life insurance companies advanced into business in the wider world. There was a lot of money gathered in Japan and there weren't a lot of places to invest it in. That was the situation. So the life insurance companies increasingly had to place their assets overseas. I was at the forefront of all the new work that was going on. I set up the New York office and the London office and then I set up the Luxembourg and Cayman Islands investment subsidiaries. I continued doing such investment-related work all of that period, finally becoming the branch head of the New York office. There I did real estate investment, bond investment and all the varieties of investment that Japanese life insurers were engaged in at the time. I was one of the people responsible for the investments during all that time.

In 1989, I heard about the death of the Emperor in New York while I was branch head. I came back to Japan in March of that year, and did domestic bond investments until 1991. Then from 1992 I went to the auditing department and I did preliminary screening work there – deciding whether it was OK or not to lend money to certain borrowers, or whether we should decide to withdraw from an investment or not – I did that kind of work mainly from 1992 until 1993.

After the collapse of the bubble, I was still involved in looking at the Japanese economy and at corporations. But three years ago, we had a total overhaul of products we had had in the bubble, and I became president of a C-Life subsidiary that guarantees housing loans. I still do all finance-related work. Since three years ago I have been doing work related to clearing up the bad loans. So, in short, ever since Fiona joined the company I was always in international investment but since the bubble collapsed I have been doing domestic work and overseas work related to cleaning up the bad loans. So for the first half of that period and the last half of that period I was doing completely different work. For the first half, I was doing very forward-looking work but in the last half I was cleaning up after we lost the battle, and after the big spending spree. So it has been an extremely harsh life that I've led lately.

The harshest conditions have been, not as long as ten years, but from about 1991 or 1992 after the bubble collapsed. So it has really been from about 1994 that we actually started cleaning up the bad loans. That has been terribly hard (*taihen*). Because at the time, we didn't think the Japanese economy would become like it is now. We thought it would become better, so we were procrastinating about the bad loans, and waiting for the economy to recover first. We thought that land prices and stock prices would go up again, and the Japanese economy would become better. So of course we were making plans on that basis. But actually, the Japanese economy went downhill. So we should have done certain things then that we didn't, and now that it has got this bad we suddenly have to do it all at once. That's how the situation is. And it still hasn't recovered – it hasn't recovered at all.

Of course the bad debts all have guarantees on them, but if the value of the land is going down as well that doesn't mean anything. If the value of the guarantee is 100, and it becomes fifty, and that fifty recovers a little and becomes sixty or seventy, then that's OK and you can recover some of the loan. But what was fifty has become thirty and then twenty or ten, so completely contrary to all our plans, the wounds have become deeper and deeper, and it's got extremely hard for us.

At the height of the bubble I was overseas. As one of the things that happened in the bubble, we bought buildings in New York and Washington. C-Life was also heavily involved in foreign investment in real estate. I was the first person to buy a building overseas – we bought one in Washington. It's quite a long time ago now, but that investment went sour because we were done in by the exchange rate. We didn't make a bad investment in terms of price, but the exchange rate went from 200 yen to the dollar to 100 and something yen to the dollar. So even if the price of the building went up, the price in yen went down sharply and we were done. As long as the exchange rate stayed like that, we were finished. We tried our best, but if the yen goes from 200 to the dollar to 100 – and there was even a time when it went below 100 yen to the dollar – that situation is impossible to handle. I don't think the investments that we made were bad. For example, the building in Washington that we bought at the time of the American bubble; the price of the building did go down, but America is different from Japan. It is a system where the returns on investment are calculated, and on that base the price of the building is determined (*shueki kangen ho*). It's not like Japan, where the land itself can go up very suddenly in price. You can't expect a large price increase on the land when you buy the building in America. If there is a 5 per cent increase in rents, then the building price increases by 1 per cent and you can sell it for that. In Japan, a building might not go up even 1 per cent, but the land itself can go up in price, and you buy a building on that expectation. So now that land in Japan has crashed in value, the wounds are extremely deep. In the case of America, everything is calculated on the basis of income, and you buy on that basis. So your losses are limited. But we invested in America with capital from Japan, so we had to bring the returns back in yen. So when 200 yen to the dollar changed to 100 yen to the dollar, our returns were halved. That is the big difference. The reverberations after that were huge, so everything came tumbling down.

I was the head of the New York branch until just before the bubble burst. At first I had the impression, 'Wow, it has really come to this.' It was the same as America with a ten-year lag. When I first went to America it was just as Japan is now. Financial institutions were going belly up one by one. But what was different to Japan is that the management were all put away in prison. They were cleaning up the bad loans in about 1984, when I went over there. It was a time when American prices suddenly fell (*taika*) so in one sense I had a huge shock and from halfway through I wondered if our investments would end up as bad loans. But that has come round to Japan after a ten-year lag.

The thing that I hate most of all is that everything can change according to the exchange rate. As the Sony president has said, you can make things for a whole year on the basis of the exchange rate being 100 yen to the dollar but if that 100 yen to the dollar changes because of one person's statement in America then all of their efforts can go out the window. That kind of situation is really strange (*okashii*). We build things up one by one (*tsumi ageru*) to make a profit but the money we make from the whole year can be completely destroyed in one second on one person's statement. That is really strange.

We eventually stopped thinking that we should leave the clean-up of the bad loans until later. We tried Jusenos (a type of specialist housing finance company in Japan) to clean up some of those loans, in Japan's post-bubble clean-up. But the Jusenos began to go under, and we began to panic. It was then that intermediary organisations were set up in the middle to handle the bad loans for the Juseno. From that time we saw that there was pressure towards cleaning up the bad loans quickly, and discussion as to whether funds should be taken from public organisations, and used to clean up the loans, or whether it should be left to the private sector to clean up their own mess. As this all became widely debated, we in the life insurance industry realised for the first time how terrible (*taihen*) the situation really was. But the public funds did not come as far as the insurance industry, unfortunately, although there has been an organisation set up to buy up the bad loans.

C's story

C-Life was originally a very healthy company. It had very reliable management. It is really a great pity to think about it now.

In the bubble, I didn't think that that pace could last for ever. But the bubble eventually burst and then stocks decreased at the rate of 100 billion yen a day after that, so I experienced both the good times and the bad. I couldn't have imagined that the bubble would come like it did. At first, when the bubble burst, we thought it was just an adjustment, just another normal economic wave. There are always fluctuations; we never thought it would end up a recession like at present. We realised it really was serious when economic growth dropped sharply too. And then, when stocks dropped even further as a result. Everyone's economic vision turned negative. Company turnover fell and consumer demand slumped. And the negative spiral went on and on.

There was a sense of danger before the bubble burst. But there was no idea at all that the Nikkei, which was at 33,900 at one stage, could fall as low as 12,000. Even though it fell, it fell quite slowly at first, so that we thought continually that it would stop at the 30,000 level or that it would stop at the 27,000 level. Well, that didn't happen through a progression of natural economic factors anyway. The Bank of Japan and the Ministry of Finance loosened monetary policy all of a sudden rather than doing it slowly like America because they decided that real estate prices might increase too sharply otherwise as deregulation advanced. So it was a man-made phenomenon. If it had been a natural movement it might have been predicted. It was the government's policy that was a mistake. I think that is beyond question. It is their mistake that the bubble went on so long and to such excess as well. And their mistake that it collapsed and the economy got so bad afterwards.

In the bubble, land and real estate prices got high very suddenly. It is a fact that they went way beyond where they should have been. Until then the government had put all their concentration on monetary easing and keeping interest rates very very low. But one day, they decided they would regulate large-size loans. So that resulted in a shortage of money and real estate and land prices fell. But even after they fell they kept interest rates high. It was evident that the bubble had to burst, but it would have been better if it was a soft landing. They made the landing really hard and that is where they went wrong. Now the American economy is very strong, but they are controlling it very well with their policies. So although there will be adjustments and down periods in America, I don't think that it will be like the bursting of the bubble in Japan: it will be a softer landing

In C-Life, assets were increasing at the rate of one trillion yen per year up until the bubble burst. If you have as much as one trillion yen in assets you can't increase the amount of money you lend out (as traditional investments) that sharply. So the extra money had to flow into stocks and bonds and real estate investments. For companies to maintain the minimum fixed return to clients of 5.5 per cent (that clients were promised in policies sold at that time) companies had to be incredibly competitive against each other. So in the bubble period, each company was investing in products that were guaranteed to bring in as high a return as possible. All the insurance companies and banks and financial institutions began to invest in the same way altogether.

When the Bank of Japan limited the money supply to put the brakes on that situation, demand for money increased sharply and interest rates rose. Even when the economy was worsening the Bank of Japan maintained that same stance. Interest rates went to around 8 per cent in the end: they were really high. The American economy wasn't too strong at the time either, which was at the background of all of this. It had to carry a Japan with a strong yen. If the yen had weakened, Japan's competitive position would have strengthened and the American economy would have suffered even more damage. So they had to encourage a high yen. Even if Japan wanted to lower interest rates, it wasn't very easy for them to do so in practice. You could call that a kind of courtesy to America, or you could call it pressure.

It has already been ten years since the bubble burst. There was no really strong sense of danger for the first two or three years after it burst. I think the real feeling that something was very wrong came about 1993, 1994. Of course, in any age you have to keep track of results. In the investment department we had investments in loans, real estate, stocks, and bonds. We analysed each of these areas against the available information and tried to improve our managerial efficiency. For example, one issue we dealt with was the number of shares that we held in related companies in long-term mutual shareholding arrangements. We didn't decrease it drastically like we are doing now, but we had begun to shift our stance to one of keeping only those shares that made sense for us in terms of profits, and we sold off the others. And rather than our previous overwhelming concentration on first-rate manufacturing industries, we began to increase the weight of our investments in high-tech, electrical companies, precision instruments and new industries. In terms of foreign investment, because we had got burned so badly on foreign exchange losses through the high yen period, we focused anew on how to contain risk. In terms of real estate investment, we re-valued our portfolios. We made changes in each of the sections that we invested in.

During the bubble period, I was in the finance department. It was a period of high risk and high return although, actually, there had been very little risk management. We were trying to strengthen our risk management ability and re-concentrated on the best way to measure precisely the condition of our portfolios. We realised that we had to bring people up that could do that kind of specialised work, and we realised that in order to keep pace with globalisation we had to consolidate the international department. I was involved in this kind of planning. However, you couldn't even compare the time it took to put these plans into placc and the speed with which the bubble collapsed. And you can't suddenly get back the money that you have lent out to other corporations; if you have lent it out for five years it takes five years to get it back. So a lot of the loans turned bad.

The land myth played a large part in this. Everyone believed that land prices would always rise. So if land was the security for the loan, the loan was made on the assumption that land prices would not fall. And to loan money with the land itself as security was very common at the time. But if that same security has fallen in price to a third or even a fifth of its original value, then the security is no longer adequate for the loan. And the value of the loan is no longer covered by the security. So our bad debts grew and grew.

I don't think that C-Life could have avoided the recession in any way. The amount of money increased vastly in the bubble and if you were a financial institution you couldn't help participating in that. In some form or another money flowed in, and you had to invest that money in order to operate efficiently as a business.

I retired shortly after the bubble burst – at the best time of all probably. I feel apologetic towards those who still remain in the company. I joined the company in 1958 when the high growth period was beginning starting with the burst in demand precipitated by the Korean War and for all of that good period I was in the company. I was the luckiest of all.

Having examined the employees' attitudes towards the economy in general, and the bubble period and the recession which followed, I now discuss their views on the life insurance industry in particular.

The industry

Insurance companies are changing from mutual companies to stock-holding companies, as it is now generally recognised that stakeholder systems do not generally work very well. They lack the ability to respond to changes in the economic environment and become ossified, particularly if there is heavy government interference.

O: If I knew what I know now? Once you know the inside of an industry, well, this industry has changed a lot since then, and the winds are blowing against the life insurance industry as a whole … I probably wouldn't have come into life insurance if I had known this.

The mood in the industry is that it is in trouble. There is no leeway for it to grow as a whole, since the market is almost completely saturated, with over 90 per cent of Japanese households already signed into life insurance policies.

I: It is an age of survival, where survival is quite difficult, especially in the case of life insurance companies, and where there was a myth that life insurance would never go under. But as you know, now several life insurance companies have already gone bankrupt or failed and those are the facts now. People inside the other life insurance companies are conscious now of great danger and they are wondering how they can get by in the new economy in Japan and how to develop the life insurance industry; how to fit with the flow of the current times in the world. And they have to think about how to change the way that they do business and recruit. I think that all companies are facing this challenge now.

And, in the meantime, competition is set to increase dramatically. Companies have withdrawn from overseas markets to concentrate on business at home. Foreign companies are making inroads into the Japanese market. Yet nobody can foresee the extent to which a domestic business such as life insurance will be affected by foreign companies. There is therefore a great sense of uncertainty and pessimism.

J: All the Japanese life insurance companies only have enough leeway to see what is directly under their feet. The influence of the domestic factors is so large that they don't have the leeway to look at overseas factors. But even though they are life insurance companies, they are still financial institutions: from now on the convoy system has disappeared and they have to compete with other financial institutions such as banks and other security companies, and they also have to compete with overseas companies. If they really understood how large that impact is going to be then they have to be looking at those factors (*Mata ta ni me ga iku hazu desu yo ne*).

K: I think that the insurance industry will recover, but it's something that will take a long time. If you use public funding to sort out the problems, you can clean the bad loans up quickly, and you can help the Japanese economy to become better quickly; that's why they started doing that with the banks. But even if help does come to the life insurance

> industry, the problem is when. The government is currently saying to the life insurance industry: do it with the money you already have. I don't think it will happen next year; that would be very difficult.

The fact, already mentioned above by some respondents, that government money will not be used to bail out the insurance industry is crucial. Because aid is not forthcoming, the industry is left with little option but to withdraw from foreign markets and concentrate on its domestic business. As one analyst comments:

> To be fair, in most cases, the biggest burden has fallen on policy-holders. Unlike the banks where depositors have been universally protected, the policy-holders in Nissan Life and most recently in Toho Life are going to take some very substantial pain by being involved in a failed company. So this is definitely being played by different rules. And government, or taxpayer money is being used much more sparingly than was the case in the banks.
>
> The fact is that the policy-holders have no choice. They are being locked in. Their returns are being reduced. Basically, the Ministry of Finance has bolted the door and are flooding the room. There is no way out of this. They reduce surrender values to zero. And then they say the guaranteed rate has been dropped from 5 per cent to 1 1/2 per cent. That is it.
>
> So they are being much more severe with policy-holders then. For the very simple reason that policy-holders have very few options. If you were to do that with bank depositors, depositors at every other bank that was considered even slightly shaky would immediately pull their money and that would cause a riot. You would have the domino effect, systematic collapse, across a whole range of banks, and even banks that were not shaky would fail because depositors would be asking for their money back so the authorities are well aware that they have to prevent that kind of US 1929 crash scenario. It's not a risk in the life insurance industry because the policy-holders can't get their money out. I'd say it is a very cynical approach. It has nothing to do with fairness, it has nothing to do with contractual obligations about what people were led to believe, or whose fault it was. It has everything to do with the practical aspects that they can get away with it.

There currently seems to be a sense of considerable confusion and resignation about the direction of the economy. The overall mood is that of pessimism, and most employees are stuck, unable to move to more secure positions. After ten years of a recession that no-one originally thought could possibly last that long, C-Life employees have lost the confidence or enthusiasm of predicting future directions at all.

Y: People ask whether the Japanese economy has hit bottom yet or not. Asking whether the insurance industry has finished restructuring is the same kind of fathomless question. It is impossible to answer either.

In this section, then, we have briefly seen how the situation is regarded by C-Life employees. They recognise the bleakness of the economic climate, but are largely resigned to whatever happens. I turn now to C-Life itself, where the effects of the recession have proved even more drastic than in other life insurance companies. I begin with M, whom we interviewed just a couple of hours after he had been asked to leave the company. His case study graphically illustrates not only the effect that the restructuring had on people's lives, but also how shocked many employees were by the drastic steps being taken.

The current situation of C-Life

M: a case study in restructuring

> Our company's restructuring plan got announced on 30 November. And today is the day that my death warrant was signed (*meinichi to kan ni meijita wake desu*).
>
> There are only 2,400 people in our company, but the restructuring plan calls for 800 of them to be laid off. Before now there were such cases as Kanematsu laying off 500, or Nippon Steel laying off a couple of hundred. You hear about other companies and figures like that. Mitsukoshi laid off 300. Compared to those figures, 800 will have a huge impact. So 30 November was the signing of my death warrant.
>
> I was the first to be called. There are thirty-three salesmen in my department but I am the only one who came into C-Life from outside, who transferred from another company. I was called because I was the last person to join the company. I should be in the one of the strongest positions because I have experience of selling securities in the securities business. I can teach the stock business to other C-Life people and I have connections at the places that we have to do business. But they told me that because I had special skills it would be easier for me to find another job than for some of the other guys. They said they could see that I could find another path. They spoke to me candidly and frankly as if they had chosen me especially.
>
> That is really like C-Life. It is true that I have had a number of job changes, but I know how hard it is to change jobs because of that. The boss told me I had better consider changing jobs again very seriously. I told him it is no joke! I have been working really hard making plans and talking to people trying to get the sales targets that the bosses had set for me earlier. I told him that I wanted to go on working here. I have

already changed jobs four times. And now I have to decide again by 27 January. That is the deadline. They have ordered me to request resignation by then.

Not everyone was told to leave out of the thirty-three salesmen; it was mainly the older ones who were told. Everyone is in a huge panic, wondering if they are going to be the next. The guy who sits next to me has already decided that he will resign.

We were all called to a basement room, the room of our sales head. He told us that 800 people would be 'restructured'. It should be really big news. But they must be suppressing it because the company is in good with the *Nikkei* newspaper. At the meeting he first sat us all down and then he got out a copy of *Bungeishunshu*, a popular weekly magazine. He showed us the articles about the Nikko Securities Detainment Room Incident. They got a group of people who were the targets of a restructuring plan together and put them in one room where they were given no work until they resigned of their own accord. He explained that this was the kind of thing that was going on. It is no longer like it was in the past. No-one should be surprised that an article like this appears in a magazine because these are the times. This is how much restructuring is happening in Japan and how common it is. He said, you are among the targets of the restructuring plan and we will decide who shall be the ones to go on the basis of results. Anyone on the lower half of the graph that we draw up will be asked to leave. So think carefully about this. The meeting finished and I was the first to be called. My results were third from the bottom. C-Life had already been advertising for people to quit of their own accord, but they were advertising for people of above 45. I am still 43 so I thought that I would be OK for another two years.

I can only get ten months of unemployment insurance.

The situation in our company is very harsh. We will restructure 850 people in total; fifty of those are already retirement age and the others will be chosen from among the normal workforce. 400 are to be chosen by this spring and the remaining 400 by the following autumn. This time it is really terrible. It is anyone who has been in the company for more than five years, or who is less than 49 years old: everyone in our department fits into that category! I can't believe that such a restructuring plan was announced. It really is my death warrant.

It came intensively to me for some reason. They told me that I must be brave since I had already changed jobs four times, that I must have a lot of energy and I must be tough. They don't call the guys who are sickly and can't work a lot, and they don't call the people who are likely to rebel or to cause big problems about it. They call up people with some kind of skill. They called me up for that reason. They said: because I had the ability to find a job elsewhere. The company doesn't really care if the employees are valuable to them or not. That is really

> Japanese. It is the last-in-first-out principle. The last guy in apart from me is sickly so he didn't get called.
>
> I do think that it can't be helped considering the condition of the company. But people have been saying that the company is in danger for five or six years now. In 1997, when Yamaichi went bankrupt, I thought the end was near for us as well. But we survived that and I thought that perhaps we were going to be OK. And then all of a sudden this huge restructuring plan! I was really surprised.
>
> I thought that I would live my whole life out in C-Life. Because it is easy … If I can find a way to remain I would still want to do so even if the atmosphere wasn't very good after I tried to remain.
>
> But then there is the risk of the company going under as well … I have to take that into consideration too.

As these last comments suggest, the restructuring plan has come as a shock to C-Life employees because it involves laying off an unexpectedly large number of employees – 800 people – and because this number includes a very wide range of people – those only five years in the company upwards. M's dramatic account of his experience gives us some valuable insights into the principles underlying the restructuring, and the attitudes of the employees to it.

One of the most striking features of the plan was the fact that the company was laying off people with skills or older people. They were less likely to drop sickly people or those likely to rebel. Those who would find it easier than others to find a new job were expected to make the sacrifice. The company therefore adhered to the principle of putting the group above the individual even at times of such crisis. The value of the person to the company was not the primary factor in choosing whom to fire, but only one factor among others. Thus, there is an emphasis on the group even when choosing whom to fire, although, as we shall see, avoidance of responsibility by the bosses during the firing was also a factor. Paradoxically, of course, the fact that all the able people were laid off while those without the skills necessary to find a new job were retained could hardly help the already ailing company's performance.

Officially, the restructuring is not an order, but in reality the employees have little choice. This is why M makes such paradoxical comments as: 'They have ordered me to request resignation'. The way that M's boss introduces restructuring by showing a magazine article illustrates several points of note. It is a shock tactic to bring home how severe the situation is. He emphasises that this is the nature of the times, and that the same thing is happening to all kinds of people and companies. But it also contains a veiled threat. The example given is meant to signal to employees that bullying and ostracism are the likely outcome for employees who defy the request to hand in their resignation.

M's response to the restructuring, on the other hand, displays little attachment to the company or any depth of loyalty. It is based entirely on his wish for security. He wants to remain in C-Life 'because it is easy'. He wishes to remain 'even if the atmosphere wasn't good after I remain', meaning that he realises he would have to suffer some kind of ostracism or perhaps a transfer to an undesirable job in the company. He is prepared to suffer this in order to achieve the security of staying. This strong wish for security by staying inside the company is balanced against the risk of losing the opportunity, afforded by the restructuring plan, of leaving the company with increased retirement benefits before it goes under.

The experience of M, then, illustrates both the shock felt by many employees at the announcement of the restructuring plan and the effect it had on those who suffered through it. In the next chapter, I discuss the restructuring plan in more depth. First, however, I consider the situation before the plan was announced. What was the atmosphere like in C-Life at the time, and what did employees think would happen to them?

Inside the company

The 800 lay-offs were the culmination of a series of measures taken by C-Life's management to try to reverse the ailing company's performance. One of these, introduced a few months before the restructuring, was a company-wide pay cut.

Q: So at the moment, has the company not decided to make everyone suffer together, by having a 6 per cent pay cut across the board?

K: Well, making that pay cut may mentally be a backward-looking idea, but I think we have to try a lot harder with the way we manage.

At the end of 1999, on top of a number of pay cuts over the previous two or three years – first, cuts for directors, and then further cuts for all management – C-Life implemented a 6 per cent pay cut across the board for all employees. This proved to be very distressing for the C-Life employees. For most employees with families to support, the men's pay packets went straight into the family account and were controlled by the wives. In turn, they received a certain amount of pocket money, also dispensed by their wives. This amount ranged from around 6 per cent of the pay packet to 15 per cent in some cases. Thus, for some families that were operating on a tight budget, a 6 per cent pay cut more or less meant that spending money was no longer available as it had been before. Among my *doki* (members of the same year-group), for example, there were families with three young children with educational expenses and a hefty mortgage on a house bought at the height of the bubble for exorbitant sums of money. These families were suffering in earnest from the size of that pay cut. However, many employees accepted that the pay cut was fair, and that management had been driven to it. Employees are, in general, far more concerned with security than with material rewards such as high pay; and the union accepted that it was better for everyone to have less pay than for some people to lose their jobs.

Y: Is all suffering a 6 per cent pay cut together one of the demerits of the life-time employment system? Well, whether you call it suffering ... it is something that we have to do in order to win. It is harsh on the individual at the level of his everyday life to cut his salary. But there is no way to win without doing that. So the salary cut is to enable the company to regain its competitive edge. That is economic principle; it is directly connected to competitiveness. It isn't necessarily the case in Japan where consumer spending is so low that cutting salaries would harm things even more now. You have to match the policy to the circumstances. Restructuring is about trying to make the parts of the company that are growing grow more while rearranging and cutting the unprofitable sections. That is what we are trying to do now. The pay cut is just one of many things that the company has to do to make itself profitable. There are probably many more things that the company could do but I think that they are thinking of them and looking out the ways.

Ex-employees who have left the company as a result of restructuring are, by contrast, less accepting of management's handling of the situation, and suggest more drastic measures that could have been taken.

H: I think it's completely normal that C-Life pay has been reduced in the bad economic conditions. The results of the company are bad – I think that they have to do things even more drastically – to tell the truth the best thing to do would be telephone marketing – fire everyone in the finance department and put in telephone marketing. That would be the cheapest thing to do or get rid of all the sales women and put in young people but they can't do that because it's a co-operative body (*kyodotai*).

Only a couple of months after the pay cut, the restructuring plan was announced in early 2000. The company planned to ask 800 people to 'voluntarily retire'. In effect, this meant that 800 people were to be fired. Even for those not directly involved in the restructuring, the news brought home the fact that the company was seriously in trouble. For around two years, the media had outlined the problems of life insurers, with particular focus on C-Life, which had dropped from its previous ranking among the top eight in Japan to a position well down the ranks, among smaller, more precarious companies. C-Life employees were subdued as they pondered the implications of the plan. Despite the extensive media coverage of the company's problems, many employees inside were still shocked by the suddenness of what was happening.

K: The retirement age at C-Life is 60, so I have two years to go. I had hoped that I would be able to retire at the end happily, but it doesn't look like it. I worked in this company for thirty years, and right at the very end is where your last memories remain from. Rather than the good times in the middle, you are left with a stronger impression of the years at the end. I will be leaving the hardest tasks to my juniors, and I think that that is really tough (*tsurai*) to think about as well.

Employees are aware that the restructuring at C-Life is simply part of a wider pattern in Japan. All around them there is evidence of lay-offs and restructuring, in the media, and even in the streets, as the numbers of homeless have increased sharply in Tokyo as the recession drags on. But as no clear pattern has emerged regarding what the C-Life employees can do in practical terms about increasing their skills; many of them are left in a stressful situation without many options.

E: There are men now who have lost their means of livelihood. People have for many years been inside the seniority system, where not only ability but a lot of other factors were counted. People who had high salaries inside that system are now being cut in the name of efficiency. And that is how it must be. People are talking about a new system based on ability, but we don't yet have a system based completely on ability.

Under these circumstances, it is hardly surprising that the atmosphere inside C-Life during my last bout of fieldwork was one of enormous tension and anxiety.

Y: The age has changed. The situation is much more competitive and culture and customs will no doubt change along with that. It is happening and there is nothing you can do to avoid it so you have to accept it in the end. There is a sense of crisis or danger at the moment I would say. The insurance world is really harsh. It used to be secure to be in a large company and there was a feeling of stability too. Now there isn't. But that is why we have to work to change that, that is why we have to make the reforms. I don't think anyone expects to find stability and security in companies any more so it is beside the point somewhat that the sense of security has been badly eroded.

J: As far as the feeling of insecurity inside C-Life now, I think that other life insurers have come to the situation that C-Life is in now as well. It is very natural for everyone to be insecure. It is not only the medium-sized C-Life; it is even the huge companies, and most of them are mutual companies so there is no possibility that they could suddenly be acquired. If they merge with foreign companies the standards are all going to be changed inside the companies and the way in which work is done. I think everyone in practically any company now is very insecure. There is insecurity that the jobs will change in content and insecurity that the industry itself will change drastically and suddenly. In Japanese companies employees are rotated from position to position, and there are always cases where people suddenly go from sales to planning or from planning to public relations, where the type of job that they do changes. So I don't think that there is insecurity about the type of work changing because they have always had rotation. In a nutshell, they are terribly insecure that the company itself will go under.

In the confusion, employees had radically different views of what was happening. But only a minority of employees were actually doing anything about it. Some were actively scouting around for other jobs, some were preparing their resumes. In fact, during this period I was inundated with requests from C-Life employees who – after having been interviewed for the film during the daytime at the company – would call me at home at night to ask me surreptitiously if I could correct their English resumes for them! Almost all the employees gave at least a casual glance to the pages in the paper advertising jobs for mid-career transferees and followed the topic with interest: who went where, how much did they get, and so on. Others were pessimistic about the industry and depressed about the forecast for C-Life, but were still unable to move because of the lack of alternatives.

H: Whichever path C-Life takes it's certain that a harsh environment is awaiting them. Well, I think that C-Life is approaching the status of a Titanic and I don't think that can be helped. Young people inside the company are quitting. Young people who are really motivated are leaving the sinking ship already. So the people behind are there because it can't be helped, because there's nowhere for them to go.

T: The interim balance sheet is already out and same as before the really harsh conditions are continuing. How dangerous is the company exactly? Inside the company they are saying that it is an emergency … that it is an emergency situation. And that is getting even more severe now. Even in normal conferences inside the company they are talking about emergencies. I don't think that they can sit tranquilly any more inside that situation. I think that they already know what the situation is. Or rather than saying that they just know about, I think that now everyone in the company now has the clear understanding what the situation is.

It was immensely difficult to judge what people were really thinking about C-Life's chances, since their actions always suggested that they had hopes for the company's recovery. However, the situation was actually very unclear. The president failed to give clear-cut messages in his speeches and the employees themselves were unable to take action.

T: Do the bosses at the conferences mention the situation or initiate action? There was the president's speech a short while ago. The present president's speeches talk about how harsh the situation is. But it is not a situation where people can just quit and go somewhere else. So it is hard to say whether the pace of people quitting is still really increasing. If people had somewhere to go that would be OK. But only those younger than about 35 have somewhere to go. For older people, unless they have incredible abilities, it is really hard for them to go anywhere else.

A minority of employees maintained that the company would recover, and it was up to the efforts of the employees. They were in battle mode, determined to do their best to save the company.

T: How is the insecurity inside the company? Well, I quit three or four months ago now ... but when you go out drinking that kind of topic comes out. Everyone still has their own work in their own areas to do and you can't just live in total insecurity every day. And for the people for whom lack of trust of the general public in the company reflects on their everyday work – for example, the sales people – the public bring out all kinds of magazines (and challenge them) – that kind of information is now in the magazines and the customers know it ... I think it is really really difficult for them to do their work now.

The salesmen had to spend their days reassuring customers that the company was in fact perfectly all right. It is not surprising that many of them were the most fervent believers in the company's eventual recovery. Nevertheless, they were perhaps not alone in their basic convictions. I think that a majority of C-Life employees, even those who were choosing to leave the company, basically believed that the company would survive. There was also considerable divergence in opinions regarding the responsibility of management, and whether management was aware of the true state of the company. I don't believe that many C-Life employees had really considered the possibility that management really knew whether the company would go under, but was not giving out any information to the employees. But industry analysts thought this might well be the case:

> They are already dead but they just don't know it. I would say that senior management is probably very well aware of the present-day reality; equally, continuing with the gambler analogy they still believe that their luck will change for the better and that they have just got to hang on in there and that it can still go right. So I think it is triumph of hope over experience. They recognise that, yes, they are down, they are in serious trouble and the wife is going to give them hell when they get home. But they know that just one more roll of the roulette wheel could

turn it all around and maybe it'll come right and because they have no choice they have to believe that it could come right. And there are chances. If the TSE goes to 40,000, interest rates go to 4 per cent, real estate values start to recover, it could still work. It is not that it is impossible for C-Life or any of the other companies that face difficulties to recover. I just say that it is unlikely.

The general mood of optimism probably had something to do with the fact that the company had been in trouble before but always survived; it thus may have seemed not unreasonable to suppose that it would do so again. The company, together with a number of others, had been narrowly saved by a sudden and unexpected increase in the benchmark Nikkei stock index the previous year. C-Life, like other insurance companies, had massive amounts of money invested in domestic stocks that had been bought at high prices during the bubble. The valuation of these stocks affected the company enormously and a sudden plunge in the Nikkei could have brought them down very quickly.

T: At the point of time of March last year (end of fiscal year) there were rumours that the company might go under. There were really harsh conditions last year in March. But at the last minute, a divine wind blew, and the stock prices suddenly shot up right before the end of the fiscal year just within two months. Because new regulations (*kinyuzaiseiho*) came in, foreigners began investing huge amounts in Japanese stocks and it boosted the market sharply. The Nikkei had been hovering around the 15,000 level. If it had fallen to around 13,000 it would have been really dangerous for the company. It could have gone under. And it could have been the case that the company was unable to pay its debts. The company was also OK in September (at the time of the interim report). Because the stock prices have gone up, the situation is better even though land prices are still falling as before. There seems to be a pause in the situation. In March, if the accountants can't pass the company's books it could go under.

This vague belief that things would probably turn out all right rested uneasily with the determination of some employees to do everything they could to save the company. In the following comment, we can see this curious mix of battle attitude – whereby the employee seems to suggest that they all need to fight together to see the situation through and survive – and a surrendering of responsibility in a firm belief that management are probably doing their best.

V: As to how C-Life is, that's a really delicate topic. There are a lot of delicate issues connected with that; it's hard to comment. It's really harsh in the company now, really harsh. But it's now an age of survival. So it's a case of thinking about how we can live through it. You have to think about whether you're going to live through it alone or with other people. It's an age when you have to think very seriously about these matters. I think that everyone is thinking very seriously about these things. I'm not a member of management, so I don't know the actual details, but it is inevitable that they're thinking about it.

Some employees were very realistic about the company situation, and accepted that whatever would happen would happen. These employees were invariably those who were in safe positions, however. The following comments are by an employee in one of C-Life's investment subsidiaries, which, being a separate company, would survive even if C-Life fell.

Y: I think the pace of restructuring is reasonable. I think it is an adequate pace. There is the possibility that my company will restructure as well like other examples in the media lately. We don't know what will happen yet. As far as I am concerned, I think that if it is the logical thing to do that they will do it. It is economic rationality that will decide that. If the environment changes and a company decides to merge with another for rational reasons then the individual should accept that. Nothing can even begin if the individuals involved say no to that. I don't think that Japanese are necessarily opposed to mergers anymore. The age has changed now.

There was, then, a surprising mood of optimism at the time of the restructuring. At the same time, however, employees were beginning to think seriously about management styles and about what should be done to save the company. In the harsh circumstances under which sales people find it increasingly difficult to sell, C-Life employees were reassessing the aims of the company and how they should be doing business. C-Life employees had been accustomed to doing what they were asked without thinking too much about the efficiency of what they were doing. Larger questions were left to top management. But one can say that the primary aim of the company, as indeed for other companies too, was 'pure expansion': growing in terms of policy numbers without necessarily trying to increase profits. This became glaringly obvious in the post-bubble period, as policy cancellations became more numerous, which meant that the number of new policies being taken out was no longer a reliable measure of how the company was doing.

S: Our everyday goals are aimed at us becoming number one (among C-Life branches). But there are all kinds of things to become number one at – the number of salesmen, the turnover, profits – from now on I think it's the most important thing to become number one in profits. To be number one in the number of people you have or in turnover is nonsense. Sometimes we obtain two billion yen worth of policies. So what? We could have two billion yen worth of customers turn in their policies tomorrow and then we'd be back to zero. There are customers that come in and there are customers that surrender their policies.

The employees showed a new realism and interest in larger issues such as the future of the industry as a whole, or in what capacity C-Life might survive.

A: There is both the competitiveness of the industry as a whole and that of individual companies that need be considered. You can't just take C-Life as a single company and say: 'Let's make it more competitive. If it doesn't become competitive then that is carelessness and lack of preparation.' You have to also think about how the life insurance is competing against other kinds of financial institutions. With the financial phenomenon called 'Big Bang', you have to think about whether the company can remain inside the financial industry in its current shape. I think it would be hard for it to survive just within the category 'life insurance company'.

This level of consideration of the issues meant that employees tended to be quite stoical about the steps taken by management to save the company. There was a real acceptance of the fact that the company had to restructure. I saw no evidence of militant positions against the restructuring, even from former and current union members.

K: There is more pain than there was before, so the people who are quitting early have suffered less. As far as C-Life goes, basically, we have a necessity to protect the policy-holders. If the company goes down, or if we decrease dividends, the policy-holders will make losses. We are not the only life insurance company – of course there are other life insurance companies as well, and foreign life insurers are coming into the market as well, so it will get increasingly competitive. Basically, you have to pay the guaranteed dividends properly. And then it becomes a matter of how you can hold back expenditure, and you can't cut expenses just by using one less light bulb or one less pencil. Of course we are economising, but it's not enough. Because life insurers are people-based companies, the personnel costs are big. We are fundamentally different from manufacturing companies.

C-Life employees also accepted the need for the company to consolidate departments and make the structure of the company more efficient. They were conscious of the negative aspects of Japanese management and were able to discuss the reasons why the economy had gone downhill. They accepted that the company had been inefficient and needed to change.

E: In the life insurance industry ever since the war it has been protected by the bureaucracy, but now we are on the eve of Big Bang where the industry will be liberalised. So until now we had an at-home kind of atmosphere and we kind of arrived lazily to here. But from now on, we have to become more efficient to cope with a more severe atmosphere and to restructure.

All the former international department employees whom I talked to said that, although it was a pity that they themselves could no longer work in the international department, it was natural that the company had had to do away with it.

K: We had been investing in securities both internationally and domestically out of separate sections until the bubble. But it is now an age where domestic information flows overseas very quickly and overseas information comes in as well. If American stocks go up, Japanese stocks go up as well, so if there are walls between different sections it is strange (*okashii*). So we needed to handle foreign stocks and Japanese stocks together. We changed eventually to the form where if we were dealing in securities, we treated international and domestic securities in the same way. There is still a problem for the personnel department over how to treat staff in the foreign offices, but for investment itself I think there are few companies now that have international stock departments, international bond departments or international loan departments separate from the domestic sections.

There was quite a difference between the employees still inside C-Life and those who had left. The latter were more realistic in summing up the sorry state of the industry and company, and more vocal in their criticisms. But they were talking to the employees still inside, and I think that they were having some influence there. One employee who has quit the company talked to one still inside as follows:

H: I am telling you to hurry up and quit. And by that I mean that if you are going to make the same effort then you might as well make the effort in an environment that is growing. In other words, the whole insurance industry is shrinking and so no matter how much effort you put in and no matter how talented a salesman you are you can't get the sales. There are many growing businesses among the internet businesses. If you go to that kind of a place and make the same effort you will get the business; that is a personal choice. It is hard to just jump in by yourself but if the company is pushing you out anyway it is a real chance if you look at it like that.

The older members of the company expressed a lot of regret that people were fired during the restructuring without having the chance to prove themselves in other sections of the company, which is what they would normally have been allowed to do.

K: At the moment, the current trend is that all you need to do is to concentrate on making your own section good. And if you don't like that section in the company, rather than continuing to persevere in the company people think that other companies might be better. Before, if you couldn't use your abilities adequately at one post, you could go to another post in the company. Or you would change your attitude, or start off with a fresh feeling (*kibun tenkan*). People would tell you to try your abilities somewhere else in the company. In a good sense, there was leeway for people to do that. Now, if one section is bad, people are just cut (*pon to kiru*). Rather than talented people going to the next section and experiencing hardship again from the very beginning, they just change companies and increase their pay and think it is better to do that. That's an American trend. I think it's a pity that the trend is going that way. That might be the solution for the individual, but I think it's really a sad thing (*zannen*). The Japanese system of rotation is really important in developing people (*sodateru*). In America, at the time I was there, really good companies also rotated people, and brought them up to be real managers. There were quite a few companies like that, although of course there were also companies that would just cut people.

Starting off again with a 'fresh feeling' is an important concept. I often saw employees at C-Life, faced with a situation that they could do nothing about, do an about-face and make a conscious decision to accept the situation and do their very best at it anyway.

In this chapter, we have seen what the atmosphere was like in C-Life at the time of the restructuring. It was highly confused: there was a general feeling of optimism, that the company would pull through, but this seems to have had something of a paralysing effect, with most employees doing little about the situation apart from glancing through the job ads each day. At the same time, there was much questioning of the traditional ways of doing things and discussion of how the company should be saved, and the steps taken by management to help the situation were therefore largely accepted. Nevertheless, the restructuring was a shock to many when it was announced. In the next chapter therefore I turn to a discussion of the effects of this plan on employees.

4 Restructuring

In the last chapter, we looked at employee views of the current situation with regard both the Japanese economy and to the state of C-Life. In this chapter I turn to the restructuring itself. Once again, my aim is not to describe the plan itself in detail: it is to look at how it affected the employees, and how they personally reacted to it.

Restructuring and C-Life

As with the pay cuts, many people accepted that management has little choice but to introduce the restructuring plan. Many others, however, believed that management were at fault for getting the company into such a mess in the first place. The following comments illustrate some of the prevalent attitudes.

K: It's in the newspapers now that we need to carry out a really large restructuring. We haven't done it that dramatically yet. But in order to respond to the present environment, we can't carry on as we have until now, playing the same game with extra innings after extra innings. I don't think we'll go as far as Nissan did, but I think that if we don't do something close to that then it'll be extremely difficult. I think there's no choice but to cut people, because the basic problem is high personnel costs. If you don't get those down then there's no hope. They may initiate 'recommended retirement', or they may ask people if they want to retire. But even asking people if they want to retire is likely to get smaller numbers than we need to cut, so there is a need to cut the personnel costs of everyone as well. So it's likely that everyone will suffer together no matter what else happens. In the end, I think it will have to be a joint decision of everybody, ultimately. At the moment everyone is suffering together through pay cuts – that has applied to everybody. But the people who have quit until now have quit early with bonuses paid on top of their retirement money.

I: C-Life has to cut people or they will go under. It's the management's decision who actually does it. If things continue the staff may become angry. At the moment they're trying to make everyone poorer together. They should be like Nissan and cut heavily in certain places and do things well with the people that remain. They say that they are reducing a certain number of people but it's not going far enough at all: it is half-baked (*chutohampa*). In a financial institution, trust is a big issue and they need to build a back-log of trust. So the present management corps should all be fired. If they don't do that they will just go on and on and on (*zuru zuru*) and everything will eventually blow up.

P: I don't know the standards that they will use when they restructure – I wonder what kinds of structure they will use.

V: It is probably the case that there are no clear standards. When I put my proposal to C-Life to go overseas to study, my boss at the time had lived in Los Angeles. When I had been in the company for two years, he said that he wanted to make the selection criteria for sending people overseas open and clear, and he asked me to do that – that was extremely unusual, that kind of person is extremely rare. It's very rare to find someone who wants to make criteria like that open. Almost all people apply to go overseas, but because the criteria are so abstract you can say anything to anybody about why they were not selected. Although they have something they call standards, you don't know if they really are standards. In that sense, things have gone backwards, back to the normal environment of a Japanese company. People think they know what the criteria are, but if you ask if they're really clear – no, they're not.

P: Is it not better that things aren't very clear? I think it is better that they aren't. I think that is the same in either East or West. If an American company restructures do they really have clear standards? And do they persuade everyone according to those standards so that everyone is satisfied that they are going to be fired? Are there any standards that can satisfy people in those circumstances? So that they will be satisfied and say, 'Well, yes, I guess that I didn't work very hard?'

V: No, that is not the case. The real difference is the form of the objective standards. In Japan it is the length of the years that one has worked that decides it. So it is the people that have worked the least number of years that are cut. It is all decided on that.

P: Yes, that does happen, doesn't it.

V: If you ask why that is, it's because everyone has a basic salary (*shokumukyu*), so if you have been working for twenty years or if you have been working for five years you still get the same base pay. However, if you are going to get fired it is the people who have worked for five years who get fired first, and then the people who have been working for twenty years are the last ones.

P: Yeah, that is the case, definitely. Although not all cases are like that. There are some companies that cut from the people that have been there the less time.

V: It is not the age that a person is; it is how long they have worked in the company.

P: Well, there are companies like that in America, yes. If you ask how it is in Japan it is all about balance. So if you have a chart of the population profile of the company … you know a chart that looks like a bell, with few people at the top and a lot of people at the bottom. And they look at that and try to take the balance in Japan. So if the graph looks like the shape of a person there are places that stick out and places that go in. And the Japanese company tries to look at that and shape that up. Well, not really shape it up, they want to make it appear flat.

V: They cut the places that are sticking out.

P: So they try to make it flat. It is not really that they are trying to make it the ideal life-time employment pattern. They are trying to make it flat. So they say, for example, let's take the people above this point and smooth out this protruding point. Or this place is narrower so let's not move them very much. And this is sticking out again so let's cut there. And they look in that fashion at the whole organisation. And then within that they probably look at ability.

V: But ability isn't the only thing.

P: They look at ability and various factors, I think.

V: No, they don't think that much about it. They don't complicate things that much.

P: And after that it is all pandemonium (*fukumaden*). Because it is completely subjective after that. As a general outline they say that they want to make it into this kind of form. They say that they want to make the waist, the bust and the hips all the same. So if there is a place that is sticking out dramatically, then they try to cut people from within that generation. But when they cut, even though they try to set it on objective data, it has to become subjective. For example, they look at the past results, or how a person has fulfilled their work … and they put an evaluation on that. In any company they would do that … and anyway they have this kind of evaluation every year anyway. So the result of that evaluation might be C out of A, B or C. And if a person had all C's, they might be evaluated badly.

J: I do think partly that it is a pity that Japanese management may disappear. For anybody, if their own company was to disappear it is as if their hometown were to just disappear. Of course, it would be much better if that never had to happen. I think that was the same for the people from Yamaichi Securities that went under a couple of years ago.

As a general rule, the older the C-Life employees are, the more strongly they identify with the company. There are many ways of expressing this identification: the name card that introduces the employee to the world as a C-Life man, the time they spend with company men and the degree to which they sacrifice their private life to the company. Loyalty – and identification with the company – is an essential virtue.

P: For a Japanese salaryman, it's important to be able to hold their name card out and say, 'I am so-and-so from such-and-such a company.' It's a matter of status – it's a kind of brand. Japanese have a strong tendency towards liking brands. Unfortunately that's very strong. Isn't it the case, that even universities, even junior high schools and kindergartens have brands? They even have murder cases over brands.

As the comment below demonstrates, loyalty is always linked to the ability of the employee to leave, that is, the degree to which they are dependent on C-Life. The less dependent an employee is on C-Life – that is, the more skills they have that would allow them to find a new job if necessary – the less loyal they are likely to be to the company.

J: I think that it is a little bit the case that because people are attached to the company they fear that if the company disappears, their identity will as well. But if you put it a little differently, if there are people working in C-Life that had a father who had assets or was a billionaire and they could eat without working and have an easy life anyway, even if the company disappeared I don't think that they would be insecure. It is not really the attachment that people have to the company after all.

J: If people are restructured, I don't think that they're all that sad. I don't think that is a big part of it at all. For normal people, it is because their income is going to disappear that their insecurity is the biggest. It is that rather than any kind of sense of attachment.

Part of the problem in the restructuring plan was deciding who should be laid off.

P: The present system (of deciding whom to fire) won't change as long as they don't get certain standards for cutting people; if it doesn't change to a pay-based system where a certain job costs so much per year, for example, and in order to get someone to do that job you determine how much you should pay him. If it doesn't change like that then basically it is still the life-time employment system. So you look at such things as whether people are at the end of their 30s or in the middle of their 40s and if they have children or not. Well, if I was the person in the personnel department responsible for making the firing decisions then I would really wonder about what I should do. It is easier to cut people in their late 20s or people in their early 30s – just cut the ties and cut them off – even though they have ability. Because those guys aren't going to be in as much difficulty (*komaranai*). Also, for example, they look at whether the spouse is working in a really stable place, men or women.

One of the problems for C-Life at the time of the restructuring, as we have seen already in chapter 3, was that the personnel department instinctively wanted to fire useful people and protect those who wouldn't be able to survive elsewhere. So instead of improving the overall quality of the workforce, they were actively undermining that quality by weeding out the most useful people. Of course, the primary aim was to cut the pay packet massively in order to have an immediate effect on the balance sheet. But from a long-term perspective, the personnel policies during the restructuring looked as if they would cause problems for the company in the future.

V: And it is also people (who are fired) who are not very useful in the company! If not the company would be thrown into confusion. Some people are 'tapped on the shoulder' (*kata tatakareru*). Those kind of people have to start thinking about their own livelihood first of all. I don't know what kind of conditions they are presented with. But they have to take a careful look at those conditions. And they have to think about how things would be in the company if they remained. They have to look at whether they would be promoted in the future in that company if they stayed. They have to look at the total situation. And some people decide that they will take what is offered.

To be tapped on the shoulder is to be given a very strong hint to put in one's resignation. But as the individual cannot be fired directly; he still has the choice of whether to decide to quit or not. As we have seen, the individual in this case must look at his options. He must ask himself several questions. Can he make a livelihood elsewhere? If he remained, what would happen? Would he be transferred? Demoted? Bullied until he succumbed? Made into a 'window-sitter', someone with no responsibilities or duties, and thus earn the ridicule of his colleagues? Or could he remain in a bearable position, but perhaps with less pay and less responsibility? Would remaining in the company under those circumstances leave him with a black mark against his name in the all-important personnel file? Would it mean he was off the career ladder in the company permanently, even if the company should recover? These questions are largely unanswerable, as there is considerable variation between employees.

Moreover, the employees do not really know whether they are being asked to leave because they are untalented or because they were easier to cut due to personal circumstances. It seems that in the majority of cases the bosses say that the person has been cut because they have such and such a skill and the company is confident they can find work easily elsewhere. This was the case even in situations where, talking to the boss afterwards, I discovered that it was nothing more than a story given the employee.

P: There are people who don't take what is offered; who say, 'This is all that I have. I want to stay here whatever the case. Whatever kind of work is OK but I want to stay here.' You hear for a fact that there are people like that. It is never the case that those kind of people are forced to quit. Well, it would be a big problem if that were the case, wouldn't it? So, in that situation, the type of work that they do might change, but it is OK with them that it changes. Some people just want to have a stable life and get their pay every month regardless of the content of their work. For example, people who used to get 500,000 yen a month might not care if their pay drops to 400,000 yen a month or even 300,000 yen a month, if they can go on supporting themselves on their pay. Some people don't care even if they are hunted, or chased into a 'window-side seat' (*madogiwa*), or even if they have to work as porters or doormen. Some people want to remain in any case, although in fact there is a lot of individual variation as to that. It is certainly the case for some that if they object to submitting their resignations that they are gradually chased into a window-side seat. In that sense, Japanese companies are also more or less rational. In that sense, if the company decides that a person has no ability, then a 'window seat' is often the end result.

The need to cut people caused genuine trauma for many of the bosses, especially as most were old enough to be members of the generation that recalls the social welfare system in the old C-Life with a great deal of nostalgia.

K: It's really hard to cut people, so the management is really suffering hardship (*kuujo*). Behind each person there is a family. So if you cut the person, it is the same as cutting four or five people. The company does, to a certain extent (*ichioo*), think about the family of the employee. If the company weren't like that, I think that would be a pity; it would be really troubling (*komaru*). It's not just a simple matter that you can cut people and then everything will be OK.

In fact, making the decision about whom to fire brought the management back to the fundamental dilemma of the Japanese company – whether they should all suffer together or whether they should let some people be sacrificed so that the rest can survive. Until the '800 List' was produced, the company had adhered as far as possible, as we have seen, to the strategy of suffering together. The successive pay cuts that were implemented were precisely about that. The employees and management were both generally happier with everyone suffering together through the pay cuts than having to risk losing their jobs themselves or deciding that others should have to go. Ironically, it was often the very same age group most vulnerable to losing their jobs themselves if restructuring was implemented who had to be involved in the firing of younger employees.

K: If you make a decision to withdraw from some areas, then you don't need as many people. But behind those people there's a family. So of course it would be better not to restructure; but naturally, in order to survive as a company, when we have to think about what we need to do, it becomes a matter of how we are going to suffer the pain all together as a company. I think it's necessary for management to take some responsibility; but if we do the same things that we've done up till now, it becomes a very difficult decision – whether we'll all go under together, or whether just some of the people will go under. If the whole organisation goes under because of a small number of people, then that is the same as striking out the company altogether (*massatsu*), and that is the responsibility of management. If we have to decide what to do from now, then I think personnel is the biggest thing. But we're not a society like America where people can move freely from job to job. However, neither do I think that life-time employment is sustainable any more.

Underlying the dilemma was the reluctant recognition that life-time employment was on the way out – and restructuring was thus justified. But the bosses also had to live with the knowledge, on the other hand, that many employees removed in the restructuring would be placed in terrible positions.

Having introduced some of the problems facing those responsible for the restructuring plan, I now consider the attitudes of the employees towards it.

Attitudes to restructuring

An important issue in assessing employee attitudes to the plan is the paucity of information given to them by management. The company has disseminated very little information about the state of the company and exactly how bad its situation is, and this has increased the sense of anxiety inside C-Life. The employees see reports in the media about other companies where the employees have only learned that their company has gone bankrupt from the papers the morning after it happens.

E: I am still inside, so it is hard to tell, but even in this situation the company hasn't been forthcoming with information. This is since a couple of years ago … our company results started to go downhill … it is kind of like the announcements during World War II. So and so regiment won a great battle at such and such a place. They told us that kind of information but said nothing when we were defeated or annihilated … C-Life not telling us the real story is the same kind of situation as that. They told us the good side but hid the bad side from us. Even inside the company … we gradually realised that this was happening. We thought, 'Hey, something is not right here (*nani ka chigau zo*).' It has been like that for about three years.

The lack of clear information has fuelled the sense of insecurity. And employees are frustrated that they have not been made part of the battle. This situation is sharply at odds with the popular view of the Japanese company.

E: We read the media reports. But when you are inside the company, you just hear the company side and everything happens according to that. I thought that if they gave us better information it would have galvanised us to action, we would have thought a bit more and done what they wanted us to ... It was as if they didn't trust us, they didn't have confidence in us. So when they wanted something to happen they just gave us directives from the top. They said that this is the situation and so this is what you have to do. I guess that is what an organisation has to do. But I feel that there could have been a better way, they could have given us more information, especially to the people who had to deal with sales (and answer questions about results). It added a lot to the general sense of anxiety. For a long time, there has been a lot of anxiety. Some people feel it more and some less ... but it is there....

They tell us the same as they tell to the outside media. A few of the finance people at the very top know the full financial situation of course ... When they decide how to let information out they do so in response to some situation or another and that is all they let us know ... But if they didn't keep things under wraps it would have been disastrous.... We still don't know if the company is giving us the correct information. It is not mistaken information that we are getting. It is just that there is probably more that we should know that they are not telling us. Like how on earth the bad loans got this bad ... They say that they have dealt with the bad loans ... I think ... but we don't know....

When a Japanese company goes bankrupt, the reality of the management structure is revealed in full. The president and the directors are generally the only ones who know that the company will go under. Ordinary staff learn what has happened from newspapers. Even high-level officials are kept in the dark. When Yamaichi Securities Co. Ltd – the first major securities company to collapse in the recession – went under, only five people in the company knew about it before it happened. Many employees reported stories to me like this, of harsh treatment that greeted the employees of bankrupt companies. This just highlighted their own anxiety. Employees were worried about their housing, and housing loans, because both are often connected to the company, and about getting another job before the unemployment benefits ran out. National unemployment insurance is determined by the amount of time that the employee has worked, but even so, the maximum amount of time is just one year. After that, no more benefits can be claimed.

A: When Nissan Life went under, it was OK if you were in the company dormitory but if you were in a rented house, and your landlord knew that you had been working for Nissan Life, some of the people were told to leave their homes because their company no longer existed. Because they no longer knew if their pay would come in every month – they were told to leave. And banks would ask the employees whether they were going to be able to pay their housing loans as well. So it was really pitiful.

W: Because we are all adults, no one inside C-Life openly says anything about the people being rejected. But it is the first time people have had to face this so there is a lot of anxiety. I am fairly anxious too. But I have experience of having changed job. What is going to happen is going to happen so I don't think about it too much and believe that if I make an effort a way will appear for me.

In this atmosphere of uncertainty, C-Life employees still inside the company had all begun at least to consider the very real possibility that they would be restructured, or that the company might go under and they would lose their jobs.

H: If you look at the population structure, companies used to be like pyramids. There were only about twenty people in the same year. They only had to shut up and they would naturally progress to becoming directors. Once you were inside the system, you got juniors underneath you and you really didn't have to do much to keep advancing. There are lots of directors in our company that we can look at and say, why on earth is he a director? Ability wasn't one of the required traits to be a director. That was the same for most large Japanese companies. Because there weren't so many people at the top they could all get some power in the end. However, in the younger generations there are 40 or 50 people in each year's intake. The company doesn't need them all and the left-over ones have to go somewhere. This has happened very quickly and it is dramatically different to the situation until now so everyone has been surprised by it.

Employees started to look anew at the population structure of the company and analyse where their *doki* were in the context of that structure. Those who entered during years with large numbers of *doki* realised that they were the most vulnerable. This may explain the fact, which surprised me at first, that most people did not consult their *doki* about the restructuring. Some of this, I believe, was caused by the intense competition between the *doki*, although this competition was always masked by the *tatemae* (appearance) of co-operation and friendship. In this atmosphere, fear of being fired could be seen as an expression of weakness.

Admitting these feelings to bosses could be a sign of inadequacy at a time when the bosses were deciding whom to cut first.

K: We talk about restructuring among *doki* but it is not something that we can do anything about by just talking about it. So it is not a subject that everyone gets really into (*moriagaranai na to iu kanji desu ne*) … it is not a topic that really incites everyone to talk.

Most people, despite these worries, still had only vague and unformed ideas about what, in practical terms, they would do should they be made to resign. They mostly expressed the ideal of being able to work at something at which they were skilled, to use their abilities in their work. But this idea clashed with the fear that they did not have the skills to be re-employed in a good job.

W: I am already 48. It is not a time when I can be saying that I am a specialist or a generalist. I would like to have something that I can call my life work. If I could do anything with the knowledge that I have I think it would have to be to create a company of my own. I don't want to work under someone else, so I'd like to have my own business. I would like to be able to ride on the present wave and be able to use my personal connections and my specialist knowledge. I'd like to be able to work at something that only I can do.

By contrast, I found the families of the C-Life employees to be surprisingly unconcerned about the details of the company's demise. This reflects the great separation between the spheres of home and work typical of Japanese companies. The main concern of most wives seemed to be that their husbands had a job, not that they enjoyed their job or that they could use their skills.

H: I think that my wife is probably uncertain about me having moved to my present company but she doesn't say anything as long as the pay keeps coming in. If the pay stopped I don't know what would happen then.

E: My daughter is 13 now. She says it must be hard (*taihen*) about the company. When I was saying I have to find some kind of work she told me that there was a notice at the local supermarket advertising for part-time staff. I just said, 'Oh yes, that could be a way.' I think she is just scared that her allowance will decrease.

The employees expressed various concerns about the practical aspects of being laid off. First and foremost was concern over their housing loans, which are typically very long term in Japan.

H: I have a lot of loans at the moment. I probably have another twenty years to pay off. I am 47 now so I probably have another twenty years to pay.

As the reality of the restructuring has sunk in, I have found that C-Life employees have become more and more critical of Japanese management, and more open in expressing their discontent. Thinking about restructuring suggested categories of workers who were more or less likely to be restructured, and this brought home the emphasis on what kind of skills they had or how different categories of people were evaluated.

E: The sales ladies are not laid off at all. They only have an income if they produce anyway so they are completely removed from the restructuring. Their basic salary structure is completely different. They have a really low base and a high commission base. If they don't produce they usually quit by themselves. That kind of work is refreshing (*sappari shite iru*) because it is clear and clean and you know where you stand.

Employees showed a lot of emotion about being on the list, but in general, after an initial outburst, they accepted the situation well. This could, however, mask deeper emotion. One woman was interviewed for my film the day after she found she was on the list. She did an hour-long interview telling me how grateful she was to C-Life and to her seniors for hiring her and for letting her work as a general worker. It was not until the hour was up that she broke down and admitted that she was on the list. It was evident that she was in turmoil about her mixed ideas of the company as, on the one hand, a supportive organisation and, on the other, an impersonal body that could fire her without even letting her know the criteria for being fired. When I talked with her a week or so later she had realised that, even had she wanted to, there was no-one to whom she could complain. As we have already seen, the personnel section is shrouded in mystery. No-one knows what the evaluation criteria are or who decides such things as a restructuring list. She asked her direct boss to verify the criteria by which she had been fired, but as her direct boss also had a hand in the decision she was unsure how helpful this would be:

E: About my being on the list, I might just be stubbornly trying to be strong but I think even if I consult people (*sodan ni notte morau*) it isn't going to come to anything anyway, I know that, I feel like I have come to understand that. Well, I am a manager as well (*kanrishoku*) so I understand the company's view. I could ask other people to talk with me about it as well, but however many I ask it will be the same.

Many difficulties were faced by minority groups in the company, such as mid-career transferees and women, but the restructuring plan gave them new problems as well. After the international department had been shut down several years earlier, some mid-career transferees, who had originally been hired into the international department from other companies, were transferred to domestic divisions. Rather surprisingly, they stayed in the company even then. One was transferred to a subsidiary but eventually asked to look for his own job. The other was stationed in a department selling group insurance to domestic clients; a job that he had never done before and in which he had no experience whatsoever. He told me that he wanted to try something new and he wanted to stay in C-Life to see how the situation panned out. But when the massive restructuring plan came out, and the state of the company looked like it was becoming worse, he moved to a foreign bank.

H: I think that employees in Japanese companies are going to have to change a lot, especially young people. I think that the people in the hardest position are the middle-aged and older people – people who are going to be re-structured. They have a lot of loyalty towards the company but they are suddenly being told 'Sayonara' as if they were being forced out. I think the most pitiful people out there are the middle-aged and older people. I think my case is pitiful as well but I had an idea that I might quit. I didn't think about it that much but for people who have never thought about it, if they are suddenly released, it is a great shock for them and there are a lot of cases lately of people jumping in front of trains because of that. People inside the company are reading magazines that talk about the bad results of the company. They think it's terrible and they are really troubled by it. Young people are quitting the company. If they're young and they have abilities they're quitting. In practice, all the people who were working overseas in the London and New York offices that were under 40 have almost all changed jobs to foreign companies – also the ones that took MBAs. They've gone to places like GE Capital or UBS.

For the female general workers who battled to be the first generation to be accepted in the same position as men, restructuring has been a harsh experience.

V: As far as women are concerned, I think it is easy for them to become the victims. They might be told that either they or their husbands should quit the company.

However, although it seemed evident to me (and to the women themselves) that women general workers were being asked to quit to protect their male counterparts, the C-Life employees argued that this was not just because they were women, but because they had alternative sources of income.

V: Are the people still left in C-Life satisfied of the logic of who has been chosen to quit? No, I don't think that they are convinced that it is reasonable either.

P: However, well, it is a strange thing but for example, not every woman is asked to quit in order to shift the loss to the weaker members. That is not the case. Shifting the loss or carrying the burden is something that comes to everyone in the end. In a Japanese company there are usually two categories; of general workers – who are almost all men – and office workers. They have to cut both the general workers and the secretarial workers (*ippanshoku*). They can't just cut the secretarial workers, because it won't result in lowering costs very much. So they have to cut a certain percentage of each. They have to cut so that not all of the burden of bearing the losses comes to the women. But if a woman has a husband, they often say, 'Well, you have a husband, so you should be OK.' That is unfortunate for her, but that is the way that it is.

One woman general worker who was cut without explanation said:

E: It is because it is still the men who are the main providers of families' income in Japan and are supporting the women in society. This is the culture that we are in amongst, and if something happens then it is easier for companies to cut the women first. If you get married and you are both working there are two pillars (supporting the household), so you get psychologically secure. The company is likely to say that if you have another income in your house then you will be OK. I think that that kind of cutting happens. I don't know if you can say that they are cut just because they are women, but the surrounding culture says that men go outside to work and women stay inside to protect the home, and this has been the way through generations of history. It would be hard for that kind of thinking to die. Now, I still have the dream that I want to advance and become senior (*erakunatte iku*) like the guys. But in C-Life now, even if I rebelled and stayed on (*muri o shite nokotte mo*) I would be off the ladder to the top and that is not what I wanted. In that case, it doesn't really matter which company I am in; it is all the same. And in that case, if C-Life will be helped by my quitting then I might as well quit.

The situation for restructured women general workers is grim. It is very unlikely that they will be able to get another job as a general worker in another Japanese company. And they generally don't have the skills required to move to a foreign company. And after being a general worker, the thought of working as a secretary is unappealing.

E: I think it would be hard to work 'as a woman' now that I have spent all these years working as regular staff. But I'll get by somehow (*said with a breezy laugh*). I'll just try to stay optimistic. Something interesting might come up in the next year or so even if it doesn't come up soon.

But the lack of good work for middle-aged women general workers means that they have to change their aspirations and aim very low indeed.

E: I couldn't stand to be in the house all the time. I have to find something to do. C-Life is not the only company … If it is just to work I can do anything, even work in a supermarket, if it is just to earn money…

These conflicting reactions are all illustrated in the following case study, of a female employee who found herself on the restructuring list. She is, at one and the same time, bitter towards the company and sympathetic to management who have been forced to make this decision. As a result, her account is disjointed, wafting between these two points of view and worry about what she is going to do.

E's story

On 27 January each individual has to make their own decision about whether they will quit. Then the whole circumstances – who is on the list – will become open to everyone when the personnel orders come out at the end of February.

The company formally put out the restructuring plan in the middle of November. We have a union inside the company, and there were various kinds of negotiations. The list finally came out on 20 December. And the interviews started in December. So the interviews have just started and there are 800 people to be cut. The 800 people come from all over the country from Hokkaido to Okinawa but it still ends up being one person in three. So which three persons will they be? Each person has a different view on that. Top management also has their view. They just have to draw some kind of line and arrive at 30 per cent. I just have to accept that I was unlucky (*en ga nakatta*). There is incredible unrest inside the company.

In order for the company to remain as a company it has to trim its excess fat. I can totally understand that. At present, it is too heavy to move so it has to shape up and become slim. If not, it won't be able to survive. But if we think about how it should become slim, there are no fixed criteria in place as to how that should be done, no criteria that everyone would be happy with, it isn't possible to have criteria like that.

The list is not openly known. Only the person on the list knows for sure about it. It has an actual shape and form but only the department heads and the individuals on the list know about it. The gossip is incredible. Because of the numbers involved … because there are so many…

People won't know who is on the list until the end of January, which is the close of the present deadline. No, even then they won't know … Nobody will know for sure until the end of February when the annual work assignments (*jirei*) are decided. Everyone is basically given their orders on the same day … So everyone goes out drinking then to gossip. They all go out before it is announced to talk about who is going to go where … there is a high degree of tension then … And when it comes out? There are happy people and sad people, bitter people and defiant people…

If any group gets together now – if, say, eight people got together – then two or three of those people are no longer going to be there next year. So you can't help but turn to the subject of who it is going to be. And that really becomes clear only as time goes on as people get interviewed one by one. Some people come out of the meetings saying that they are relieved that they weren't told they were on the list, and some people say, 'It has come to me! (*Kichatta*!)'. There are all kinds of ways to say it…

I heard that it is Personnel who made the list – well, it must be Personnel in the end. There are a lot of people on the list who you would think, but why him? Why him? But if you start to say that there is no end to it. You have to have a line somewhere. Debating about exactly where the line is when it is to divide two on one side and one on the other is impossible. Well, the president had to approve the list in the end. (This is very hard for E because the president was a great supporter of her in her career.) If you think about it too hard it would be even harder (*ki ga kurushikunachau*).

They say that the way they are deciding is on the *gyosekihyo* (results sheet). I asked them what the criterion was and this is what they said. I asked them if it was done on age or on sex – well, of course they couldn't say that it was. Also, I heard about some other women in the head office (*tantoshoku*). There seem to be a lot of women on the list. So from what I have heard already I would say it is biased towards women. There has been some news like that. They have to reduce costs somehow and people who are older cost more and management costs more as well and because it is a Japanese company, rather than cutting people who are supporting a family it is easier to cut people who are not, like women who are working as general workers. If I were on the management side I would probably think the same. Anyway, I think that we are in a pretty dangerous position. I think that the fact that we are women is a significant factor.

But I still have a lot of sympathy for management. I understand that section chiefs have a quota that they have to fulfil so they have to do what they do but even so, some of them tell the people in a really horrible way, such as saying, 'Congratulations! You have made it onto the Eight Hundred List!' I think there is really no call at all for doing things like that.

I think that there are a few department heads that might be on the list but almost none. A lot of people will be older people who are not management. As far as the personnel structure of the company goes, in the 1965 oil shock period the company had few people and after that people increased until the bubble. So, if you imagine 1965 as the waist of the company, then the population of the company looks like the figure of a buxom girl. That is good for a girl, but it is not a good shape for a company. So to drastically cut the parts that are protruding is the first necessity.

I am actually in the waist of that structure so I think that in my case there were other factors involved as well. As I said before, I think it is a combination of my age, the type of work that I am doing, and the fact that there is another person supporting my household. I don't think the company will come out openly and say that because they are not able to come out and say that legally. But I understand why they would feel that way. My husband is working in the real estate industry and through the bubble he has experienced really harsh conditions. Three or four years ago they already began restructuring. My husband was one of those involved in doing the restructuring. So objectively, the cutting is done on factors such as age and places that cost a lot are cut first. But as an organisation they can cut without any heartache (*kokoro o itamezu ni*) if they know that another person in the household is working.

I am really bitter about it, and I don't know what standards or what criteria they have for putting me on that list, and I would like them to tell me that and I plan to ask them. I am still discussing things with the department head, but when I asked him what kind of criterion it was, he told me that he didn't know either, that he had just been told by the personnel department. And I was quite angry about that. So he said that he would go to the personnel department before the week was out and ask them.

I don't think that I will be able to do anything if I find out what the reasons were for them having chosen me. But I still just want to know for the sake of knowing it. And because I plan to go on working in Japanese society. I half feel that I would like to cling on. I loved C-Life for a long time and it seems really foolish, but at the time that I was hired, I really felt that I had 'picked me up' (*hirotte kureta*) among any number of other good candidates. And there are really people that I owed a debt of gratitude. I really wanted to go on working in order to repay that debt. I haven't yet told that person that I am indebted to that I have been asked to resign.

Yes, I am really bitter about it. The personnel department has made the list and they give out the list to each department head and under the responsibility of each department head, the individuals who have been selected to quit are to be 'persuaded' by the department head. That is what I think is happening.

I am quite forceful so I asked a few of my *sempai* (superiors) including the one who was most influential in my career. He said, 'I am sorry I couldn't be of more use to you' (*chikara ni natte yatte aganakute gomen ne*). But I was happy that he said that to me. He was one of the directors. So this case is beyond the influence of any of the individual directors – this huge wave engulfing C-Life.

The guys around … I don't know what they are thinking. I told them about me from the beginning so they know. But we still don't know about each other unless the individual speaks out himself. I told the people close to me. No-one knows about anyone else. It is really really strange inside at the moment.

There should be other people in the same section but I don't know who they are. There are nasty things happening as well. A lot of gossip and in some places the *bucho* (department head) is putting a lot of pressure on the guys in their departments who are on the list to quit.

I do know about one *doki* (member of her year group). I know because I wrote in my New Year cards this year something about my own situation. And I got a phone call from a *doki* to say that he was on the list as well. I think there are other *doki* as well but not everyone is as open as I am about it. That particular *doki* was in the countryside and he had a lot to think about because he has a wife and kids. He wanted to know what I knew. Because he was in the countryside he didn't have a lot of information. He wanted to know what would happen if he didn't resign. I think that he would immediately get a job transfer. Anyway, he wouldn't be able to stay in the same job.

Quitting isn't compulsory (for those on the list). It is you who have to make your own decision. If you decide to quit you write your own letter of resignation and hand it in. If you decide not to, you will still be there for the next round, which is in September this year. But then they will treat you as being fired, which gives you less unemployment insurance and benefits, so it is more like getting laid off than resigning.

It is also hard to judge how many people will actually resign. Whether the number of people that the company actually wants to resign will come forward, or whether it will be oversubscribed. It is impossible to tell. Then the next session is in September. So it could be even stricter then.

I think that there are a lot of people who are waiting until September to see what will happen. But I thought about that and thought that they are likely to transfer people to a department where it is obvious that they were transferred there for that reason. And that is not the road that I want to travel. I asked my boss what would happen if I didn't quit and he said that I would move but it is not sure where. So they might make a department especially that has no real work attached to it. Or it is most possible that they will send people back to sales offices.

It is also unclear whether failing to quit when you were asked to will remain as a black mark on your record the whole time that you remained in the company. Even if the company recovered and went on about its normal business after a period of time, this period and this list would still be an issue.

I think all general workers would get a transfer if they tried to hang on. The deadline for giving our decision is 30 January. The retirement money is really very low. I don't think that they have the leeway to put a lot of extra money onto the retirement package because there are 800 people – so many of them. I don't think that there are people around in the company who would dislike it, or put on a bad face, if you refused the company orders and didn't move. You're not troublesome to them. It is just that the company has got too fat and has to be shaped up. And it just happens to be me who drew the short straw.

As far as my own feelings go, I am more or less decided. I talked with a number of people inside the company but it was pretty clear that what I wanted to happen was mostly an impossibility. I talked to some of my *sempai*, and also to a few *doki*. They said all kinds of things but I guess the recurring theme is '*Shoganai ne.*' It can't be helped. It isn't anything that my *doki* can do anything about. And in the end, even the *sempai* that I consulted can't actually do anything themselves either. And it can't be helped. If I went on thinking it would just be tiring. I actually feel relieved (*sukkiri shita*). Now I just have to think about what I am going to do. That is a lot easier.

We'll see if I will be able to carry on with my dream of having a career or whether I will have to put work for the sake of my living standard first. Whether I will now work just for money and separate it from my self-fulfilment (*jujitsu* and *seikatsu*). I haven't thought about what kind of work I would do. Even if I thought about it, if there isn't such a job I wouldn't be able to do it. It is still the case that most companies won't allow women to work on the same basis as men. If they don't allow it, there is way to try to persuade people like that.

The company has offered to help me look for a job but I don't really trust it. They can't even place the guys so I think it would be difficult to go through them. It will be easier just to move by myself. I can ask the help of various *sempai*, people who have retired from the company and gone to other companies is one option. Also there are people that I was close to when I was working in the sales offices. I will be able to use all the connections that I have built up over a life as a company person.

I thought that I wanted to work as part of this company until the very end. If the company told me that I had to leave as part of the restructuring plan then I think that that would be a great pity. But I still love C-Life. I want to continue to love C-Life. In that sense, to be told that I would be restructured would be like shedding blood! It would take away the pain though if the person who is thrown away might still think that they want the company to live on and to fight back and to win. No-one really knows whether the company will survive or not. Of course, we all gossip about it. But there is no way of knowing. It is a gamble. You might go this way and fall over, or you might go that way and trip up.

At the moment a special compensation package is paid out on top of the normal retirement benefit. But the bitterness doesn't necessarily disappear from that. I think it is the opposite to that actually. I think that might be one difference between men and women. It might be strange for me to say so but in my case it is not only the salary ... Of course I would rather get a salary than not get it ... but because money is not especially important this decision is especially difficult for me.

I have the feeling that I would really like to stay. But the company really doesn't have any leeway. And until now, although I had the handicap of being a woman, the company was quite generous in the way that they treated me (*oome ni mite moratta*). So there was nothing in which I felt disadvantaged as a woman. And in some ways, because I was a woman I got special treatment. So, if that was pointed out to me, and I was to continue, I would have a different kind of stress on me. In a situation where there was no leeway at all, I wonder if I would be able to handle that kind of situation. I don't think it would be the same as it had been until now. I don't know if I would be able to handle that. But if I was able to stay here ... if I was able to continue here ... if the economic environment changed for the better, if the company recovered a little, I might think that I was really glad that I had continued. It is a gamble so I am in a quandary.

This has been given to me in the form of a decision that I can make for myself. But if I said that I don't want to quit and rebelled, I think I would probably just get an immediate transfer, probably to the provinces. That is what I think, anyway. It would be really troublesome so I think it would be easier just to quit.

So how does it feel to receive such treatment? Well, I am really bitter (*kuyashii*). However, I don't think that the company had any choice but to put out such a plan. It is not as if anything is going to happen right now and it is not as if it is going to go immediately bankrupt. But one or two years from now – in the period of huge turbulence that is going to follow (in the Big Bang of the financial industry) – in order to remain through that, they have to do what they have to do. I have been given the information that the company will go down if it doesn't do this restructuring now. So, in that sense, I don't think that it can be helped that I got caught in the middle of this painful adjustment.

Taking responsibility

A question discussed frequently by my respondents was who was responsible for the situation now facing them. Indeed, being confronted with the likelihood of their own company going bankrupt made the C-Life employees think anew about the question of responsibility in general. This is especially so in the current climate where companies are going under one by one, and the traditional method of 'taking responsibility' has reached new heights. Suicides are at their highest rate ever in Japan; the media is flooded with stories of company presidents committing suicide to take responsibility for the failure of their company and employees taking their lives after they have been fired. But in the C-Life environment where the employees have been left to deal with the aftermath of the bubble – now that it is their own company and their own situation – they are re-assessing the very concept of responsibility.

A: It is hard to say what responsibility means when you talk about who takes responsibility in a Japanese company. For example, there are people who say, 'I am quitting to take responsibility.' But is quitting taking responsibility? I wonder … Responsibility means grasping clearly the reason why a problem has occurred and putting a policy in place so that that doesn't occur again. I think that is when you can say that you have fulfilled your responsibility. If someone says, 'Well, I was the auditor responsible at the time of an occurrence and so I will quit.' If you ask if everything was cleared up by the person quitting, no, the company will just do the same thing again.

But having said that, the C-Life employees are at a loss over whom to blame. Some are critical of the government and the fiscal policies in place at the time of the bubble. Others blame the previous president who had quit C-Life two years before, after fourteen years in office – all through the bubble and its aftermath. Some, as we shall see later, put the primary cause down to Japanese management and its failures. Some even blame the failure on the foreign exchange losses that the industry endured when the dollar moved against the yen as the bubble collapsed. Some theories are quite outlandish. Foreign analysts, for example, ridicule the belief of one C-Life department manager that the movement in the yen had been part of an 'Anglo-Saxon conspiracy':

> Every loser in the casino believes that it is a conspiracy. Do I think governments are even capable of manipulating exchange rates over any significant period? No, too many have conspicuously failed to achieve that. Even if the government wished to manipulate the exchange rate from 80 to 140 back to 100 – even if that was the game plan – I don't think they would be capable of doing that. And I can't for the life of me

think why they would wish to! What would be achieved? So I don't buy into the conspiracy theory. No, I don't think there are dark forces at work here that have conspired to bring down an otherwise great life insurance company. They made some bad decisions. The market went against them. They decided to bet in one whack in overseas assets because the yield was higher. Why on earth did they think the yield was higher? There are no free lunches. The yield was higher because there was an exchange rate risk. And they got caught. It is no good blaming a conspiracy.

But most of the C-Life employees have a sense of helplessness about the whole period. More than anything else, this is because the whole of Japan had been in the same situation at the same time, giving rise to a false sense of security.

H: Now loans are already discontinued as a business but at the time we got a lot of interest from that and we also made a lot of investments in foreign bonds. But we should really have hedged the foreign exchange risk, and unfortunately we didn't, and so when the yen began to rise dramatically we lost money on foreign exchange. That was about the same situation in other companies too. There were some large companies that were hedging the foreign exchange risk so I think that there was some unevenness among companies as to how much risk and how much losses they made. But whether it was large or small, everybody got done by the exchange rate. There was a feeling that if we all crossed the river together we didn't need to be scared because everyone was in the same boat.

I: It was 'portable shrine' (*o-mikoshi*) management. Everyone went together towards the same goal, all jostling together. However, if a mistake is made or a failure recorded, no-one takes the responsibility. If you go on and on in that system – if you don't stay with the momentum – you will feel like a fool. So everyone gets on the same boat together.

(*O-mikoshi* is a shinto portable shrine that is carried at festivals on the shoulders of a large number of men. Because so many people carry the shrine, it is hard to say who is really supporting the weight and who is only appearing to carry it.)

The question of who was actually responsible was further obscured by the internal dynamics of C-Life and the murky lines of command. Also, the continuous moving of employees in and out of departments every two or three years ensured that no one really knew how much a person's current results were affected by the performance of the people before him, and how much he himself would contribute to those who came after.

Again, it is not always clear whether a person has followed out an order given to him by somebody else, or if he has taken a decision or implemented an action of his own accord. In the former case, it is difficult to say whether the responsibility for that action lies with the senior or with the junior.

T: C-Life's results are really in a depression. It is hard for me to talk about it because I was in that section myself. But it is not at all clear who has the responsibility for what. Even for one bad loan, you can't tell at all (*mattaku*) where the responsibility lies for that. Well, I think there were a lot of different movements (transfers of people) stemming from the personnel department. But in the end we don't really know what happened. For most ordinary people in the company, they have really no idea about what goes on … the matter is dropped without coming to a decisive conclusion – it is as if everything is left unclear (*uya moya ni sareta kanji mo shimasu shi ne*) … So there is no-one who can say no to the top people. And even if they could say no, people won't be fired even if they are at fault.

C-Life employees are rather forgiving towards the people who were in positions of responsibility for investments in the bubble. There are several such employees left in the company, in the positions of department head. I did not hear any direct blame put on these employees specifically. If any blame was assigned to actual people, it was invariably toward the former president, who had by now left the company, or towards the former directors.

A: I don't know if my company is taking responsibility or not, but the real problem is why the bad loans were created in the first place. We need to think about why that happened. Japan as a whole was involved in the bubble – was floating – and how the bad loans are going to be handled is our present responsibility. The top management is thinking with all their might about how they can clear it up. Even if you blame the people who made the bad loans at the time, the bad loans have already been created so there is not really any point. They thought they were doing the right thing at the time, didn't they? They didn't do what they did knowing that the bad loans were going to appear.

One important idea illustrated by this comment is that the managers at the time are not regarded as responsible because their bad investments were not *deliberate*. In many areas in C-Life I saw this same idea: that people are only responsible to the extent that they are aware of what they are doing. I believe this concept underpins the idea of responsibility in other areas of Japanese society too. For example, it underlies the openness that is displayed during drinking sessions. If a person is drunk and does not know what he says, then he is not responsible for his behaviour.

Another idea we can gather from the above comments is that it is no use to chase up responsibility now, as it is an issue now in the past. Responsibility is not handled as an absolute crime, but as a situation-specific matter. If the person responsible resigns from a troubling situation, that act puts a lid on the matter and the issue is concluded, although this situation is rapidly changing and former management increasingly is being held to account. Many employees are caught between the two poles of believing management to be responsible, and believing the whole thing to be something that could not be helped as all of the insurance companies had been in the same boat.

> E: I am bitter mostly towards the past management … towards the past management who were too optimistic: the management at the time of the bubble. But having said that, all of Japan was dancing (*odotte ita*). It couldn't really have been helped. They may have thought that they were doing the right thing at the time, but they got very badly burned.

Foreign analysts generally take the latter view, but put the blame on the government for having created the situation where individual companies lost perspective:

> I think you should probably assign the majority of responsibility to the policy makers. If a company gets itself into financial difficulty then it is the management's fault. If almost every single company in not just the life insurance industry, but almost the entire financial industry are in financial difficulty, I think the only people you can blame for that are the people who were setting monetary and fiscal policy. You can't blame every manager of every bank and every life insurance company for making a stupid decision. How come everyone was suddenly stupid all at the same time? Well, because the circumstances were created where it was highly likely that everybody was going to behave in an irrational sense. So in that sense I think a great deal of the responsibility rests with government. Of course, individual decisions were made by management that resulted in specific losses but I think the personal responsibility for those decisions is actually quite light. Where there may be a heavy responsibility on management would be the case – and we have seen this in the banks – where they fraudulently concealed the consequences of those decisions. Where they got themselves into difficulties they then proceeded to lie about it … Now that places a great deal of responsibility on management that I don't think is really excusable. But it is excusable having got themselves into trouble given the extraordinary circumstances created by mismanagement of the economy.

The managers themselves, despite putting blame for the situation on various other people, such as the government, or the top management of the time, also feel a considerable sense of responsibility for their own actions. But they do not express this by formally admitting responsibility, although they may admit to feeling this way in informal circumstances.

K: I carried out the foreign investments for C-Life, and we got done on the exchange rate. There were things that we did well, and things that we did badly. There were a lot of bad loans for C-Life as a whole. In response to that, minor management or office workers can do what they like; but if you are a section chief or a department head, and have done all the investments all along – because I am one of the people who was stamping the approval for those decisions – I really feel my responsibility, unfortunately. There are many things that I look back on and wish I had done differently – many things. But I think that's the same for everyone. There's first and foremost a certain atmosphere in the surrounding world. You look at the overall environment as management corps. If there were people among management who thought the world was strange, or if there were people who said so out loud, and if, for example, it was the president that said that, or if there had even been a majority opinion that the situation was strange, then we could have made fewer bad investments. It was the same for banks and manufacturers as well – especially for banks – as it was for insurance companies. At that time stock prices were going up and up. Land prices were sky-rocketing. There was a feeling in the whole of Japan that if you didn't get on top of that wave you would be a great fool. So it's not really a case of whose responsibility it is. If you ask whose responsibility it was after the bubble burst, well, banks are asking now whose responsibility it was. But at the time everyone thought they were doing the right thing. I think that people should be blamed who did things above and beyond the necessity of the time, but that certainly isn't everybody. People were saying towards the end that the bubble was getting really strange. But there was nobody who dared to say in a loud voice, 'Well, let's get off now.' If you had said that, you would have been treated like an idiot, judging by the atmosphere at the time.

Both C-Life employees and foreign analysts, then, distinguish between the companies that followed the wave of euphoria into investment chaos, and those companies that went a step further into clearly irrational, immoral or illegal activities. C-Life employees believe that, at the time, a surprising number of companies did just that, including major corporations and banks.

K: I think the biggest problem was not how much we lost because of greed or the desire for money. I think that we should put the blame on

> the fact that we lost our sense of reason (*ronrikan*), because it's the result of our having lent money to places where we shouldn't have lent money. I think the people who did that kind of thing were bad. If you lent a certain amount of money and did it properly, I don't think that would be a problem. But for example, people were lending money to companies involved in buying land and hiking up its price to resell at a profit (*jiage*). Even in large companies, that kind of thing was happening. Of course they didn't admit to that on the surface (*omote*): they would use a subsidiary company to do it. Even the Long-Term Credit Bank of Japan (Chogin) did that. When they were finally investigated, everyone was in a panic because they realised it really was a serious issue (*taihen da*).

We can see from the above comment that, because an established institution such as the Long-Term Credit Bank of Japan was involved in the shady practice of *jiage*, other companies got a false perspective, thinking that if the bank was doing it, it must be all right. It was only when this institution actually got investigated that other companies regained their perspective and realised where this practice lay in terms of moral and legal ground. As we shall see later, there were some rare C-Life employees who did say, at the time of the bubble, that they did not want any part of some of the lending practices that had become commonplace. One of my *doki*, who quit the company at that time, said, 'There was work [in the department that handled corporate loans] that I didn't want to touch'.

X: Basically, I think that people who did things that they shouldn't have done should take the responsibility now. I think it is a matter of degree. When I think of how I did I don't think I did anything that went against logic (*ron ni han suru*). I think that is the basic issue (*kontei*). It was the jusenos (housing loan companies) that first did things like lending and borrowing money with gangster groups. I don't know if it is really true but the president of one juseno had been doing this for ten-odd years and had so much money he built a huge mansion. For those kind of people a bubble is the best time of all. But now is the time to pay back the money. I don't think it was the presidents of these companies that were bad. I think it was the other guys (gangsters) that induced them to do that kind of spending. Even companies that were not doing those kinds of things were being influenced by the companies that did, as was all of Japan, so innocent companies were also influenced.

There is, then, uncertainty over who is responsible for C-Life's current state. It is frequently very hard in C-Life to assign responsibility in general, and this is particularly so in this instance. The rash of different theories seeking to explain C-Life's – and Japan's – current parlous state simply reflects this.

In general, most people are willing to forgive whoever was responsible, and look to the future, to which I now turn.

Visions of the future

Even if they aren't doing anything about it, C-Life employees are at least thinking about how the company and its practices will change in the future. They generally predict a more positive scenario for Japan after the present recession comes to an end. But they invariably believe that Japan as a whole needs to restructure radically in order to achieve that improvement. The globalisation of the economy and rationalisation of business methods are expected to cause far-reaching changes in all areas of society, especially in the education system.

C-Life employees are generally quite well read on business matters and news. They do have clear visions of what they believe the company should be like, and how to achieve it. It is curious to compare this to the inactivity of most employees over making decisive steps towards that change, which we have already seen in this chapter, and which I will address further in the next chapter.

There are positive comments on Japanese ways of doing business, but these are often voices of nostalgia for an age that is, without question, changing. There is no sense of active rebellion against the coming changes, or an active clinging onto the past.

W: My view of the future is that, at present, the population is at its largest in Japan. There has been a lot of competition lately as far as costs go, but if we don't change the industrial structure now then employment won't increase any more. I think it's a period of great transition. We have to change to a society in which there are a lot of service industries. In order to support that, you need ventures, and to support ventures you need to change the nature of financial institutions accordingly, and you need to change the education system. You need to bring up people like they have in Silicon Valley or in Boston. We have to create that sort of environment. That should be the future image of Japan. You need to respond to the aging of society. The burden on young people is huge. You have to consider how to change that. I have to think very seriously about this. I think that it's important for Japan to think about how to change the structure of industry. It's an information society, and it is information industries that will support those changes.

The C-Life employees are increasingly critical of management. When they speak of 'management' they use two senses of the word. The first refers to *all* management, right down to the first rung – including the section chief status that was only recently attained by my *doki*. The second sense of management generally means the president and directors of the company.

When E said she was bitter about management for their incompetence during the bubble which had culminated in her being asked to leave, she was talking of the president and directors. When the C-Life employees are critical of 'management' it is generally that layer to which they are referring.

The C-Life employees suggested a number of steps that the company should take in order to recover.

H: I think that the management steps that C-Life needs to take now are to hurry up and take management responsibility and give the company over to people who have management ability. The company should decide whether they are going to merge with a bank or whether they are going to be taken over by a foreign-capitalised company and if they don't get their trust back – if a financial institution doesn't have trust they can't do business – and they should be thinking about that above everything else.

Employees generally feel that after the euphoria of the bubble, when the company stopped focusing on selling life insurance and instead branched out into risky areas, and lost money, it should retreat and re-focus on that core business.

S: But now that the overall environment is bad and stocks are going down it is important to be getting good results from insurance and to sell the type of insurance that is going to result in long-term customers. If we look after our main business, the stock business and getting profits on our stock investments or real estate is plus alpha. But the important thing is to look after our main business – we have been hearing that since three or four years back from the bosses at the top. However, it takes time for that idea to penetrate right through all the sales areas. We have to keep on reaffirming these ideas. If we don't hold these ideas as important the salesmen's salaries won't increase and even though we hire them they'll quit right away because their salaries aren't increasing.

K: So how should Japanese companies respond to American economic dominance? Well, I think we have to return to our core business and strengthen our base (*ashimoto o katame yo*). Our basic business (life insurance) is our foundation so I think we have to put money back into it and restart things again from scratch. Banks also have ceased their overseas business and are now focusing on domestic business. I think it is that kind of trend now. Although we had neglected the domestic market to send money overseas to make money – now we have to turn our tails and retreat (*shippo gaeshi mo ichido kaerimasho to*). We closed the international department, or if you use a finer phrase, we 'withdrew in the interests of further development'.

W: After the collapse of the bubble, in our industry, and in the financial industry as a whole, there is no more extra leeway. Consumers have deserted. In that situation both the Japanese economy and the bureaucracy have to follow a course of internationalisation but I feel that we are actually following the opposite course. That is because adjustments in employment are still not finished. We will still be going the wrong direction until we have finished resolving employment issues. When companies are shrinking they don't need specialists.

K: If you ask me personally how I think Japanese management will change in the future, I think the most important thing is to think about how we can shrink the areas that we developed in the past that have already outlived their usefulness. We need to develop a mutual understanding about the direction we need to go in. And that includes issues of education in Japan. We need to cut our fat and become muscular once again. We need to develop again from the very beginning … You need to make a decision, to focus on it, and to gain strength towards that. We need to strip off our outer layer, to go to the plastic surgeon and get rid of the excess blubber, and start again from the very beginning. We need to go back to our core businesses, and I think that's one part of it. So I think that restructuring is, of course, part of that.

The emphasis here is on consolidation, retreating from the excessive expansion of the bubble years and focusing on the core business of selling life insurance. The C-Life employees are much more aware of the importance of chasing quality now rather than quantity, especially those involved in the sales areas of the company.

S: After cancelling out the pluses and minuses you have to end up with a plus. That kind of idea is going to be really important from now on. There was a period where we just took and took and took insurance. We were always increasing sales. Among the sales staff you have to have a stance that you are always growing. If you don't have that then you can't increase your profits, and the company won't continue. That doesn't mean getting numbers just for the sake of getting numbers. You have to get the kind of numbers that turn into profits. If you follow methods that make no sense the salesmen are just going to give up and you have to question you own sense of morals then. You can't just behave as though anything goes any more. Profits really became the main focus for all our life insurance companies only about three or four years ago. When things were going well a lot of profits were coming from stock investments because stock prices were rising so even though our main insurance business was bad and wasn't producing profits it didn't matter.

Japanese businesses have a strong tendency to concentrate on quantity of business rather than quality of products. And because the Japanese economy was so strong, this only became seriously problematic when large-scale cancellations began to occur in the period after the bubble, and when competition exacerbated this trend. The C-Life employees who were of a positive frame of mind toward C-Life during this latter period still seemed to feel individual responsibility for improving that quality. They talked earnestly and at length about how they should strive to improve the company. Their emphasis was most often on quality, not quantity.

Y: Do I think that it is a pity that the company's results are so bad when I have worked hard investing for so many years? Well, I think that I have to make an effort to improve those results. I think each one of us needs to think hard about the way that he is working. That is the last means that we have available to us really. That is what the president is saying as well. We need to concentrate on quality instead of quantity. We need to improve the quality of the work that each one of us is doing. We should have targets but they should be something that each one of us has for himself. That is not something like coming an hour earlier to work: that is about quantity. It is about the content of the work. I think it is really difficult. I wouldn't know how to do that apart from in my own work … There are good and bad sections in C-Life now. The bosses are trying to get the staff to see that they need to change the way that they are working and improve the quality of their work. They tell them to turn their thinking from a level ten up to a level fifteen. If there is something that you want to do in work you have to start thinking about how to do it. Then you turn to acting on that. In order to act on it you have to think of the best way to do it. And that is where what we call work really happens and it is that part that we need to not just talk about but actually strive to make better.

This seems self-evident, but stating formally that quality should be improved is a long way from actually outlining what specifically should be improved, and implementing steps to ensure that this happens. This process only really became faster as the recession dragged on. However, we still see that even in the tenth year after the bursting of the bubble, and as bankruptcy becomes ever more likely, talk among the employees remains very vague. The bosses tell their underlings to 'turn their thinking from a level ten up to a level fifteen'. But, apart from fine words for a speech, what on earth does this mean? The C-Life employee above was unable to tell us immediately. However, along with the new focus on core business, and quality, one positive step stressed by the employees was the need to put the customer first – although this, again, was expressed vaguely.

A: Our ideal is to make a company that is ideal for the customers. And to ask ourselves what is best for them and to fulfil that. I think that life insurance companies somehow changed from the style where they were working for the customer to where they began to work for themselves. It somehow changed. And I think that is why they began to lose trust. I think that for banks, and for insurance companies, and for all financial institutions there has been a big loss of trust. I think that that is maybe because they stopped doing things for the customers and started doing things for themselves ... started doing things for the sake of money itself.

The employee here describes another basic business principle. But in many ways, actually to implement it into C-Life as a strategy was a revolutionary move. The employees were not really used to seeing the company as an organisation existing for the sake of the customers. Rather, the company existed as a real, solid entity for its own sake, a group made up of a society of individuals. Of course the customers existed and it was the business of the company to sell to them, but the thought that they were all *employees* of their customers – which is the actual situation in the case of a mutual company where the policy-holders own the company – rather than villagers in a village that simply existed, was a rather unfamiliar thought to them.

The next quote illustrates the impact of a sudden jolt into awareness of what business is really supposed to be about – the search for profits – from the perspective of one C-Life employee who worked for a time in New York.

J: One movie that I really like is *Wall Street*, with Michael Douglas. In that movie he plays a character called Gordon Gecko. There is a shareholders' meeting for a certain company that Gordon Gecko is trying to acquire, and the present managers are trying to get the shareholders to object to the plan. Gordon Gecko isn't a good guy. He says that if the company is acquired it definitely won't become better. That is what the present management says but Gordon Gecko has a chance to speak, and he says that the total shareholdings owned by the present management is only 3 per cent, so if you look at it that way they haven't really succeeded at all. If the company makes money it doesn't follow that the management does. He says, 'Greed is good, greed is right, greed is it.' That is a part I love in that movie. I like it so much I feel shivers down my spine! I think that movie came out in about 1987. From about that time, American companies brought in a kind of management that responded to the greed and the desires of the employees. Put simply, if the company makes money your pay rises. The ESOPs or stock options and the bonuses are not fixed like they are in Japan but increase if your results are better. The management put in a lot of incentives like that and both management and normal employees decided to put in their best efforts (*yoshi gambaro to!*) and make the company better and increase earnings. If each and every person has this mentality then the company's vitality and competitiveness becomes very strong. And that is why I think American companies are so successful. In Japan it just doesn't work that way.

After some agonising, this employee left C-Life after his return from New York, and joined a smaller, more risky, foreign-capital company. Here, although his pay was not that different from C-Life (according to him – but he knew that his *doki* would read this account and so may have wanted to avoid seeming boastful), it was directly related to the results he achieved. He was not alone in his realisation that the company should be trying to maximise its profits, however.

H: Because the company is a co-operation the final aim is not at all that of making a profit – they just want to all carry on together (*minna de waiwai yatte iru no*). That's where the big mistake is. They have to put profit ahead of everything else. If they bring profit to the forefront they'll realise that rather than having the older sales women they should bring in young women to do the sales. It is obvious that they should do that. So they should fire the older women but because they've all worked together till now they don't do that. So that kind of co-operative body doesn't suit the age we're in now. In the age when the economy was growing rapidly they had the leeway to do anything they wanted but since that has disappeared they're now heading rock bottom and now they have to really focus on profits.

The general view of employees is that competition will increase in Japan. Opinions differ, however, as to how much Japanese management will come to resemble America.

Thus, employees have strong ideas about how the company should change. They have learned the lesson of the bubble that a life insurance company should focus on life insurance rather than property speculation, and they are keen to import Western capitalist ideas such as an emphasis on quality of products rather than quality, the idea that customers are essentially their employers, and the need to maximise profits.

One of the main issues connected with the future of C-Life is globalisation. The C-Life employees take a keen interest in developments in other Japanese companies at the forefront of internationalising. The issue of the global is on everybody's tongue.

H: For a while, Japan was a closed country where they thought that all they had to do was export but now Sony or Honda … they have all left and gone overseas. They know that they have to globalise and if they don't they won't be able to survive. As a repercussion of that, from the companies with good results, companies have been globalising. In that sense, C-Life is a company that did not follow the global flow.

T: I think that Japan is in the process of becoming a more competitive society. I think we are in a stage of great transition. Inside the transition everything is very confused and companies are cutting people drastically. In the last five or six years, I think that things have changed dramatically.

C: If C-Life doesn't globalise too (implement global standards), it won't survive against international competition. It is simple fact that if you put an efficient person against an inefficient one, the efficient one is going to win. The competition has become global now.

The C-Life men told me that the new view current in Japan of 'internationalisation' was completely different from what it had meant at the time I joined the company.

I: The internationalisation that we were thinking about at the time – fourteen years ago – and what we are thinking about now are quite different. At the time, we were just thinking 'Internationalisation! Internationalisation!' If we didn't get on the same flow as the rest of the world we would be left behind. So there was a real hurried quality to our thinking. However, when we actually began investing overseas, if you ask whether we had adequate results with that, we didn't. And we lost a lot of money and made a lot of bad debts overseas. So we actually failed in our asset investment. So amongst those various experiences, we realised that it is not enough just to think 'Internationalisation! Internationalisation!' and barge ahead like that.

Together with the interest in globalisation is the concern over mergers, regarded by some employees as the only way the company could survive. The big question in early 2000 was whether the company would merge or not, and if so, with whom. All around C-Life, as we have noted already, insurer after insurer had tied up with foreign companies or other Japanese financial institutions. The other options for C-Life were to declare bankruptcy, to de-mutualise or to be swallowed up by another institution.

At least some employees, and certainly analysts, were unsure whether it was not too late for C-Life to merge with anyone. According to rumours in the company at the time, the government was looking behind the scenes for a partner for C-Life. A European company was hinted at. C-Life employees told me the gossip was rife inside the company regarding who the prospective partner might be, but this particular gossip did not hit the media.

H: I don't think there's that much point in merging – I wonder what they will do. I don't think anyone wants to have C-Life. But I think that because C-Life can't change from the inside, the company either has to go under or it has to merge. So the picture that I have in my head is of the form of Toho Life. Only the new departments will be formed into a new company and the C-Life employees hired by the new company. The main insurance contracts would remain behind in the body of C-Life. I don't know what kind of people would remain in the company if that happened. And I don't know which would be better; to remain or to go.

Among the speculation, the C-Life employees were generally at a loss to say what they thought would actually happen if C-Life took such a radical – but understandable – move as merging with a foreign company.

Y: I can't imagine the company after a merger. I think it would change but I can't imagine how. A capital injection from a foreign company is the most realistic scenario. How will the insurance industry be in the future? It will all depend on the company's strategy. I don't think there is anyone alive who can answer how the world will be in five years' time. It is a really hard time to tell ahead.

T: I think that everybody has the clear understanding that C-Life can no longer go on in business alone. So it is not official, and it is not certain, but people are expecting some kind of movement towards a merger. So there is a lot of gossip inside the company. For example, even in magazines and journals it writes about the possibility of merging with a foreign company. There was one book that came out speculating on this, and a company that seemed to be C-Life was referred to in that book.

That came out about six months ago. The president has clearly said to all the employees that there will not be a merger like the one that happened to Toho Life. He said that about a year ago. That he wasn't thinking of that kind of merger. I have never talked with other company employees about the possibility of a foreign merger. I can't imagine what would happen … not at all. Well, there is the previous example of Toho Life but it is completely impossible to imagine the actual case of us being in that situation. What on earth would happen?

Many of the employees are quite dry about the idea of a merger, and even see it as advantageous. But as with other issues, employee opinions differ according to their positions in the company. Essentially, and unsurprisingly, those who would be likely to benefit from a merger are generally in favour of it, while those who stand to lose their jobs are apt to be hesitant about the idea.

Y: I think the other people in my generation are also as rational as I am in thinking that if the company has to merge to survive it will have to do that. That is economic rationality.

J: If C-Life were to merge with a foreign company, what would happen in that case? It is like saying how many fish do you have to put into a group of fish to make them start moving actively. I think a merger would really light a fire at their backsides. If an American manager came in and decided that salaries would be according to work performance, it would become a situation where everyone would have to try really hard. I think that everyone would forget their laziness and get a really fierce look in their eyes and start working hard.

For the C-Life employees, the first thought when they consider a merger with a foreign company is how it would affect them. Employees didn't mention opposition on the grounds of a potential merger partner being foreign. The primary consideration seems invariably to be first and foremost their own positions. After that, they consider whether the move would be likely to save C-Life or not.

J: As to whether employees don't want to merge together with a foreign company because it is foreign, I think that is a complicated issue. The moment they hear the words 'merger with a foreign company', they think of other companies that they have known about. What happens is that the pay structure changes dramatically. And in some situations, there is large-scale firing. That is the first thing that comes to their mind. So they take it as quite a negative thing. It is not a question of internationalisation at all. Merger, even with a foreign company, doesn't necessarily mean internationalisation. It is a merger – it is a question of living or dying – and not a question of internationalisation. Older people in the company? Normally the older that people get, the harder it is to change jobs. So in that sense, the older the person is the greater the degree of insecurity. That, and, it is the people with the highest pay base who get fired first in restructuring. Or people who are not working very hard or are not very efficient that are cut the first. So it is the oldest people who are cut first. If a merger happened the company would have to restructure. And at the very forefront of that is firing people. So in that sense, maybe it is like the old Japanese saying that they are 'agreed in principle but opposed in detail (*soron sansei, kakuron hantai*)'. Companies must merge together with foreign companies in order to grow. But if that actually happened, people are thinking about their own positions and if their positions were to disappear and they were to be fired. And in that case, they are opposed to it, of course.

Foreign analysts are invariably far more pessimistic about the fate of C-Life than C-Life employees. And they generally regard a merger as the only possibility left for C-Life to continue in the same form. We can see the contrast between the clarity of the analysts and the vagueness of C-Life employees:

> I think it is very difficult to see a change that C-Life could make now that would wipe the slate clean. I think there has to be some form of financial reorganisation in there that allows them a fresh start. At the end of the day, they have to do what every other management has to do. Do they make an adequate return on the capital invested in their business? And if they are not making an adequate return they need to either withdraw from that business or find a way to make an adequate return. Because there is no long-term future without an economic return on the capital employed. If they can't earn it they should be forced to step aside in place of a management who can make an economic return on those assets. And if no-one can make an adequate return those assets should be handed back to the people they belong to who can choose to go and invest with a different set of managers who are capable of earning a return by the old invisible hand of Keynes. This is capitalism; this is how it works. It doesn't work by design; it works by the invisible hand ... I think (C-Life) should be negotiating with the government over a possible restructuring, and with anybody with money over a possible restructuring ... They are not telling me if they are in talks with foreign buyers but I would be very surprised if they weren't. I mean there are a lot of potential foreign buyers. We have already seen four deals from GE Capital to ManuLife to Aetna to Axa. There is a long list of foreign companies who do want to get into the Japanese life insurance industry ... What are C-Life's objectives? Do they want to continue providing employment for their staff? Having their staff transferred to another company and leaving their existing business behind in a run off company which will often become a burden on the rest of the industry and the taxpayer may well be the best option to preserving employment and continuing what remains of C-Life. The consequences are not very pleasant.

In sharp contrast to what one might expect if one held the view of the Japanese company as an organisation where everyone works 'for the sake of the company', most C-Life employees are remarkably unconcerned about the idea of the company itself going under. The overall view from these interviews seems to show that C-Life employees are not really working 'for the company' but to repay debts to specific seniors, or to surpass or not be left behind by their *doki*, or for the sake of their families. Employee loyalty to the company is, at root, essentially a function of the employees' own desire for security. When the company's situation becomes so dire that it may not survive, employees' need for security will inevitably override their loyalty to the company.

In this chapter, we have seen that many employees emphasise the need for certain changes if the company is to remain competitive in the future. However, nobody seems very keen or competent at actually doing anything about this. I consider this in more detail in the next chapter, in which I address what lies behind the issue of change and management in Japan: why have companies such as C-Life found it so hard to change in response to fluctuating economic circumstances?

5 The company and change

In the last two chapters, we saw how the employees view the current state of the economy and their company, and how they have reacted to the restructuring programme implemented by C-Life's management. We concluded chapter 4 with a discussion of their views of the future, in which they advocate certain changes to the company and the way in which it does business. Why have these changes not been implemented? Why is the reaction so slow? These are the questions addressed in the present chapter, where I discuss employee views on why the company is so resistant to change.

Japanese character and change

Why has C-Life found it so hard to adapt to changing circumstances? Why, despite their awareness of the need for action, have most employees been unable to do much about the situation? In this section I look at how the employees approach these issues. I first examine some of the reasons why the company has been unable to change effectively to deal with changing circumstances.

Change

A primary point raised again and again during my fieldwork was why C-Life had not responded more quickly, and why it was still not responding adequately to the changes in the environment. Various reasons were put forward by the employees. The first was that companies and individuals both lacked experience in dealing with this kind of situation.

W: I don't know why the company doesn't move faster in doing something in response to the danger that it is in. It is a difficult question. I think it is because they have never faced this kind of experience. Politicians have not, nor bureaucrats.

H: That is the problem with management now – it is firmly in their heads that they have been successful until now – they have only had experiences of success. Since then, the world has changed but they only know how to respond to the world in the same pattern. And that is the mistake that they are making. Many people in Japan don't know what is going on in the rest of the world … because we live on an island … That could be the big reason why the Japanese people can't adjust to the world change. Now for the first time, economic growth has slowed down, competition has increased, people are trying to look after themselves, and what we really need is management that can use their heads and manage. The US and Europe are already at that stage, so since global competition really started and the doors opened, Japan is getting done in.

W: Japanese companies are really having to compete for the first time since the last world war. So they are lost and don't really know what to do.

This in itself, of course, did not explain why management did not at least try to adapt to new circumstances. Employees therefore suggested that the company was too indulgent, too unprepared, too inflexible to respond to the times.

J: The amazing thing about American companies is that even when their results are good they still try and restructure and make the company better. So they are always thinking of making things a little bit better. When times are good, Japanese companies forget all about things like that and become too secure and just have a peaceful existence in those good conditions. For Japanese life insurers there were also good times but they didn't think ahead very much about the way the world would change. So now they are in a really serious state.

V: I think that the question of why Japan doesn't change easily is a very relevant one. It is because it didn't need to change, to be honest. I think they are trying to change now – towards the West – but it won't change overnight. From a seniority system it is changing slowly, by degrees, towards an ideology where people are judged on ability.

One contributing factor was the lack of *desire* among top management to change. Contrary to my expectations, many employees were very vocal (and critical) about the desire of present management to hold on to power as long as possible, even at the cost of obstructing the recovery of the company. Once more, the individual held priority over the group, not vice versa.

H: Why doesn't Japan change? Because an inefficient system for companies or countries is a very efficient system in the eyes of the people who are holding the power.

Q: Do you think C-Life is changing fast enough for the world?

J: I don't think so. But it is not just with C-Life. It is all life insurance companies, and the whole financial industry in Japan. It is really slow to adjust to global change.

Q: What do you think is preventing them from changing?

J: It is a good question and a tough question. The minds of the people. It is just that the speed of the change is too fast. That could be the biggest one … the one biggest reason … the speed itself.

Q: So Japanese companies can only change slowly?

J: Yes.

Q: What do you think C-Life should do to change faster?

J: The management should change. They should invite outsiders into their management, into their company.

Q: Why doesn't that happen?

J: Because they don't want to lose their jobs.

H: I will tell you why Japan doesn't change. It is just like the situation of Samaranch and the Olympic Committee. He says he is changing the Olympic Committee system so that there will be a retirement age for committee members but it will be only from the new members and won't apply to the ones already in. That is exactly the same position as the present Japanese company directors. They don't want change. As long as the company doesn't go under, anyway. They think that they have to make changes but they don't want themselves to be part of those changes so they try to put them off as far as possible. So they devise restructuring plans that involve everyone but themselves. They want to try and wait until they reach retirement age safely themselves rather than rocking the boat and risking something happening. That way they retire with their retirement money intact. It doesn't matter what happens after they have got their retirement money. The people who are affected are those that are younger and that have to take the brunt of the restructuring plans.

Even if the top management did intend to make C-Life efficient, even at the expense of their personal security, the C-Life employees said that the whole system prevented management from getting the right information on which to base decisions. This is seen by the employees as a particular fault of the Japanese system of management. And indeed, we have seen how difficult it is for information to flow freely through the company. Nobody is aware of the full picture of any situation.

I: Only the good information would go up towards the top. So decisions were made on the basis of the good information, and that's why mistakes were made.

J: I think that it is very often the case that the opinions are not getting to the top from below (*shita kara iken ga suiagerarete inai*). But because it is a large company some of that probably can't be helped. But in America even large companies do take the opinions of the people at the bottom into account. I don't think that the top has enough information about the situation and conditions overseas or enough information in general.

The amount of knowledge that the older people in the company have about the rapidly changing environment is questionable, as is their knowledge of how to respond. Most importantly, because the information flow generally goes from the bottom up, or the middle up, and there are many stages along the way that an idea can be vetoed, or toned down, or manipulated to someone's advantage, much information is diluted by the time it gets to the top.

J: The question is why doesn't C-Life change? I don't think that the situation that all the powers are gathered at the top will change. American companies are the same. It depends on whether the people at the top have power to take in the opinions of the people below them. And I think it is a problem as to whether the system is in place that would allow them to do that. In the case of C-Life – and I think it is the same for all Japanese companies – they don't know what is happening outside the company or they can't or they don't see what is happening outside the company so they don't really know what to do. I think that is one reason why they can't change.

I: If you're talking about one company or one department, they always have their own customs. And there are problems of human character. Whether it's a problem of human nature or a problem of customs – if one person tries much harder than the others, they will be seen as a heretic. So if the entire department doesn't change its customs altogether, a new world will never arrive. That is a very difficult thing to achieve. I don't think it will become like that in a morning and a night.

J: I think there are a lot of people who think that Japanese management is bad but they don't try to change it. Instead of that they either put up with that or they run away out of the company because those are the only choices.

Why is leaving the only choice? Because it is too difficult for one person to change the company. The fact that everyone changes positions in the company quite frequently, together with the fact that all decisions are taken jointly by a large number of people, greatly limits the effect of any individual on the company. Also, if one person makes moves on their own they are likely to run into social problems before they can achieve anything.

J: I think that there are some young people with the strength to change the company but the pressures that are keeping them down are probably stronger.

Even a former director had this to say:

I: I tried to reform things to the best of my ability when I was in the company, but there are all kinds of walls in the road of change. And there is nothing you can do with only one person's strength. Those kind of people (who want change) need to gather together, and the group needs to have enough strength. If that doesn't happen, I think it's really difficult to effect change. If everyone around you wants to work in a harmonious, refined kind of atmosphere….

It is even harder for middle management:

E: When we get together as *doki* we do talk about the times. We are all becoming middle-aged now. So we are each in sections that are important to the company. And from where we can see from different viewpoints how we can approach the future. And we talk about how we think things should change.
I think we are at the age where we have to be able to change the company ourselves. But I don't know if we are of the age that we can change the company ourselves. I wish that we were asked that more – but in order for us to be heard more we need to get our data together properly and present materials that we can use as the basis for discussions, and proceed on that basis. If we are heard our ideas can be effective, but if our seniors are not listening then it doesn't matter what we say – it is no use. Whoever listens to what you say also has to move on that. There are a lot of people on the management side: conservative people and also aggressively active people. It all depends on where you take what you want to say as to how effective it is going to be.

The above comment shows that even members of the middle generation in C-Life are unable, in practice, to have their voices easily heard by senior management. This employee outlines the way in which middle management must proceed if they want to try and implement change. They must gather data, and present material to their seniors that will go up through the ranks after discussion at each level, a slow and laborious process. Alternatively, they need to be able to target the right people at the top to get their ideas across directly – also a slow and laborious process, and one that they must take on in addition to their regular work.

Management values highly those juniors with the ability to present ideas, to promote new ideas and, once approved, to implement them. But, as the following comments show, there is a great discrepancy between the need for young employees to change the customs of the company and their ability to do so in practice. Younger employees are not given clear directions about coming up with their own ideas and selling them to their seniors. Some C-Life employees – especially the less successful ones – seem not to be very aware of what their seniors really want. Whilst playing the role of a good and obedient employee, they lack the initiative, energy and foresight that the seniors really want of them.

I: How actually to change the customs of the company is a really difficult question. The kind of employees that C-Life needs now and the way that C-Life needs to change its customs is as follows. Rather than clinging on to C-Life for ever and ever they need to think about what they want to do ... what they want to proceed with ... they need to have a certain image that they hold and to make a challenge. If they are not able to do that inside C-Life they need to go to another company and make their challenge on that new stage. They need to change toward that kind of free thinking. Before, if you got into C-Life you would spend 35 years there, all the time until retirement. So you had to choose that road; there was no other. But now, people like J, if they think that they can make use of their abilities in another direction, and if they have the confidence, they can change and make a success in another direction. There are a few people like that now. Of course you really should explain that sort of thing. And the personnel department should tell the bosses to explain it properly. And they should try and put that policy in place. So I think there are quite a few people who don't know why they can't advance at the same rate as their *doki*, and who are feeling insecure. But I think they do have some kind of feeling about what is really going on (*usu usu wakarunjanaika*).

Finally, C-Life employees suggested that the inability of the company to change is exacerbated by the recession and the subsequent personnel moves. We have seen that, as many talented and forward-thinking members of the company leave in droves, either of their own volition or in as part of the restructuring plan, many of the untalented remain. The general result is that the remaining personnel are more domestic, less talented, less risk-taking and more conservative. Moreover, many new employees are surprisingly conservative, probably because of the intense insecurity of the times.

H: I have the feeling that conservative types of people are coming into C-Life still – even the young ones. The people who were in the foreign

> corps in C-Life or who were stationed overseas have all quit now. Even people who have remained behind in Japan are quitting too. So it has become harder and harder to change what remains … So the older-thinking kind of person remains behind to face the tidal wave. C-Life is not really like the Titanic – it is more like the Battleship Yamato! Everyone on the Battleship Yamato died!

There is, then, a variety of reasons behind the company's inability to change. Besides these, however, the employees identify a certain resistance to change as inherent in the Japanese character. I consider these points next.

Japanese character

In the lead-up to the bubble, many positive aspects of Japanese management were famously ascribed to Japanese culture in the '*nihonjinron*' literature – the 'theories of Japanese-ness' literature. Books such as Ouchi (1981), Christopher (1983) and Vogel (1979) sought to account for Japan's success in terms of those cultural factors that supposedly made the Japanese unique. The Japanese are unique, according to these authors and others like them, in their consensus approach to human relations and decision-making, and in the harmony and co-operation between members of the group, minimising conflict. The group is seen as a hierarchy with paternal and benevolent leaders and loyal followers. And practices in modern organisations were assumed to have grown out of traditional culture. We shall encounter this portrait of 'Japanese-ness' again in chapters 7 and 9.

But now in the tenth year after the collapse of the bubble, I found that C-Life employees ascribed many of Japan's economic woes to the very same traits that had once been thought to be part of the secret of the country's success.

W: Because we are a uniform people (*tan itsu minzoku*), when everyone goes in one direction, you can't stop them.

H: Because Japanese were never capable of accepting variety, they can't achieve a balance, because everyone is equal. If somebody says 'Go left,' everyone goes left together. Japanese society is like a see-saw. If one side starts to get heavy, everyone goes there in one fell swoop. It changes 180 degrees. I was predicting this.

W: And one of our national characteristics in response to a first experience is a waiting stance. Basically. That is a Japanese characteristic. So there are few people who just get up and initiate action.

K: As far as the recession having lasted ten long years I think it is a special characteristic of the Japanese that everyone tends to have the same ideas, so after all everyone ends up tending together, but after a time everyone all had huge confidence together. Japanese tend to all lean in one way together.

In the intense uncertainty, and even while the company is accepting the inevitable changes, some employees expressed their belief that Japan is only reluctantly going along with changes that it would not otherwise make if it had any choice.

C: Japan was not allowed by law to have more than twenty life insurance companies. And as you know, in the convoy system, the bureaucracy protected each company and allowed them all to remain floating (despite the bad condition of the weaker ones). I think the bureaucracy wanted the stability as well. I don't think Japan as a society likes drastic change.

H: I think that people who don't want to change are much more common in Japan than would be, for example, among Americans. I think there are people in the world who want to change the existing system and people who don't want to change it and people who lie in the middle. If the anchor is the people who definitely don't want to change the system there is a large brake operating against change and they take on the role of being this brake. I think this kind of person is quite common in Japan – people who take on the role as stabilising factors. I think when C-Life employees change to another company for the first time, their thinking has to change. If they don't have any need to change then they don't change – it's easier not to change if you don't have to – unless there's pressure from outside then they don't change. The thinking of average people is that they just want to maintain conditions as they are at present – they just want to get their salary. Even if their salaries are all being reduced together they have a 'warm-water' kind of thinking. They pretend that they are still doing work and think that as long as the company is still paying them then it's all right to go on like that. I don't think that even now they are liking the changes that they are making.

(The reference to warm water is from the story about the frog basking in a saucepan of warm water, which is gradually heated up: the frog doesn't realise what is happening until finally it is boiled to death. I heard this same example from more than ten C-Life people. It seemed to be almost a communal metaphor that was used to sum up Japan's woes.)

Under these circumstances, C-Life employees frequently told me that the only real way to change the company was to bring in pressure from outside, as it was impossible to change the company dramatically from the inside. They used all kinds of metaphors to illustrate this. One was the example of World War II, and the amount of force it took to change the direction of the

Japanese nation. They pointed out that in that situation too, once the nation was forced to change, it did so totally and dramatically.

We have already seen how the possibility of a merger with a foreign company was considered. Here we see one of the reasons why some employees thought such a step necessary. They believe the system in the company to be so geared towards stability, and to have so few mechanisms in place to introduce change, that they consider external pressure to be the only way to achieve change on the necessary scale. This is seen as a typically Japanese characteristic.

H: I think it is all Japanese groups that only respond to pressure from the outside. Basically, they don't want to change. From the companies with good results, companies have started to globalise and in that sense, I feel it is a kind of outside pressure that is causing them to change. Japanese organisations can't renew themselves because as a national characteristic Americans – who are the descendants of people who came out from England who wanted to transform things – include a lot of strong people. There are conservative people as well but they are more in the minority, and there is a larger percentage of people who like change. In Japan, there are a lot of people who don't like change, who like stability. In American society there is not much stability so you have to be used to change.

J: Some people say that it is impossible for Japanese to change gradually – something has to be broken completely. Otherwise change is impossible. I am almost wholly in agreement with that. Somebody told the tale about the frog in the bath. After the frog got in the bath the bath was heated up slowly and gets warmer and warmer. And the frog doesn't really notice the change. In the end, the frog gets boiled to death. I think that in Japan we are in that situation now. If we don't actually face death (*saigo wa ittan shinde shimawanai to*) people won't realise that they were mistaken. I think you can say the same about the company. I think that C-Life has tried to implement changes – putting in university graduates as sales women or Japanese who spent their childhoods abroad or foreigners for example. But even though you say that they put in foreigners it has no meaning to put just one or two into the company. That doesn't mean they are trying to change the way they are thinking. It just looks good in the eyes of the world. That was the level that those changes were at. In other words, it is just sleight of hand – it is just a performance trick. If they were really going to change something they would invite a foreigner to be part of management, onto the board itself. I think that you have to go that far.

In cases where these unusual types of foreigners were put in, the tension between surface-level change and the unchanging culture underneath caused endless conflict both within departments and between departments. As in that case, the C-Life employees believed that the attempted change was not large enough.

P: The international department was called the 'international', but except for one or two guys, it was actually a very domestic department. Even if one international guy turns up it doesn't turn the whole department international. It is becoming the international age, but that doesn't mean everybody is into wanting to try and be international.

If one accepts the idea that change must be on a scale large enough to break down existing structures entirely, this does not explain why the change must be from outside, or specifically 'foreign', as the C-Life employees seem to suggest. The next section describes the case of Nissan, which was taken over by 'foreigners', and the thoughts of the C-Life employees about it. I focus on the case of Nissan not because of its inherent significance in the context of the Japanese economy, but because it was so important to the employees with whom I spoke. The fact that a Japanese company had been taken over by a foreign one, and turned into a success, made an enormous impression on them, and they mentioned it repeatedly.

The case of Nissan

C-Life employees were generally fascinated by the situation of Nissan, as indeed were the media. Nissan Motor was the first case of a really major company – seen as truly representative of the past glories of Japanese manufacturing – taken over by a foreign company. It had a merger with French car manufacturer Renault SA in 1999. Since then, all eyes have been watching the company's fortunes. This was especially so as the company implemented a number of radical management and policy changes, including installing a 37-year-old foreigner, Carlos Ghosn, to head the company. Ghosn proceeded to run a tight management ship with only a handful of key figures involved in decision-making, and promoted large numbers of women.

The new president turned customs upside down in unexpected ways. There has been a long tradition in Japan of *sokaiya* – mafia-connected extortionists – disrupting shareholder proceedings on behalf of key shareholders, who pay them secretly. Alternatively, they may be there on behalf of management, as a threat to any shareholders who might want to ask the management embarrassing questions. They do this by shouting the shareholders down – on the pay, ostensibly, of the company. At his first shareholder meeting of Nissan, the new president was berated by *sokaiya* and not allowed to say anything, but he withstood the onslaught for well over an hour until he finally managed to speak.

The fascination of C-Life's employees with Nissan Motor is understandable. Since the French company Renault began running the company, operating profit for the first half of 2000 doubled. Koji Endo, auto analyst at Credit Suisse First Boston (quoted in *Financial Times* 31 October 2000), said: 'Nissan is basically run by three Renault people. They make every final decision and then execute it … It's completely different. A completely different mentality, different attitude. I don't think any Japanese manager could have done this'. Carlos Ghosn agreed (in the same article) that recovery would have been impossible for Nissan without the alliance with Renault.

For C-Life employees who were critical of C-Life's management, Nissan became a key case against which they mirrored the defects of C-Life and came to conclusions about what should change. I introduce here the opinions of a number of C-Life employees in full and summarise the points they make at the end of the section.

J: In order to produce any kind of real change it would have to be done from the very top. You have to bring somebody in from outside and put them in the presidency or somewhere nearby to effect real change, like with Nissan and G E Edison. For example, if a foreigner came into C-Life bringing foreign-style ways of doing things, then I think it would really change.

P: I think that it is the case in the very tight form of a Japanese organisation that it is difficult for things to change slowly. Things have to be completely broken down and a new start put in to initiate the changes. So now Nissan has put Ghosn in they are making a new start. If it isn't a success, that company is going to see a lot of tears. But I think that they had to do that.

C: It is not that Japanese companies are so many years behind where they should be; it is that the timing of the response is slow. You can say that they can't bring in genuine revolution without entrusting it to a foreigner. That is the same for everywhere. Japanese corporations all have the same weak points.

H: If you want change it has to come from outside like in the case of Nissan. That chairman was both clever and not clever. He knew that real change had to come from outside. So he brought in the foreigners. It didn't matter who the foreigners cut because they had no relation to anyone and no-one said anything back about it. If the chairman had done that degree of restructuring himself his private life would have been miserable. He would have been ostracised (*murahachibu*). So he didn't want to do it himself: he got someone else to do it. If they did the same at C-Life and brought in foreigners, everyone would just say it can't be helped. If they did it themselves they would meet concentrated opposition and they wouldn't be able to face up to that individually. If

> they do nothing they don't have to take the blame. And that is why nothing changes. Japanese directors are most self-righteous about quitting. They think that someone else should quit for the sake of the company but that it should not be them. If someone like Ghosn of Nissan puts everything back to zero, and only rebuilds the really necessary things then a really good company can be born. Japanese organisations can't renew themselves. You need to start again from zero (in the Japanese company) because the rules about what has to happen in each department in the company are built up into thick manuals … Japanese managers will open the manual at such and such a page and tell you that it is written there, so you can't do it, and if you ask why, someone old will come out and say it is because it was decided a long time ago and it ends there. To avoid that kind of contradiction you have to throw away the manual and cause a revolution of management. You have to have the kind of head that can decide something in the morning and turn it over by nightfall. If you don't do that, you can't get by in this industry … If only old-thinking people are left inside the company they can only drag on (*zuruzuru*). But before they drag on too long they will merge or be acquired and people will be fired. That is the fate that is awaiting them. If you do something like Mr. Ghosn of Nissan, the people inside the company would be forced to change at a pace but that is actually a type of foreign pressure (*gaiatsu*). If you don't put foreign pressure on the company or pressure from outside then it's impossible for it to change. This is the theory of the boiled frog. A frog is soaking itself in a warm bath and then you warm up the water little by little and it is quite comfortable and happy – but as it gets gradually hotter and hotter, it boils to death before it even realises it. If you put it into the hot water from the beginning it would jump out of there quick smart. But if you warm it up slowly it doesn't know what is happening – that is the theory of the boiled frog!

We can sum up a number of principles that can be seen in these comments. First, change must be implemented from the top or it conflicts with the existing culture. Because the existing structure of C-Life ensures that those with the power will not relinquish it and will only implement change from below their own level of management, radical change is impossible to implement unless it is from the very top.

Second, change must be radical and dramatic. The change needs to be complete, to allow the organisation a fresh start, rather than confusing the old systems with the new. Third, change should come from outside, because it is easier to blame the resulting chaos on an outsider, and it seems that the people involved in the changes will accept it if they see it as a situation that cannot be helped. If someone Japanese were to implement radical change himself, he would be ostracised and his life made miserable. It is easier to blame change on an outsider. The clever way to achieve this is for top management to arrange the change behind the scenes and blame it on the outsiders.

The pressure for change is '*gaiatsu*': foreign pressure. This is a common expression usually used by the media to describe situations in politics where Japan does not change until it is forced to do so by outside pressure, usually from the USA. Such situations – from trade relations with the USA to deregulation of the domestic insurance industry – are often the result of such foreign pressure.

Throughout this section, we have seen the employees' views on why the company has been unable to change, and what should be done for the future. In so doing, much has been said on the topic of Japanese management in general. I turn therefore to a detailed analysis of attitudes towards Japanese management. What, according to the employees, is Japanese management, and how does it differ from management in other countries? What are its good points and its bad ones? And finally, how is it going to change in the future?

Japanese management

C-Life employees generally agree with the anti-*nihonjinron* literature, the authors who wrote as part of a backlash against *nihonjinron* – especially after the collapse of the bubble and, with it, the belief that there was some inherent quality or qualities in the Japanese that would guarantee them success more or less indefinitely. It was now felt that Japanese 'traditional' management is not actually traditional at all, and that the *nihonjinron* authors had, to one degree or another, been hoodwinked. They had mistaken the rosy descriptions of Japanese life reported by their respondents for the real thing, instead of recognising them for an imaginary ideal. As we shall see in chapter 9, this dismissal of the *nihonjinron* literature is both unfair and premature, at least in part.

Indeed, during the bubble, the *nihonjinron* literature was very popular in Japan, and my respondents often referred to this period as the days of 'Japan as Number One', from the famous title of Vogel's 1979 text. At this time many Japanese were quite happy to overlook the fact that Japanese management practices were a quite recent innovation. Now, however, together with the backlash against the *nihonjinron*, there seems to be a general acknowledgement among C-Life employees of this fact.

V: I think that traditional values from a traditional age are colliding with the present situation of work as it is now. But even though we say traditional thinking, what we call traditional thinking in Japan is really only since the Edo period. Sometime during the Edo period, Confucianism came into Japan and took root and the world of the Samurai – the world of the warriors – took shape. And a pseudo-world like the world of the warriors then came in after World War II. As long as that type of pseudo-warrior feudal clan arrangement existed in society and there was a clear hierarchy and it was going well like that, there was no need to cause waves or to break down that value system. However, if you have that value system, in a time that you can no longer protect the organisation, I think that the organisation has to decide which to choose. It would be OK if you could choose to go the traditional route and still survive. But I think there are few companies that will be able to survive that way.

What is Japanese management to the C-Life employee? For one thing, they take C-Life to be representative of Japanese management in general, and segue between the two fairly indistinctly. And when they speak of it, they tend to do so in terms of a dichotomy between 'wet' (subjective, human-relations-based management) and 'dry' (rational, objective management).

C: If you analyse the Japanese economy piece by piece, you can see that between what they call 'wet' or 'dry' management in the US, it is definitely 'wet.' And it is often said in regard to whether you see humans as cogs working a machine or not, then in Japan the human element is emphasised.

Good points of Japanese management

Many employees considered Japanese management techniques to have been responsible, at least in part, for the great success they enjoyed during the 1980s.

C: I do think that it was the characteristics of Japanese society that helped make Japan the success that it was, as described in 'Japan as Number One'. And there was a time that America was trying to copy various things, from the way Japan made cars, to life-time employment.

K: As to whether I think that's a sad (*zannen*) thing that management will become more American – I think that you have to make the clear decision (*warikitte*) that the company is a place in which you do work. It's a place where you come from 9:00 in the morning to 5:00 at night. It's a place where you behave in an office-like manner, and it is enough to get your pay. When I went to America I realised this; that the people who are working are really working. The popular stereotype of American workers (that they don't work as hard as Japanese) only refers to a part of America. Now I think it's actually because the people who work really work, that America was able to recover.

E: The fact that everyone is in it together is the good point of Japanese management. People like me with no particular talents can have the others cover for me (*kabaa shite moraeru*) so it is really good. There is such a thing as individual talent … but in order to do something, if you do it by yourself or with others, if they have different skills to you, rather than one and one being two it can add up to more than two. Like the Japanese example. We started out copying things and in the process we got good at it and went on further than those we had copied from … We could go further because we all did it together….

Behind these comments is a nostalgic view of Japanese management as a bygone era. There is also a self-indulgent air. The last comment – 'people like me with no particular talents can have others cover for me' – is from an employee who has been asked to leave the company as part of the '800 list'.

J: As far as the relationship between companies and employees goes I don't know how it is lately but for my generation in the company the relation was a mutual relationship with the company. You looked after the company and the company looked after you (*mochitsu motaretsu*). If you look at it in terms of stockholding the employees in the company are shareholders in each other.

Most of the employees found good things to say about Japanese management. Most were nostalgic about particular elements of it, whether they were reminiscing about an ideal or recalling an actual reality. But in all the comments there was a realisation that that style of management was no longer suitable, that it was out of step with the present times. Employees in the company could see other 'better worlds' outside, and those with the relevant talents were tempted to move.

K: I think that the method of management will be really important from now. Before, everyone had the spirit of always trying harder and harder. Even though the pay was low, there was a lot of motivation in work, and that's why you did it. You did it to make the company better. But now, among young people there's hardly anyone like that left. So I think that management must change their mindsets towards a new type of management. So I think it will become more American, and that can't be helped, because the young people are getting that kind of education (before they come into the companies).

'Japanese management' existed as a unified, monolithic structure. The inability to move encouraged single-minded focus on the company, groupist education inside the company encouraged co-operation and competition among *doki*, and low pay coupled with high potential rewards for long service encouraged employees to resign themselves to life with the company and be ambitious within that framework. But, as the above comment states, the present employees coming into the company are a different kind of people with different expectations. I therefore now turn to employee criticisms of Japanese management.

Criticisms of Japanese management

With the confusion of restructuring and the pessimistic atmosphere in C-Life, employees have grown more and more critical of Japanese management. The criticisms read much like a list of the traits that the *nihon-jinron* literature claimed were the key to Japanese success. First, life-time employment is sharply criticised as a total system because of the tendency of the system to fossilise and become rigid. Inside the system, C-Life employees felt that change was not possible.

W: Especially in large companies, they had life-time employment until now so anyone who tried to initiate a revolution was certain to fail. Even if they had some success they didn't get very far.

The stereotypes of the life-time employment system had stressed harmony in the workplace, everyone working for a common goal, and so on. The C-Life employees, in analysing the company, conclude that the Japanese company is not as harmonious as it was promoted as being.

H: In the company I am in now it is such a small place that everyone is together and our aims are also the same. So in that sense, we are a collection of people with common values. We are totally different from the random selection of people that have been gathered together in the Japanese company. There is an enormous amount of difficulty in just getting a random number of people together like is done in the Japanese company, as you can see from the kinds of problems that are happening now. For example, in investment subsidiaries they should have professionals – people with a sense of direction (*hokosei o motta hito ga*). But instead they have all kinds of random people gathered together (*yosei atsume mitai na koto o yatte iru*). So amongst those, there are people who don't fit the work and there are people that are doing the work even though they don't like the work. And there is also the opposite. There are people who really want to do stock investments but because they have already become older they have to stop doing what they like doing and become managers and manage other people. Those kinds of problems occur all of the time.

In particular, the employees found that the Japanese system of recruitment and arbitrarily sending people to sections regardless of their liking for the work or their own desires was, in the end, problematic. Or at least, that this was especially problematic in this age as it does not fit the environment surrounding the company where young people are encouraged to be increasingly individual.

The pay schemes were also criticised. As the employees saw more and more of their *doki* – their contemporaries – in other companies go into more competitive positions where they were rewarded for merit, they had begun to question the necessity for equality in wages in the Japanese company.

C: Among my doki, unless you were a real loser almost all of them became section chiefs, but in a competition-based society people start to think 'I have ability and he is a loser; why should he be getting the same salary as me?'

In the case below, the employee questions for the first time the idea that pay is not directly linked with ability. Like 'skills' and 'efficiency', 'ability' (*noryoku*) is another key word for the age. Employees with skills are starting to demand pay based on their abilities, and they are willing to move to a different company to get the pay that they expect. Fourth-year university students whom I interviewed for the NHK programme were adamant in their desire to work for companies that would reward them on the basis of their abilities.

C: From the point of view of the workers, the family ideology type of thinking – the livelihood benefits, the family allowances, getting pay in areas that had nothing to do with your work you got extra pay – were good. Our lives were stable. That was the good side. However, from the management side it is a strange phenomenon to have to pay out for things unrelated to the results of the company.

The employees accept that they could have done something about these problems. They regret sharply their lack of analysis and action at the time that the problems were beginning to surface.

E: It is probably not just us, other companies as well, but for a long time we have been languishing all together in each other's company – as if in a warm bath – and now we have to stand alone, nobody is going to look after us, there is a storm approaching … We were too indulgent (*amae*). I think that has become realised now … We can't really say that the company alone was in the wrong … but we were too indulgent; as a company. But we were able to be indulgent then and we could get by like that. If the company had restructured like it is now then … I think the timing was indulgent … everything was indulgence …

The following comment illustrates this new awareness of the outside. The companies are no longer introspectively looking in on themselves, but are looking at the outside world, at how foreign companies work, at how the more successful of the international Japanese companies work, and trying to learn lessons from that analysis. There is a new understanding that employees *inside* the system were unable to see their own positions clearly; that once one is *outside* that insular system, one's perspective changes dramatically.

H: Since the war ended, the growth rates every year were 10 per cent or 20 per cent. In that kind of situation you can maintain a collective body and things went well as they were. I don't think many people inside C-Life are really aware of the situation because they're right inside it and they can't see clearly. French people who call Japanese ants are right in some way … because it is a socialist country … the salary men in Japan are really pitiful. If you get out of the midst of it you can see that. If you are inside it is like the frog in the hot water concept so you think that the warm water is comfortable. But the real reality is that your individual life and all of your individuality is sacrificed.

This last comment is particularly telling. There is a 'real' reality, one apart from the company's reality. The company's reality stresses groupism. The 'real' reality is that one's individual life is sacrificed to that groupism.

H: Because C-Life is a Japanese company like everywhere else I don't think they really think about the happiness of the employees.

The vocabulary of individualism is invariably used when the C-Life employees criticise Japanese management: they talk of happiness, personal skills and ability, and achieving satisfaction at work. For example, they see the system of scattering employees throughout different departments in the company as problematic in terms of their individuality and individual goals.

H: In the case of a Japanese company the personnel department is separated from the other departments where the work is actually done. The people who hire are the personnel department and they hire according to their own thinking about what kind of people they should hire. Then they implant the person into the organisation. The person who has been implanted didn't necessarily want to be embedded in the situation they have been put in at all so they start off with a victim mentality. The section into which the person is implanted didn't necessarily want that person either so they also have a victim mentality – especially the section chief of that section. That is different from American companies … In the Japanese company the personnel department sends people to the department that they have taken upon themselves to just go and hire (*katte ni sayo shita*). So in the sections they don't know what sort of guy is going to be sent to them and find themselves in great difficulties sometimes, especially in the case where they don't actually need anyone coming in. So there are a lot of problems caused by that and that really came out into the open in the 1990s and it is one factor that caused everything to go wrong.

Efficiency is the buzzword of the age for C-Life men. The word is used in every possible manner, to justify changes being made, to explain why Japan had done badly, to explain why global standards had to be adopted.

C: Because there is a lack of competition, Japan is stable on a social level. I mean, you don't see new banks springing up here, there and everywhere or anything like that. On the reverse side, Japanese management is lacking in competitiveness, and I think there are elements of inefficiency.

The employees thus identify a great deal wrong with the system of Japanese management. What do they think will happen to it in the future?

The future of Japanese management

This is what a foreign analyst had to say about the future for Japanese management.

The EPA has said that Japanese management is nothing but a hindrance ... That sounds like a gross generalisation to me, and what are they going to put in its place? Some Japanese companies are not acting in the best interests of their own companies, their employees or the wider social good. But I think again, to blame an entire class of people is to miss the point. People ... They react to the circumstances in which you put them....

People used to say Japanese management could be a new type of capitalism. What I would say to that is that pride comes before a fall ... There was no Japanese management paradigm that delivered of itself exceptional returns. I think what you did have was a number of companies that excelled in particular fields and were world class companies. But I think there was a lot of confusion between what were in many cases maverick companies and their success was in some sense confused with a management structure that delivered long-term economic success.

I don't think that many people believe that Japan has found the correct balance any more than I think that Europe believes that it has found the correct balance. But I would think that most European politicians – particularly left-of-centre politicians – would believe that there is there a better balance and that they are closer to finding it than, say, the Anglo-Saxon or the American free market model. Clearly Schroeder in Germany believes that government intervention in companies, rescuing them, directing them, deciding who should take them over, is a good thing for the wider population, for the country. I think that Japan believes the same....

So have the Anglo-Saxons won the war? I would say that the Anglo-Saxons may have won a battle. I am not sure that the war ever finishes. And I am not sure at what point you can decide who wins it. I don't think in 1930, post the crash on Wall Street that you could say that the capitalist model was looking particularly victorious. It has had a very good decade. And I think that the belief in a unique Japanese economic model – or Asian values or any of that talk – has taken a tremendous battering. But human existence isn't over so the war isn't over.

The C-Life employees largely agree with these 'dry' views – without emotional overtones – of foreign analysts. They certainly don't believe that either Japanese or American management was superior. They have a balanced view, seeing both as having merits and faults. This is obviously a considerable change from the thoughtless over-confidence and pride of the early bubble days. However, it is recognised that Japanese management – as it was – has had its day. It was well suited to past economic conditions, but not to the current climate.

H: Since the end of the war, Japan has changed from a place where it was difficult to find things to eat. In the fifty years since the Second World War everyone became able to eat. So companies have contributed to that prosperity. However, now that everyone has adequate food, housing and clothing, the companies are no longer able to respond adequately to the times. There are things that each age requires. Japanese companies were OK for the past age.

J: The reason that I changed to a foreign company is because I don't think that the way Japanese management is done will be effective in the age we are in from now on. Foreign companies – especially American companies – have a system that brings out the utmost of the people who work there – of each and every employee who works there. If you look at the pay system, it is one in where each employee's strengths can be developed to the utmost. I started thinking this way since I went to America. It is now one year and nine months since I came back from America. In America I found out about various kinds of methods of American management. I think it was probably from about that time – I wonder when it was exactly – that I decided to quit the company. I think it was five or six months after I came back.

However, employees don't see Japan as moving wholly towards an American model of management, which is not, in any case, wholly new. Nor do they think that this would be the most beneficial pattern for Japan.

C: I don't think it is exactly the case that Japan is being dragged unwillingly into being like America. Even thirty years ago, they were trying to introduce the good points about American management. Japanese are good at trying to bring in better things. The problem is that they are lacking in creativity.

J: I don't think that American management is the only good style of management and I don't think it will come unchanged to Japan. Like a lot of people are saying, I think the best thing is to combine the good things of Japanese management and the good things of Western management, although I don't know how that could practically be done....

They do not believe that Japanese management will be wholly discarded. As the analyst above said, 'What would they put in its place?' This would suggest that some kind of new system, influenced by an American style, will emerge. But the employees seem to find it hard to imagine what such a system would really be like.

V: As to whether companies that have become slim and healthy again will return to a seniority system....

P: If you look at the Edo period, I think that the present situation is like the latter days of the Tokugawa era. The Meiji government had just been created and a new hierarchy was in the process of being created.

V: I don't know whether that was a seniority system or not. But the seniority system is very widespread. It will be very different to the West, whatever form it takes in the future. However, it will not be the same as it is now.

P: I don't think it will be the same as it has been. But as to how much it will change it is hard to say. How much it will fuse or merge with the West is hard to imagine.

Throughout my fieldwork, I heard various comments or wishes hinting that perhaps Japanese management would reappear if the times were better. Some employees, at least, wished for a return to Japanese-style management as soon as possible, and saw the current turbulence as a temporary phenomenon to be endured and overcome. This was by no means limited to the older generation. I was particularly interested to find, in interviews with university students who were looking for jobs at the time that I did my fieldwork, that many wished for a secure, group-oriented existence in a company with life-time employment. Indeed, the C-Life employees noted that new people coming into the company were in some ways quite as conservative as their seniors, in the sense that they were passive, unwilling to make decisions and wanted security more than other factors in their jobs.

One foreign analyst has summed up the view that whatever new style of management evolves in Japan, it will be quite unlike what has come before, yet nonetheless different from American-style management.

> Have the Japan as Number One myths been thoroughly debunked? Oh, I think they have been kneed aggressively in the groin. I think Japan has taken one hell of a beating over the last ten years. I think there are very few managers or just people in Japan who believe that Japan had discovered or has discovered some unique form of economic management that delivers superior economic growth. I am sure there are people that believe that there is somewhere a better balance between capital and labour, or whatever you care to call it – a third way in the European context – that offers a better return between the interests of capital and the interests of labour – the interests that involve the company – than the pure capitalist model – and that may well be true.

Throughout the discussion in this chapter, I have focused on the future. Employees are uncertain what to expect from the future, but, however nostalgic they may be for the past, most of them are aware that it cannot be resuscitated.

In the next chapter, I provide a number of detailed case studies of my *doki* in C-Life. These are eight people – seven 'types' – who were selected to be filmed for an NHK documentary. Looking at these 'types' gives us a fascinating insight into how change is occurring in Japan now on the micro-level; on the level of employees' lives.

6 The flowers of 1985

In the previous three chapters, we have seen the current situation of C-Life from the employees' point of view. How are they responding to these changing, uncertain circumstances? This is the subject of the current chapter. Here, I discuss the employees profiled in the NHK television programme. The focus is on the different strategies being developed by employees to cope with the changing economic realities facing them. In the programme I aimed to examine what was happening with mid-career employees at a large Japanese company after ten years of economic downturn. In this period of enormous change and turbulence I expected the employees to be facing difficult choices about their work and future careers.

The interest in the programme from a Japanese audience's point of view was to get the 'real' story from present employees in a major Japanese company on the verge of bankruptcy. In actual fact it is practically unheard of for employees who currently work for a major company to appear on television to talk about their relations with their company. These Japanese 'salary men' in their thirties are faced with enormous change and very hard choices, and there is little precedent to help them make their decisions. There is overwhelming interest in the choices that are actually being made and why. Thus, our programme drew considerable interest from the television audience, and 2.5 million people tuned in to watch it.

We looked at all of the fifty employees who entered the company in 1985, the same year as I did, which meant that they were my '*doki*' or members of the same year-group. We interviewed them all extensively to try to identify the ways in which they were responding to the recession and the pressures of restructuring. The first point of interest was that fully half of the *doki* had quit C-Life by the time that I finished my fieldwork. Among the *doki*, there were a number of patterns of response that showed that these employees were responding to the changes in very diverse ways. In the absence of any clear direction in the changing Japanese employment situation and economy, sharp differences were evident in the way that different individuals interpreted the changes, in their ideas and strategies for dealing with their work and for dealing with the possibility of changing jobs or being laid off.

Once we identified the main patterns among the *doki*, we chose the ones who were most representative of each type and singled them out for more extensive interviewing and inclusion in the actual documentary. We chose seven types, and eight people for the programme. What follows is their individual stories, summarised from the interviews, and an analysis of the ways in which they have chosen to respond to restructuring. I discuss each case briefly following the interview, and sum up the themes uniting and dividing the *doki* as a generation in the summary at the end of the chapter. These studies, together with the company environment described in chapters 3 to 5, provide the material on which I base my discussion of economic strategising outlined in chapter 7.

Unlike in other chapters, I have here referred to the *doki* by their full names, since their identities were broadcast in the television programme.

The generation of *doki*

The generation I chose to film was employed by C-Life well before the bubble got underway. It was an unusual time for the insurance industry, as the laws had been revised to allow a sharp increase in overseas investment – as discussed previously – and the hitherto domestic-oriented life insurance industry was poised to join the international financial world. The generation of 1985 included many who would otherwise have joined more international companies, and were thus unusually talented – hence their nickname, the 'flowers of 1985'. This generation – especially those in the loans and investment departments – was entrusted with unprecedented responsibility for their age during the bubble, just three to five years after they had joined the company. This proved to be a problem for some of them, as is evident from their interviews.

Following the crash, this talented generation has struggled through sober times, with many pay cuts, and now with the threat of actually being laid off. At the time that we finished making the programme, exactly half of the fifty *doki* who had started in the company together were remaining with the company, an astonishing number for that age group in a major Japanese company such as C-Life. Doing a cross-cut study of the generation we chose was of particular interest because it hovers between two sharply different generations. The *doki* described the generation above them as 'group-oriented' and conservative, sacrificing, company-oriented, more concerned with company than with job. This is the traditional image of the Japanese employee, commonly described in the Japan literature to date. The younger generation is described as individualistic, self-oriented, more occupied with career than with company.

These *doki* sit uneasily at the dividing line between the two generations, and, indeed, among the types we chose to portray, there are those who have remained with the older generation in values, as well as those who have been pioneers in steering the younger generation in a new direction.

Uesaka and Takemitsu

Uesaka and Takemitsu were among the first wave of *doki* to quit C-Life and move to another large Japanese company. At the time the trend of quitting and joining other companies was just beginning. They were pioneers for their age group. We interviewed them together because they were close friends, very similar in their views and had gone from C-Life to similar companies. In C-Life they had been in the same section at the time that they quit – the group insurance sales department. Uesaka quit C-Life three years after he entered, to move to a publishing house; Takemitsu went to a different publishing house two years later. They had a lot of bones to pick with C-Life and were not afraid to express their grievances.

U: I am selling magazines at a publishing house. There are people assigned to each of the different magazines and we decide how many of each magazine need to be printed and where they will go. I deal with the distributors. I didn't always want to work at a publishing house.

T: At publishing houses you read a lot and find out about a lot of things other than just work. You find that even games or anything you touch in life becomes part of your work, so your world expands a lot. You have to look at all kinds of things for work, and study a lot. I read all kinds of things for work that I would never have picked up and read if I didn't have to. I have a different world-view now. My kids like Pokemon, and I can bring them home things that I have worked on at work. Everything has contact with our work – we find ideas from everywhere. Even going shopping is a kind of information gathering. I was doing group insurance sales in C-Life in the same department as him and with two more of our *doki* (including Aoki who appears below). We were all very close because of that. I was very much influenced by Uesaka quitting because we were so close. Uesaka quit two years ahead of me to go to mass media, where I wanted to go. I thought that if he could do it then I could do it too.

U: If you ask why we went to an insurance company in the first place – well, we were university students and I thought that I would become a businessman as a matter of course and, in fact, I didn't really have that many other choices. But after I got in I thought that I could do it seriously and become a person that society respects. I did it for four years. But when I got confidence in myself I began to think seriously and realised that it wasn't what I wanted to do. So C-Life, in the end, was a kind of work training school for me.

T: I didn't know what I wanted to do either as a university student. But when I was playing hooky in C-Life I was always in bookshops standing and reading books. I wanted to quit after about three years. I realised that working in mass media was what I really wanted to do. I wanted to do something that suited me.

U: When I started out at C-Life, I didn't have any real image of how I would be in the future. My image of how I would be was so stereotyped it is hardly worth recalling. I didn't know anything about society. I thought that I would be married with kids in the suburbs with a house. I didn't think about the prospects of the industry or the company, just that the pay was OK.

T: We were in a dormitory. There was a company dormitory next door with middle-aged people living there. I thought I would be like them – balding, going shopping with the family on the weekends.

U: I wanted to work in Tokyo. I hadn't really considered that I might have to work all over the country if I got into an insurance company. That was a bit of a shock.

T: I think C-Life was very effective as a work training school. At university we had no idea why we were doing what we were doing, we just got into a big company with name value and pay. After we actually got in we felt a big gap. I don't think that I could have got into my present company straight from university. I don't think I had what it takes. For that reason I am grateful to C-Life. In terms of work it was good because of the bubble and because insurance companies were at the centre of attention then. There was so much money no one knew how to invest it fast enough. We got good results and gained confidence. We learned how to sell.

T: Having quit I can see the benefits – but I would never do it again, not if I had ten times the pay! It was hard – you had a feeling you were hunted (*oikomareru*). To play a good boy role all the time – how is that bearable?

U: The work was also hard: it's a hard objective for a university student, to go from door to door to sell insurance. The insurance bag weighed ten kilos and we had to walk everywhere with it. The skin on your legs all got rubbed off, and the skin on the soles of your feet. You had blisters on your hands. In the first year it is really miserable (*mijime*) in an insurance company. From the worst houses we got salt thrown at us (a purification rite to ward off evil spirits!). We just went on working hard because we didn't know what else to do.

U: I could bear it because of my *doki*. There were people who you could talk to with *honne* (one's real feelings); but we were also all rivals. We were all in the dormitory together. If that hadn't been the case we would all have gone under with the pressure (*tsuburete iku*). We knew each other inside out, but it was competitive – with some *doki* we thought, there is no way that I am going to lose out to him! We all went through the same hardships. We still see our *doki* from C-Life, and we have such a close understanding with them. We feel comforted when we meet.

U: There is an *uradokikai* (shadow *dokikai*) that the early generation of quitters set up. It is not quite the same with the later generation of quitters. Some *doki* suited C-Life, like Aoki. I think he could work well anywhere. Why is he still there? Well, you need to ask him. I think he could do anything and he has confidence in himself. I think that he likes C-Life. Actually, I really want to ask him that myself – we are really curious about what he will say to you. We used to talk a lot, all three of us together. He always said from the very beginning that he would never quit, that he would always stay in the company. We said that if the company doesn't change, we will. But he said rather than change, he will stay and change the company. I wish him luck! He is a *doki* that we really like. But it would be good if he were saying something a little different now, not just the same as he was saying all that time ago. We still drink sometimes with Aoki; he hasn't changed, he is still Aoki. It is fun drinking with *doki*, we know each other's weak points; we talk about memories. There is a big line between the people who quit and didn't. We don't talk about C-Life now; it is a bit taboo. So we talk about the past – that always goes down well. And about our kids and families. The environment is harsh so talk about the company is taboo. We can't really say: 'Why didn't you quit the company, why are you still there?' We could have said it at the time, but not now because now it is serious. Before it would have been a joke but now it is quite serious. And now my *doki* are in positions of responsibility.

T: In the group insurance department we got to see different companies by visiting them on sales trips and I got to know what different companies are like. I started to think about stretching myself.

U: If I were advising university students about getting a job … Well, although we did change jobs, university students don't know anything about jobs or industries. If they find a job that suits what they want to do at the outset, that is best, but I would tell them that if they don't find it first off they don't have to stay stuck in the same company all their life. Until you are actually in a company you don't really know what it is like. If they don't like it they can get a job elsewhere. University students are amateurs at making job decisions. I don't think that even I could choose easily again now; can 22- or 23-year-olds really choose? I don't think so. I might have been like this from the beginning. I might have just realised half-way through. But I do have love for the company, all the same; it is just that it is for the company that I am in now and not for C-Life. I am happy when we get a best-seller on the lists or when our magazines sell. I still have a feeling of love for the company. It is just a case of which company and whether I feel I fit it or not. I said at the time that if the company doesn't change then I will quit. I didn't have a wife or kids so I could quit easily.

T: By the time I actually quit, I had already been accepted by my present company so I was relieved to be going. I was excited that I could write my letter of resignation. I made a copy of it! I thought, this is the only time in my life that I am quitting the company; I had better keep a record of it! It was my second life starting. I couldn't even imagine having stayed on longer. When I stopped I had already reached my limits. I thought I was killing myself in all kinds of ways.

U: My physical condition was bad. My head hurt, my blood pressure was high; I was stressed. It all went away as soon as I changed the company!

T: Uesaka was my rival and it was an eye-opener for me that he quit. I realised that I had a choice too. But I didn't want to lose to him when I changed jobs; I didn't want him to laugh at my choice. But then I saw an ad for a company that I had wanted to work for when I had first graduated and to which I hadn't been accepted. If I hadn't got in then I might have continued at C-Lfe. I might have given up the idea that I could change companies. Seeing Uesaka succeed at changing companies felt like you might feel when you see that someone else has won the lottery and you want to win too. I spent about a year looking earnestly through the newspapers every Sunday. So he was the guy who set the pattern for me. Of course, it is not a question really of winning or losing but I felt pressure anyway – I knew that I would know him all my life. We make fun of each other and tease but all the same I didn't want to be criticised in earnest. My family was upset that I quit. But I thought, why shouldn't I change? Should I persevere and put up with it for another forty years? I didn't have the feeling I wanted to be all my life in the same place, but I didn't want to go to a worse place either. Changing jobs was already becoming more common. When I got a job out of university the Japanese economy was struggling under the high yen and it was harder to get a job than four years later in the bubble. Then companies that people hadn't got into the first time around were advertising again and so they had a second chance. I was very confident at my interview. I knew that with what I had learned in C-Life I could get through that easily.

T: I had no hestitation and no regrets about moving. I was depressed at the time, psychologically. I knew that it was the right step for me to change so I was relieved, but my family and people around me opposed it. I told my family that this is my own life. I didn't ask them for advice, I just told them what I planned to do. They thought it was a waste. My family thought it was a catastrophe. Well, they have different values.

T: In C-Life, I got sick of being 'a good boy' (*ii ko de iru no o*). Toeing the line (*gaman gokko*).

U: We were told we were bad (*furyo*) salarymen; that we were cheeky. I believed that I was bad too. We were like a different species (*ishitsu*) from the others. So we quit. You have to stay in the mould in C-Life, and that is the only freedom that you have. We said our *honne* (true mind) and got into trouble. We had to be 'good' (*ii ko*); that was the biggest pressure; it wasn't bearable. I felt isolated because there wasn't a lot of *doki* in the section where I was working. I felt like a salaryman instead of a businessman.

T: We had to always say 'good boy' (*ii ko*) things that showed we were toeing the line. If you said those kinds of things, 'good boy proclamations' (*ii ko hatsugen*), at my present work people would say: 'What the hell do you think you are saying!' But it is because we say our *honne* – our real feelings – at my present work that our opinions are regarded as having value.

U: The bubble period was crazy. C-Life got money in and invested it at 8 per cent while the loan department was lending money under prime at 5 per cent. No matter how bad you are at mathematics you could see that something was seriously wrong there. C-Life obviously couldn't support that and that is why it is now in its present state. We couldn't understand what was happening, why a situation like that could happen. But the company's performance was good. We could see that it was the peak. I knew that something bad must be on the way because I couldn't see how it could have got any better than that. I wondered how, when I had only been four years in the company, it was possible I was given work on the scale that I was doing. Well, we did the work; but was it because we were really good at what we were doing? I don't know. We did such big work right from the beginning of our time in the company because of the bubble – there was little left to achieve.

T: Because we were in sales, each year our targets all went back to zero, to a blank sheet. It was a feeling close to terror for me. I thought that the industry would go downhill because it had nowhere else to go. So I could move companies without hesitation. I thought it was a chance. I think the timing was right – there is a timing of these things. I was in the department that lent money to corporations at the end in C-Life. I could see what the situation was. There was work I didn't want to touch. Normally work goes from the bottom up in a Japanese company but this work came from the top down. There was work with an underside (*kage*), work that I didn't want to sign my name to. I didn't want to have to deal with issues like that. I began to wonder what would come of it. I wanted to protect myself and have a straightforward life. Some money shouldn't be lent to other companies. If you are asked to do things like that by the company it is immoral. Those orders that come from the top down cast a shadow on my heart. We had to follow orders but normally the work should have been bottom up (ideas created at the bottom and passed up for approval). I felt a contradiction, a splitting in my mind (*bunretsu*). The financial industry calls for logical action, but this was completely apart from any kind of common sense. I really changed then. I realised there are things that I wanted and things that I didn't. I became able to separate those things. But I didn't tell my *honshin* (real mind) to others. I wanted to be able to have that separation in my life, in my career path.

U: I can't believe my *doki* are really section chiefs. I wonder if they didn't just make their name cards themselves to use at bars to show off! We got left behind our colleagues when we changed jobs. We knew that that would happen from the beginning. We have no thought of really getting ahead any more from then. Joining a company from half-way through is really a big handicap. We knew that and accepted it, so that is OK like that. We don't have the ambition to get ahead now. People don't really think about getting ahead that much in publishing, just about doing the work we really enjoy. What is going to change if you go up in status that much? In C-Life we did think about promotion and life-time employment. If you were the only one who did not move ahead with all the rest you would think about it, but in publishing gaps are not so obvious. You do want the increase in pay that comes with the position, but not just to have the position for its own sake. It is the difference between working just to advance or working for the sake of the work itself. In C-life there were norms and targets and it wasn't interesting work. What is interesting about selling insurance? Now I am promoting books that I really like. It is really creative.

T: Not all my work is work I really want to do, but I do have the stimulation of doing a lot of new things. I can become involved in these new things. I can feel satisfied that I have an influence on which things get published and I can give feedback – I can express myself. In a company you want to be able to express what you feel and decide how you will contribute.

U: Our hobbies have become our work now. C-Life work was work twenty-four hours a day – we always had to think about work. That was awful! I want to have my own life and to make it rich in quality (*yutaka*). I think that my personality is suited to mass media. People told me that at university and I didn't listen. I was in the business faculty so I saw myself becoming a businessman. I get easily bored – that is my character, so mass media suits me. I don't get bored at work now because the subject of my work changes all the time.

T: I am surrounded with my magazines. I really have a lot more interests now; it is much more interesting than being in C-Life. I read literature and philosophy; things that I would not normally have been involved with. Social problems and issues have become issues that directly touch my life. I feel the merits of that.

U: I am happy that we were able to expand our selves in our companies now. Company names are like brand names, and our generation was well known for being extremely brand-conscious. I think I still behave within that reference. We didn't want to move to a company that our *doki* would laugh at. We wanted them to be envious when we quit.

T: I felt that I still needed to be involved in a company, though: I am still a company man. But the degree of my attachment to the company (*kutsukiai do*) is weaker than before. The strength of your involvement is different after you move company. C-Life wanted people with total attachment to the company. Now I am attached to the company, but not as strongly, and I am less conscious of it. I don't feel that such attachment is absolutely necessary any more.

U: In Japanese society, if you want a proper salary and you don't have skills or a real specialist area, or can't set up a business of your own, you need to stay within the parameters of working in a company.

T: I think I will stay in my current company in the future. I don't think that will change much from now. I want to be the kind of person who can express their own opinion; who can say the things I think. Even if people think that I am loud-mouthed I still want to be able to express myself.

U: The *doki* who quit recently had much harder conditions in which to quit than we did. They are already management level. When I talk to those who have quit recently we don't really see eye to eye. When we quit we wanted to criticise the company a lot. But the recent ones have already committed so many years to the company that they don't have the same negative feeling about it. I don't think they are telling us their *honne* (real feelings), and I don't think that they can. The later ones quit partly because of the condition of the company and the environment. They are investment specialists and that is different. They can quit because they are wanted somewhere else and they have skills. It is a kind of trade for them. The sales guys will be the ones to go in the restructuring, those or the ones doing office work inside the head company. There are lots of guys with abilities, but some of them didn't have opportunities to ever do specialist work. There are ten sales offices alone in Iwata prefecture (an isolated country area). The guys who are there have had their lives decided for them. People have their own dreams, but people can get laid off regardless of those dreams; regardless of whether they were able to fulfil them or to do the work they wanted. But also they have no skills, so it can't be helped. In this age it can't be helped. Whether you work for a company or work at a certain type of work is a big question for our generation. I am shocked that the restructuring is affecting people who have been only five years in the company. They are only 26, the age at which we changed jobs.

U: After we quit, there was one *doki* who didn't want to talk to us, although most of them were OK because we were really close. I was really upset about that. We did the same things – ate rice together that was cooked in the same rice pot. Even if we are in separate companies now, I thought we are still *doki*. I thought that even though our future was going to be separate, we shared the same past. To ostracise us because we left is village thinking! If you are living in the same village it is OK, but once you are out you are ostracised. While you have that kind of village thinking, nothing can change. The village doesn't accept a multitude of opinions. We didn't fit with that kind of strict thinking.

T: If I were still in C-Life I might be like them, have that kind of face. It is a kind of brainwashing; you have to believe the same as everyone else. If I had not changed jobs, I would be just like them.

U: I don't think we would be like them. I think that we would have been pushed out. We were like the '*shinjinrui*' – the new generation – people who were radically different in attitude to the previous generation.

Comment

Uesaka and Takemitsu talk of the large gap between the hazy dreams of working that they had as students and the reality that hits them once inside the company. How to resolve this gap is the first task of the company, the trainers and of the *doki* themselves. All of my *doki* have resolved the problem of this gap in different ways, and in many ways this was the biggest issue faced by the company in training its workers. Some adjust by fitting their expectations to fit the company, others by rejecting the company outright, and still others by psychologically attaching themselves to a speciality or a 'job' rather than to the company.

Uesaka and Takemitsu are ultimately unable to give up their 'individuality' in order to shift their position towards conformity to the company. Takemitsu talks about his discomfort about putting on a face, not being able to speak his *honne* – what he really thinks – as opposed to '*tatemae*' – what he is expected to say. He speaks of conformity to the company as 'killing himself'.

They represent one type among company men quitting Japanese companies. All the issues they stress are to do with individuality: work must 'fit' their personalities; work must be enjoyable; work and hobbies are ideally the same; work is not a separate part of life and they do not want to put on a face there; the content of work is important; they must be able to work honestly. They speak of 'what really suits me', 'suits my personality', 'what I really want to do'.

In sharp contrast to the general stereotype of the Japanese worker, this type feels keenly the pressure to conform in the Japanese company. These two men both resented having to put on 'a face' in the company, having to play the role of a 'good person' or having to play at being a model employee. They said this again and again throughout their interviews, saying that they were not able to express themselves, their real feelings, their true mind. They chafed at having to stay within the 'mould' of the company's idea of an ideal employee. They were conscious – in Uesaka's case from the first month in C-Life – that they did not fit in; they felt like a 'different species'. They also resent the long working hours and the intrusion of the company into after hours. They say they didn't 'have their own life', 'life was not rich and fulfilling'; their disillusionment expresses itself in physical ailments and depression. The 24-hour presence of the company in their lives results in the feeling of being 'hunted'.

Work should be somewhere where one's hobbies also come into play; there should be less divide between hobbies and work. To Takemitsu it is important that his family can understand the content of his work, that whatever he studies in his spare time is consolidated into his work. Work should be interesting and fulfilling; it should expand one's world. The individual should feel stretched at his work. This wider view of work is summed up in Takemitsu's wish to be a businessman instead of a salaryman. A 'businessman' is an independent person with a skilled job; a 'salaryman' belongs to the company and does the company's bidding regardless of the content of the work.

If the company does not 'stretch' people like this, and they find the means to quit, then they do so.

Change for the early movers was still a very radical move, inviting strong opposition from co-workers and families. Some of Uesaka and Takemitsu's *doki* did not speak to them for more than five years after they left the company. That will be discussed further below, but considering how close the *doki* are, this represents a major rift.

The bubble represented a window of opportunity for the early movers. Hitherto, they largely had no opportunity to move companies even if they desired to do so. But because of the mania involved in the bubble, companies were hiring many times their normal quota of workers and also taking on employees from other companies. C-Life hired 200 fresh graduates in the peak year of the bubble, compared to fifty people in the 1985 intake.

Because of the degree of risk in moving, and because the early movers were still quite conservative in their views of work, moving for them was dependent on whether they were able to move within strict criteria. Despite the lip service given to individuality, a primary concern for the next company is that it be somewhere that was 'better' than C-Life in the eyes of their C-Life *doki*, somewhere that will make the *doki* envious and at which they won't laugh. But such movers still constitute an early stage in the changes of the last fourteen years. They are individual enough to choose to maintain their individuality rather than change themselves to fit C-Life, but they do not reject large company life altogether. Both Uesaka and Takemitsu chose to go on to large Japanese companies not so very different to the one that they left. They realise this is a characteristic of their generation, a generation which is heavily 'brand-conscious'. They need both the large company environment and the large company name card to affirm their status in the eyes of society. They still want to be in a life-time employment situation. The ties to the company have weakened considerably, but are still very much in place.

The act of moving itself has also automatically weakened their ties to the new company. In the new company they are off the fast lane for promotion; by moving they have fallen several years behind both their *doki* in the new company and in the old one. Thus, they are no longer directly comparable to *doki*, and so have no-one towards whom they feel a very strong pressure to keep up with. They say that they no longer have the same competitive attitude because of this. This is echoed in the interviews with other *doki*. Competition in the company is fuelled by the intense half-co-operative/half-competitive relationship between *doki*. People are motivated by the desire not to fall behind far more than by the desire simply to get ahead.

Takenaka

Takenaka speaks in the tiny apartment he has rented following his divorce the previous year. It is less than three metres square with a sloping roof and is on the third floor. It is crowded with books, with a smallish table in the middle, but no sign of food. As a new bachelor he eats out. It is now six months since he left the company. He has plenty of time on his hands....

I am doing the American accounting exams in May. If I get the qualification I will be able to work as an accountant in America. There are a lot of Japanese who want to take these exams lately. They can work inside Japanese companies in Japan dealing with American companies or they can transfer to foreign companies. Now is the age that companies are shifting to using international standards for accounting and American standards are the closest to international standards. I tried taking the exams even before I quit C-Life but didn't pass. This time I studied every day for about eight hours. Next time I will try to be a little more concentrated but I think that I will pass.

When I was in the company every day I was so busy I had no time to myself. Now twenty-four hours a day I have as much as I like, so there is no stress. With such an easy life I worry about drifting away from society altogether! I spend each day doing a couple of hours of study and then I go for a run in the evenings. I don't really know what I do every day. I don't have any fixed schedule. I do some work on the computer. I didn't have time to think in the company; doing work every day, there really isn't time. Thinking about the work that you are doing at the time is already enough. I am not very good at thinking of two things at once. I couldn't really sit down and think about my situation. Once I quit I could think about my future and my future direction. So I quit without deciding my future direction.

The reason I went to work in an insurance company is because I wanted to work overseas. I thought about what kind of companies would let me do this. Banks and trading companies already have many people stationed overseas. But I am an arts graduate; not finance. In the finance industry, insurance companies were the only ones to still be aggressively developing overseas markets, so I thought I had the best chance of going overseas with an insurance company. And I was lucky to get into one.

When I got into the company I had no idea what I would be like fourteen years later. I thought that people change a lot over time, but people don't really change inside. Well, because I worked in the business world, I learnt a lot of knowhow as a 'member of society'. But I don't think that I have really changed inside. I don't think that my personality has changed.

I got employed before the bubble; before 90 or 91 when it all slid. It was an age where you could cause huge losses with one decision. It is valuable to know that this kind of organisation exists, but I know there are other worlds out there as well. I experienced both ages, up and down. The environment now is something that we couldn't even imagine then. We couldn't imagine that the industry as a whole would be this bad now. I thought when I quit C-Life that the industry won't grow any more. In that case, it is hard to do work with an optimistic forward-looking attitude. That would be the same for everyone, and that is one reason I quit. During fifteen years in C-Life I saw both the top and the bottom. I thought that it was the right timing to quit now.

My career was as follows:

Training – 2 years
International dept – 3.5 years
Sent by the company to work at the Life Insurance Association (Seimei hoken gyokai) – 2 years
Loans department – 2 years
International department – 2 years (international loan business)
Individual loan department – 2.5 years

It is the training I remember the most of those fourteen years. We had to go and sell insurance door to door in a certain area and were not allowed to do sales outside the area. We couldn't sell to our neighbours or friends so we all had to start from exactly the same basis. I learned how hard it is get insurance contracts, and how to make my own contacts. When I got my first sale I cried. That is how grateful I was. It was a really emotional moment.

At the beginning the industry was really growing and the problem was where to invest all the money that we had. We had to start investing overseas because there was no places left in Japan to invest profitably. When I first got in I was able to go to the department that I wanted to go to – the international department. In the bubble real estate went through the roof. We had a lot of problems with the high yen in the bubble period. We made money on stocks but lost it on foreign exchange. So eventually the international department was abolished and I was moved to another area. The funds that we had to manage also grew gradually smaller. It is a highly risky business to send assets overseas and we weren't making money on those assets so the department was abandoned two years ago and the personnel transferred to other places. I moved from the international department four years ago to the loan department for individuals. That career move was a bit different from what I had expected.

I was in America as a child, and after I started work I also wanted to work in America. The way of thinking there is really different from Japan – I wanted to make a go of it (*gambaru*) in America. At the time the people that were sent to the international department were all candidates to go overseas. I don't know why I couldn't go. Some people didn't get to go. If you compare Japan and the US, it is not that I am saying that America is better, but I feel a sense of freedom in America. I would like to know how far I could go in that competitive world. I wanted to do international work and go abroad to work and live there. I don't know why that didn't work out – that is the company's affair.

It was a question of age in the end. People go overseas when they are young or they go as the head of the overseas office. There were only two patterns. Once I got beyond the age that meant I could still go overseas I knew that I had lost the chance and I had a long time to wait if I wanted to try for the second type. I then realised it was impossible. That was a big reason for me to quit the company. Because I was in a big company I knew that I couldn't influence anything by myself. So I became resigned to the thought that it couldn't be helped that I couldn't go overseas.

I have never been in the position that all my dreams came true. I stayed in the company initially because I was sent to the international department where I wanted to be. If I hadn't been sent there I don't know what I would have done at that stage. At the end, I could see that I would be in the last place I was in (the individual loan department) for a long time. I had already gained enough experience there and I didn't need to stay longer. I think that I might have been transferred and sent again to a department where I had to sell insurance if the restructuring had continued and in that case I would have quit immediately. I had no intention of selling insurance.

I was a returnee school child (*kikokushijo*) – I went overseas because of my father's work. That had a big influence on my character. I was in New York for kindergarten and primary school. I acquired a different way of thinking then, I think. I was with American primary school kids – it is much more individualistic. I couldn't adjust to village life in Japan, to group thinking. I was really surprised by it when I came back. I couldn't understand why everyone wanted to do the same things, and I knew that it didn't suit me. I was surprised by the assembly in the morning (*seiritsu*). The kids in America all stand all over the place whereas the Japanese stand in neat lines for assembly.

I felt the same in the company. I was surprised by the company song: 'Power Up, C-Life!' For one month after you get into the company you have to learn a whole lot of things about the company and to become an insurance man. You get put into a sardine can with all the others and you have to sing the company song every morning. You have to sing it with energy and show that you will try hard. I thought, 'Give me a break!' although I did sing it. I wrote so at the time to my boss. We had to give in our opinions. I wrote that this doesn't suit me at all. I was going to resign then but they stopped me. They made earnest efforts to stop me (*nesshin ni tometa*) and I ended up staying somehow through fourteen years. It is hard to get off the rail once you are on it.

When I first got employed I didn't think that I would be employed all my life. But I did think I would be there for quite a long time. So I did really try and I needed to learn what the company had to teach me about (*shakaijin*) life as a member of society. But in a large company you cannot force your own opinion out (*tosu*). I felt that was frustrating (*madorakashii*). I never had the thought that I would spend the whole of my life in the company. I really wanted to quit more quickly but I wasn't able to until now. I started to really think about it about two years ago. I felt I had come to the end of where I thought I could go in the company. I had done international work all the time, but the international department had closed down.

The seeds for quitting were sown right from the beginning. I guess they flowered when the timing was right. If a company man gets an order from a senior that he doesn't really like, salarymen just have to put up with it and do it. And I did that too all the time I was in C-Life. But I really didn't like that. It was hard to put forward your *honne* (real feelings) in that company. With *doki* that you are close to I could talk and find out what they thought about things. But life inside the company is very protected. One's income is protected and wages come in automatically. As long as you don't do anything incredibly stupid, you don't get fired. It is quite hard to give that up and quit.

I had been thinking about quitting the company for quite a long time. It was a matter of timing: last year a lot of conditions came together and I was able to quit. The particular work I had responsibility for was abandoned by the company at the end of June, and after finishing it all up I was able to quit. I was married at the time, but I separated with my wife and became a bachelor again. I don't have a home loan so that wasn't a hindrance. I had in the back of my mind that one day I might quit the company and I didn't take out a loan because of that. I did some work to do with home loans in the company so I had some familiarity with how it all works. There were a lot of chances for me to buy an apartment with a loan, but I didn't. This time they didn't try to stop me quitting. They asked if I was quitting because the company was in danger, but I told them, 'No.' They might have tried to stop me this time if I had been a really valuable member of staff but they are now trying to get people to quit as fast as they can.

It was a big risk for me to leave C-Life but I wanted to try to go to a new world where my opinions count. I am glad that I quit now that six months has passed. If my *doki* came to me for advice about whether to leave the company, I would advise them that the last train is leaving. I felt a lot of pressure because of my age. They often say that the barrier for changing jobs is 35 but I think that 40 is another such wall.

I needed courage to quit the company, even though people all about me were quitting. They all thought that it was because the company was going downhill that I quit. They all thought that I had left because the company is in danger and they thought that I must have already decided on another job. Everyone was surprised that I hadn't decided where I was going to work next. Most people do decide first. They were surprised and all asked me if I were scared at not having a decided place to go on to. I told them that I wanted the time to think and decide what to do. I wasn't really concerned when I quit the company about not having my next job. I didn't do that deliberately. If I had found a job I would have had to start work at the next company immediately. I wanted some time in between jobs to think. About what I really wanted to do. Time to think at my leisure.

I thought a lot about what I would be like if I stayed in the company all the way until retirement. I saw a lot of people like that. I didn't want to live just in one world. I wanted to know what other places are like as well. There are people who retire having worked all their lives in the same company. I wanted to use this short life and see other places; to get that experience. It wasn't that I was really dissatisfied with the company itself.

There was no influence on me of other *doki* quitting although I think we all felt the pressure of age. I didn't want to quit because they did. I think the biggest asset of having worked in the company were the people that I was able to work with and to meet there. In my work in the future they will also be an asset.

I don't have a real plan of what I want to do, not clearly anyway, although maybe I should. I want to have a plan. My ideal is to contribute to society, but work is also done so that we can eat. However, if I could also taste the feeling of being able to really contribute to society that would be perfect. I don't think that accounting really suits me, but I did it for a long time, and I guess I will carry on with that. Actually I don't mean just working for money, I mean anything – volunteer work or anything; but to have a position in society. If you lose your place in society, you can't end your life with good memories. You would give up easily (*hayaku orite shimau*).

I do care about the type of work that I do. If I get a qualification of some kind then I think that I will be able to do some kind of work. But you need experience as well as just a licence. For ten years in C-Life I was in the finance department. I have that experience and I think that it would be best to use that experience. The licence that I am taking now is to increase my skills. I don't really have a clear idea of what I am going to do. I would like to be able to use my abilities. But I don't have any really strong feelings about going in one direction or another. I would like to do a different kind of work from what I have been doing now.

You (to me) quit and went to graduate school and then became a journalist – isn't the world bigger for you now? If you have skills and like the company then maybe you can be there all of your life, but in my case I think I am the type that goes on and on looking for a purpose (*mosaku*) through life. My niece does cello. She loves cello. She will graduate from university in music, and she will do cello all her life. There are salarymen like that as well that have one talent and one great love. That kind of people are lucky. I think that the age now requires specialisation. That is why I am taking the exam. It is not a good time for generalists – no-one needs them. I felt it was a risk to quit C-Life but I also felt that I would lose a chance if I didn't. If I lost that chance I thought that my whole life would be spent conforming (*dakyo*). I don't think that our age has a lot of loyalty to the company.

I thought that I would have to spend my whole life without having ever really looked for a job that really suits me. I think I am at the age that I can't do that again. If I make a mistake now it won't be recoverable. In your 20s you can recover your mistakes. I think I have to find a career this time with the intention of this being the final move. If you are setting up your own business it doesn't matter how old you are but if you are changing jobs that is something that is very important. I am also thinking about setting up a company with a friend. I could go that direction too.

Having a noodle shop is also a good way to live. Some people do that when they get older. They are good at making noodles so they set up their own business. In that case, I don't think it would have been a waste having worked in C-Life all my life before ending up in a noodle shop. That is just the way that it turns out for some people. If there is something that you like to do or to study you should do that. If the person is alive and happy with what they want to do then I think that is good.

It is best if you can achieve self-realisation inside the company. That is an ideal situation, You need to have a dream in your work, an objective. You want to be able to see how you will be at 60 or 70. I would like to be healthy and still trying my best in society. It would be ideal if I were still working then.

Comment

Takenaka was the favourite of the NHK crew. He represented what is dubbed in Japan a 'moratorium human'; a type who is unable to make up his mind about what he really wants to do and is still searching in middle age for the answers to what life is all about. He represented to them a lot of the uncertainty of this generation that is caught in the middle between two different eras and unable to decide their values for themselves.

He came across as half-idealist, half-naïve. We thought that his inability to focus on clear goals in life would strike a chord with the audience, many of whom were also company men, still inside the company, perhaps dissatisfied, and facing the same kinds of choices as Takenaka. He is rather aimless, rather lacking in confidence and direction, and his goals and ambitions are unclear. He is a little envious of others with clear goals and purposes. He has drifted through all of fourteen years of the company before he has finally summoned the courage to quit.

He is taking similar exams to Hara (below). But whereas Hara passed the exams that will enable him to find work outside the traditional large company environment while still in C-Life, Takenaka was unable to do this. After three attempts while still inside C-Life he has finally quit the company before passing so he can concentrate full-time on them. His is the only case that I heard of in C-Life of someone who had made the radical move of quitting of his own accord without having decided on anywhere to move on to.

Takenaka believes in self-realisation (*jiko jitsugen*) through work that 'fits' his personality, as do Uesaka and Takemitsu. But, unlike these two, he has not discovered his ideal work. He admits that it would have been easiest had he been able to find self-realisation inside the company. However he could not connect the work that he did as an individual in the company with the wider company goals. He couldn't bring his individual motivation into line with company's goals.

Finally, faced with the choice of giving up and putting up with something that is not his ideal he chose, like Hara, to move aggressively to embrace risk and make a last attempt to find that ideal.

He has been dissatisfied with life in a large company from the very beginning. Many of the C-Life employees recount similar rebellions in the beginning. It is certainly not at all the case that Japanese employees begin company life passively and have a high degree of motivation and loyalty from the beginning.

Takenaka disliked the 'group-think' mentality of C-Life, and the way in which work became automatic so that the years passed by while he had no time to reflect or think. He says 'somehow' (*nan to naku*) fourteen years passed him by. The urgency to quit now was brought on by the fear that it was the last chance because of his age.

Although Takenaka specialised to some extent in foreign investment and loans during much of his career, he had been shifted to a purely domestic department four years previously. This had made him fear that he would end up a 'generalist' and lose the specialist skills that make his employability elsewhere more possible.

Throughout his entire career he has made it known to the personnel department that he wanted to work overseas. Finally, he has given up on the idea as he eventually realises they have no intention of sending him. Some of his *doki* said that this had been fairly obvious to them for much of Takenaka's career. But because it is very hard to assess one's own position in a Japanese company and much easier to see how everyone else stands, Takenaka himself has gone on hoping for a transfer throughout those fourteen years. He has never been told clearly that he cannot go overseas; he has always been left with vague hopes that he might still be able to go after his yearly interviews with the personnel department.

For Takenaka, 'overseas' is also a vague ideal. One senses that 'foreign' is opposed to everything he dislikes about C-Life and is a concept that he has idealised. He positions himself, like Hara below, as a returnee (*kikokushijo*) who has lived overseas as a child; but in Takenaka's case he was very young and has some memories but no language ability.

Among the later quitters, the conditions to leave still have to be in place. These are to be divorced or unattached, and to have no home loan.

Normally, home loans are taken out through the company. But that causes considerable difficulty for employees who want to quit while still paying off their loans, as they may have to transfer their mortgages – which necessitates them finding a new company that is willing to sponsor their home loan as well as employ them. Many employees talked about being tied to the company by their home loans.

Ogihara

Ogihara is still inside C-Life but is working at a subsidiary as a specialist in investment. He was particularly keen to participate in the programme. I suspect that this was partly because his work is very different from most of his *doki* and many of them had little understanding of what he does, whereas I did, having been a financial journalist. Being transferred to a subsidiary is often a sign that an employee is out of favour or lacking in talent; but when they are transferred to investment subsidiaries it usually means that they are specialists in investment and therefore are valuable. So Ogihara may have been keen to make it clear to his *doki* that the company did value him, and that his work was really interesting. The 1980–1985 generations mark the beginning of real specialisation in C-Life. Some of the 1985 *doki* have done nothing but investment for most of their working lives at C-Life, a pattern that is becoming increasingly common.

> I was transferred to my present company – an investment subsidiary of C-Life – five years ago. There are new things happening all the time with new effects on what we do. I can never get bored. I don't have to think about the investments all the time, but I read newspapers if I can get hold of them. I look inside securities house windows to see stock prices if I am on vacation. As long as the work I am doing now is specialised then I want to do it. I want to keep on doing just what I am doing now. To have a speciality is important for all these investment areas. Especially in this age; with the type of investments that insurance companies are involved with. Without experience you don't have the knowledge to do these things. You need at least a few intensive years before you can really start to be useful. I have about a hundred stocks in the portfolios that I oversee. And as a fund manager, I have to look at all of these companies.
>
> I really like what I am doing now. Inside company life, I think I have been really lucky. I don't get bored. This kind of work just happened to match with my personality, and I was lucky to get into the pension fund department when that business that had just started and to be able to start that right from the beginning and make it into something bigger. That has been really fun and really interesting. I would rather be in this kind of environment than to be one person inside a large workplace.
>
> It wasn't that easy to get a job when I was trying straight out of university. I went to quite a few companies. There were a few companies

that gave me offers but this company was the best. It seemed that it would grow and that the industry would grow. The popular image of insurance companies were of a world of middle aged women selling insurance. But it seemed that the industry was growing out of that old image into a fully-fledged financial company. I wasn't conscious of feeling that I wanted to be in the company all my life when I joined. But neither was I thinking consciously about changing anywhere. I couldn't really imagine a work life of thirty years at all. I could see my seniors (*sempai*) above me and thought maybe after five years or so I would be like them. Now I think really differently. At 30 or 40 years of age a lot of people think about changing jobs and the new people joining up now have a very different way of looking at things. They think consciously about moving jobs. When I got into the company, rotation was still really common and that was true for all the financial institutions. You went from branch to branch and from job to job inside the company and sooner or later you became section chief and worked your way up. But now the sense that you are working at a job rather than for a company is getting stronger.

I remember the first year of training the most. When our *doki* all get together it is the talk of that time that goes off. I had to go into the dormitory like everyone else. We all had to, even though I was from Tokyo and had a home in Tokyo. We had a really close life for a couple of months. Life inside the dormitory was really fun. There were all kinds of weird characters among the guys. All guys together – it was really fun. I knew that we had to do training for a long time. I knew that in a logical sense, but actually doing it was really different from my expectations and really hard. At first I didn't know if I could do it, but it is a strange thing – we did as we were told and were taught and slowly that we could really do it; to go out and get sales. Some of us were bad at talking and shy; bad at approaching people. But at the end we could all go out and clinch a sale. It was the whole system that brought us up to be able to do that.

At first I actually wanted to do that work when I got into the company. But after a year of it I lost my enthusiasm for sales although I could probably have gone on doing it if I really had to. I said that I was willing to go anywhere in my letter to the personnel department at the end of the first year. But after training the company sent me to the investment department. I realised then that I was probably going to turn out to be a specialist in the company. I don't think there has been a lot of change in my consciousness about work in the last fourteen years. I have learnt a lot and acquired a lot of specialist knowledge along the way though.

I spent fourteen years in investment; mainly in the securities department, the stock department, and in bonds. I had to learn first how to do company research and make assessments on whether to buy or not, which is the basic work of an analyst; learning how to read balance sheets and such. Investment was the most popular area for new trainees to go to in the company. It was the age when the economy was really zooming and the bubble was gathering momentum and it was interesting. I was really happy about that! I was not really conscious of being on an elite path or anything. Stocks were still at 10,000 but they were on the way up to hit 39,000 (now they are back in the 10,000s after the bubble – at that time they were at 10,000 too, but it was before they had started to skyrocket.) More and more money was gathering in the insurance companies. I stayed there in that department until the peak of the bubble in 1989. Whatever we bought went up and we had to keep on investing the money that came in. If I think about it now we were investing enormous amounts. If the stocks went down at all we were all happy because it gave us a rare chance among the continual upward movement to be able to buy more.

Then, after 1989, I went to the neighbouring department – the corporate pension investment department – where we invest special accounts for pension (*nenkin*) money from corporations (*tokubetsu unyobu*). And I have continued that same type of work right until now – for eleven years.

I remember being transferred to this present company (the subsidiary) particularly clearly because that was a big move. When I first came into the pension fund business it had just been started and we had to do a lot of different kinds of work. We found the first customers ourselves. It was very challenging and we had a lot of early successes. I feel a little like this is my own business. We feel that we set it up ourselves, and that we are doing really well now. We have a real sense of achievement (*jujitsukan*) because of that. But I feel that I am really separate from C-Life now although as far as actual business goes, we (the subsidiary and the parent company) are not really separate. In the sense of the everyday investments that we do, we are completely separate so I am not always conscious of being a part of C-Life. There is still some possibility of going back to the head office of the company because rotation still exists as a company policy. But people here like it and mainly don't want to go back.

I decide – as a member of the portfolio management team – how much money goes to the stock team and how much to the bond team. We decide the distribution of the funds. I have to have a comprehensive overview of the investment environment. If something happens I need to know how that will affect stocks or bonds or company performance; if stocks go up, what will happen to interest rates and how will that affect bonds? Now I can see that that kind of money that was involved in the bubble wasn't normal at all but at the time it was incredible. For young people there were a lot of chances and chances came round very quickly for people. I had no experience but I was able to do really big work. When the bubble burst I was already in the pension fund department so I wasn't directly involved in the stocks then. But because I do investment work my big memories in the company are of the bubble, the crash, America's Black Monday. I was still sleeping that morning and my wife woke me up telling me that something big was happening. I got straight up and went straight to work. But with experience the big events get smaller; you stop being surprised by things. If I couldn't continue doing this kind of investment-related work in this company I would think about moving to another company. There are a lot of companies doing this kind of work. If I could do it somewhere else I would do that.

I see so much change in the stock market and in the investment world every day that the change in the life insurance industry doesn't look so big. Of course, it is a different matter when I realise that I am inside those changes and they are affecting me. I think restructuring will become even more aggressive. It is true that the speed is fast but there are still a lot of choices. People will move out of sunset industries into newer industries; that is the trend. I am not very attached to C-Life. I don't feel a pressing need to work happily until retirement and experience a happy retirement from C-Life. I don't think we are living in that kind of environment any more. Our company is reducing in size and that is a fact. The international department has closed down. Lots of people have moved out already. There are many different kinds of work and people have different aspirations. If they wanted to do a certain type of work at all costs and that work has disappeared from the company itself, then it is natural that they should move out if they really wanted to do that work. I don't really know that much about other companies in detail but I know that many other companies are doing the kind of work that I am doing now. I think that I could move if I wanted to.

I am still officially part of C-Life so the sense of insecurity is the same. But the degree of insecurity is probably different depending on the part of the company you are in. People working in some parts of the company will probably find that they will have to move jobs inside the company and many others will have to change the content of the work that they do when they move. The restructuring now is aimed at people of all ages in the company (when initially it was limited to older people). It is even directed at those in the company for only five years. I have confidence that this subsidiary is going to survive, anyway. The subsidiaries of Yamaichi survived after Yamaichi went under; the subsidiaries were bought by other companies. So I think that even if the worst happened this subsidiary would survive after C-Life went down as well.

I think that I do have a certain degree of insecurity now. In the ads in the paper the recruiting advertisements all say they are hiring people of 35 years of age or below; and we are 38. So I wonder about that. I wonder if I could have a problem in terms of age if I tried to move. All of my *doki* must be thinking about what the possibilities are of their changing jobs. The concept of life-time employment is becoming weaker, and there are a lot of people who have already moved out and are working with renewed energy or vitality (*ikiiki*) in their new jobs so they must think a lot about the possibilities for themselves. I think about it too. I don't know why I have never done anything concrete about it. If there was a real chance that came up for me, I think I would have thought about it more seriously. But I haven't had any really serious offers lately, and I like the work I do here and the atmosphere.

If I did get laid off I wouldn't think about it for long. I would act on it. I would go somewhere else and look for new chances there. I would start looking for a job straight away and lose no time about it. If I think about what I could actually do at another company, I would have to use the skills I have now. It is true that I am a specialist – well, compared to people who are doing general management. I guess that I have an advantage here.

Everyone wants the company to recover. A lot of companies are restructuring and there is a lot of pain. For the company, results will become better through restructuring and the people who remain in the company will probably feel that things will be better after restructuring. It depends what position you are in at the company as to what you feel about the restructuring. If you are on the list to be laid off you might be feeling very different about it. I don't necessarily feel relieved that we are restructuring and that I will benefit from that if I remain. The positive effect of the restructuring won't be apparent immediately. I think that if I were 'restructured' (laid off) I would try to be optimistic and just go ahead and look for another job.

If I had to give someone else advice after they were laid off, I think I would try and help them by introducing them to any job 'connections' that I might have, but it is hard to do anything else for them. In actuality, the sales people do have a lot of skills although it is not apparent to some. They are good at selling things, and managing people. There haven't been any head-hunters around lately. But there were before. There were a lot of head-hunters hired by foreign companies that were coming into the Japanese market and wanted to find fund managers to buy Japanese stocks for them. When an offer first came to me, I asked about the pay and it was twice what I was making! I was really surprised by that. It was when the bubble had already burst but foreign companies were still coming in to the Japanese market (to buy up Japanese stocks at low prices in the expectation of an eventual recovery). At that time, I asked all about the working conditions and about the investment stance of the company and I did think about it. But it was a little different from what I wanted. I thought that if I remained in C-Life I could get better chances to experience a lot of different kinds of work and investment. That was when I had only been in the company for a couple of years. I really had no serious thoughts at all of quitting the company at that time.

If you had hung on to the old thinking of C-Life from the days when it only had to compete with other domestic life insurance companies you would be swept away by all the changes now. There are foreign companies buying up Japanese companies and deregulation. There are things you have to think about: where you will go in the future as an individual and where the company will go, and I guess you need to think about the overall environment as well. I can't see clearly where I will go and I alone cannot influence the direction of the whole company. It's not true that I don't have any love of the company but it would be a lie to say that I have a lot. I think that I want it to become better in the harsh environment that it is facing. But I don't feel that I really love the company either. I think that everyone has roughly the same attitude. They do have some love of the company because they have been here for fourteen years, collecting their salary and working hard. I think they all want the company to become better. I think the people who would work hard in any circumstance are working especially hard now. The ones in the forefront of the sales area are working particularly hard as they are in the most difficult position. When we meet up with our *doki* every now and then we get reassured. We feel that they are really trying hard. If the guys at the forefront of sales were losing enthusiasm we would know that things were really dangerous. We feel that it will all be OK if those guys are fighting hard.

Where does the loyalty to the company actually come from? From doing a task and doing it well and getting a feeling of satisfaction. In my kind of work everything good that we do is returned directly to the customer in the form of investment returns. Because I do well the company doesn't do well directly, but if we get good returns for the customers, we get a feeling of satisfaction. And it is getting good results compared to other companies that is especially satisfactory; the knowledge that the decisions that I made were sound and the knowledge that they bore fruit. Well, that doesn't finish today; the need to keep working and being satisfied by getting good results goes on and on endlessly.

But pay is important in work too. If my pay was really low I wouldn't be motivated, but it is more important to know how much your opinion counts, how much you can move with your decisions. It is about whether you can do what you think – that is the interesting point of the work that I am doing now. If you take that all the way to its conclusion then you have to start thinking about setting up a company yourself. I would think about doing that if I could think of a good idea. You look at examples of people who have had good ideas and turned nothing into a fortune.

So I think that I am less loyal to the compay than my other *doki*. It is mainly because I have a different name card from theirs. That has decreased my feeling of loyalty. As far as knowledge goes I do think that the company gave me a lot in the beginning. But after those first few years most of the work that I did was new business so I think that I have given a lot back to the company. I had to learn the work from watching what other companies were doing and applying it to the work that I was developing. There were a lot of people whom I had to teach right from the beginning because we were expanding so fast. They were only a few years younger than me and I didn't really know that much more than they did. I don't really have the feeling that the company brought me up (*sodatete moratta*) but I do feel the company gave me the place in which to expand my work skills. I am thankful to the company but not incredibly so. Whether I would work really hard to resuscitate the company depends on the environment and conditions at the time. If I were told that my pay would be halved tomorrow I would probably think about things. It depends on exactly what the situation is. I am a little removed because I'm in the subsidiary but we still get the same pay rates as main office C-Life employees so we are connected quite closely. But now, I hardly ever go back to C-Life.

I don't feel bitter about the *doki* who have quit the company. They went to get chances somewhere else so that is their life and their decision. In some ways I am really separated from my *doki*. I know what they are doing but not really how hard things are for them now. There are about a thousand sales branches (*eigyosho*) in the country and they are all ranked every month from best to worst so that is a very different kind of pressure from what I experience. If I had been told that I wasn't suited to that kind of work in the beginning I probably would have agreed. If we meet up in a group of *doki* now we talk about the latest rumours about the restructuring and the company situation, and we talk about the changes and what is likely to happen. But we don't really talk about it that directly. I feel sad that *doki* are quitting but it has been happening for quite a long time now. Even in the first year there were some that already quit. When we have *doki* gatherings (*dokikai*) we invite all the *doki* inside the company and outside. It is not as if we will never see each other again if people quit. *Doki* are *doki* regardless of where they have ended up.

There are probably people who want to take the retirement pay that the company is offering now in conjunction with their efforts to get people to quit, and take the opportunity now to get out and try to grasp another chance somewhere else. That movement first started in the bubble when companies started advertising to get more staff in when they couldn't get enough fresh recruits. Some people saw companies advertising that they hadn't managed to get into the first time around and went to the interviews to see what their chances were.

I don't think that I have really changed a lot in the last fifteen years. I don't know how other people see me though. I still have the feeling that I would like to experience a lot of different things and study a lot. If that feeling changed I think it would be the beginning of the end. I really don't want that to change. It is hard to separate whether I work for the company or whether I work for a job. But in my everyday work I don't really feel that I am working mainly for the sake of the company. For sales people in C-Life, the company name is really important because they have to bring it up all the time and sell it, but it is not so important for those working on the investment side. It is hard to say what is 'wet' and 'dry' about my attitude toward the company. I don't think that I would lay down my life for the company or anything like that – I am not that wet! Sometimes we talk about the differences in different age groups. As the generation gets younger, their attitudes change from wet to dry. So the age group around 40 (us) is around the middle. The ones after us are the *shinjinrui* (new age), the ones that really had a difference in opinions to the older generation (*kyujinrui*).

The weight of work in my life has not really changed that much either. I do think about stocks and economic things on vacation but I try to maintain a policy of not thinking about work. If you think about stocks all the time you can't sleep at night. I am in a really different position to the people in sales. They have to bring up their company name thirty or forty times a day. And they have to sell the company's products which makes them conscious of the company all of the time. While I am at the company I do think of work though! I have my own life though and I want to keep that in good balance. If you lean too heavily to one side I don't think anything in your life goes very well. Although exactly where the balance lies is probably different according to different people. I don't have any kids yet but I have a pet. I have a rabbit. I have an apartment and I can't have other animals but I can have a rabbit so I do. And I like to run. I am in the running club in the company. There is a *sempai* that I really like and he has gathered a running club around him. I don't do it that much lately but I have run a couple of full marathons and I would like to get back into training and do some more.

If I weren't able to work in this company I would look for an environment where I could go on doing the kind of work that I am doing now. I guess I could be asked to go back into the main office of C-Life and asked to change to do a different kind of work. But I wouldn't want to do that. I would think about moving out of C-Life altogether in that case. But if I was offered something that would be a big plus for my career I would think about it. Career is something that is wider in concept than the company. I don't see career as being a simple ladder inside the one company and ending at the director's post. I don't work in order to advance in the company. If I get good results with my work I might rise as a result, but, as far as my image of work goes, I want to do something myself rather than just manage other people. I think that managing people is really difficult and you need all kinds of skills. Rather than polishing my skills in that I would rather do what I am doing now. I want to do what I do and if I have to look after other people as a result of doing that work, well, then that is OK but managing other people is not my primary objective. That was never really my objective. I never had the feeling that I wanted to work in order to move up the ladder. There are lots of kinds of work that you can't do unless you arrive at a certain level in the company – for example, you need to be a section chief (*kacho*) to do this or a department head (*bucho*) to do that. But investment is different. You don't need to be a section chief to do this or that in investment. So I think that my ambition to work my way up has lessened because of that. The work of investment itself is flat with few levels among employees.

As far as my age goes I think I should probably have a goal as far as my career goes. But I really don't have that now. I don't know what could happen from now. It is like a marathon. So far, up to the thirty kilometre mark I think that I have run pretty well, but who knows what will happen in the next ten or twenty kilometres? It is not that I am not thinking about it at all but I don't have a strong vision of it. I think I will finish the race whether I am slow or not. I will try to do my best and not end up walking. If I stay in this subsidiary it is easier to see myself moving on to another company rather than back into C-Life because I want to do this work and not another type of work. I don't know anything about insurance sales so it is hard to imagine that I would be asked to do that now inside C-Life again. I would like to do things under my own power as far as my work as a salaryman goes. Lots of companies do this kind of work. I would like to have a global viewpoint from which to look at my work, but I don't know if I am there yet.

Comment

The concepts of 'wet' and 'dry' come up again and again as a theme in the *dokis*' stories. 'Wet' is used to describe traditional Japanese large company management; 'dry' means what is seen as its opposite – global standards, Anglo-Saxon business methods, American management. Ogihara lies in the middle of the spectrum. Although he is a specialist he is still inside the company. He has no plans to move and is quite satisfied inside C-Life. But he has a rather detached attitude towards the company, and only limited loyalty.

Ogihara joined the company as a regular employee who could have ended up in any section of the company but he happened to be trained as a specialist. That background has inevitably altered his views on the company and puts him into sharp contrast with his *doki* in sales and other more traditional areas. Some of his ideas spring from the nature of his work in investment and have more in common with other fund managers in different companies than with his C-Life *doki*. He keeps a careful balance between work and leisure; 'you can't think about investment all of the time'. He is less concerned with hierarchy because the investment world is flat, and he has been removed to a subsidiary, and is thus out of direct competition with his *doki*. Because he is watching the markets all of the time, and the balance sheets and ratings of other companies, he has a very practical and detached view of C-Life's financial woes. Restructuring seems inevitable and comes as no surprise.

The sense of detachment is exacerbated by the fact that he is in a subsidiary. His consciousness that he is a C-Life employee has faded over the years since he moved. A crucial element in this has been the realisation that when the major Japanese securities company Yamaichi Securities went under, the healthy parts of the company – its investment subsidiaries – stayed intact. While his *doki* contemplate their fate on board the 'Titanic', Ogihara is already in the life-boat. He also says that the probability of his being recalled to the parent company is small, and he now doubts whether he would want to move back if he were called. His detached position is symbolised in his name card, which doesn't have C-Life's name on it. He describes his *doki* who have moved as 'taking the opportunity', grasping a chance elsewhere. Moving out is seen as a positive move.

Work is 'what you specialise in'. The type of work is important; 'if people wanted to do a certain type of work then it is natural that they should move out' of the company if that work disappears. He is not alarmed by the thought of having to move jobs; 'there are lots of companies doing this kind of work'. His skills have given him a base for confidence.

Job satisfaction is about 'doing a task and doing it well', setting something up by yourself, doing something challenging, achieving success and thus satisfaction. It is increased by a larger sphere of responsibility; 'how much you can move by your decisions'. He has stayed at C-Life because the content of the work is more interesting than he is likely to find elsewhere. In the investment world, the insurers are among the largest firms on the 'buy-side'. If he moved company he would probably have to go (like Hara below) over to the 'sell-side' to work for a firm that provides investment services of one kind or another to companies such as C-Life.

He thinks it important to find a fit between his work and his personality but admits that in his own case, he was lucky to have been sent to a section of the company that suited him.

In contrast to his *doki*, Ogihara has a more realistic view of the direction of C-Life. He doesn't see the sharp opposition between Japanese and foreign companies that most of the others do. He sees Japanese companies as moving fast towards the Western model. With time he sees there being little difference in working for a foreign or Japanese company.

Osaki

Osaki was the most conservative of the C-Life *doki* I chose. His views on loyalty to the company were close to the stereotype of the hard-working Japanese company man.

He had worked as a trainer for new employees for three years after finishing training himself. For each generation that got trained at C-Life, there were three trainers of various ages. The youngest was just one to three years older than those who were being trained and had just come through training himself. The person chosen for this job is the person among the *doki* who is felt by the personnel department to be the best role model of what they want in a company man. He also needs to be able to empathise with the new employees and be able to motivate and direct them, but above all, he must be a role model for the new trainees to aspire to.

Osaki is very likeable and social, a very average guy who is able to get along with everyone.

> I am working in the Kodaira Sales Office. At the moment I am a sales office head. There are a lot of saleswomen, and I have to look after all of them. I have several dozen staff and I manage them. I sell insurance along with them, educate them, motivate them, go with them to the customers sometimes, do planning, study sales, finance, group insurance sales in training. I work as long as I like each day. If there is work to do I stay and do it. I just want to do as much as I can with the work in front of me. That is really the definition of a company man. We are selling a product that is useful for society. That is the very definition of a company man. I am not unhappy with that definition.
>
> I just drifted into this work. I didn't have particular ideas about wanting to work in this sales area or that one. I really am a salaryman in that sense. Fifteen years ago, as a university student, when I had to look for a job I wanted to work in finance. So I looked in banks and finance and insurance companies. The personnel department of this company was nice to me and made a positive impression on me, and I thought I would put myself in their debt. My mother had a bad liver at the time and she had to go into hospital for a long time. I had to pay the hospital bills by dropping them off at the bank and getting money out, so I knew how much they were. I knew that my mother wished she had had insurance. I thought a job in an insurance company would be the kind of job that would be really useful for society. I wanted to do something useful for my own satisfaction – more than just for pay or such things. I was really happy when I got the offer from this company. It was the first sign that the society had recognised me as a person with potential.
>
> I couldn't imagine fifteen years ahead then. We all started together in training and survived one day at a time. For the first two years we just polished ourselves as company men; just getting through that is already

enough to think about! There is so much to learn about becoming a company man. We were all together in training twenty-four hours a day, so we know each other really well. We all started on the mark, ready, set, go (*yoi don*)! Slowly we realised that we could really trust each other. I think U is a fantastic guy. I feel safe in the company if I know these *doki* are working with me. I think it is about recognising what society is. You need to get to the stage where you can make your decisions. I grew up at home and had never left home before. I had not had any opportunities previously to make my own decisions. I think there is a big gap when you go into the company. Even if you work as a student you can use your own money and you have free time after. But when you are in a company there are all kinds of rules that you have to keep. But I didn't feel a big gap because of that. There were a lot of people – and always are – who complain that it wasn't supposed to be like this (*konnahazu janakatta*)! But I didn't feel like that.

As for my experience in the sales training … I did the work every day, going with the standard insurance bag to each home in my area, one by one, to get insurance. You get them to decide on a product. But it is also about getting them to accept you and to recognise you. I was only 23 years old and I was selling to people a lot older than me with a lot of experience in life. That felt like I was gaining recognition. The training lasted only six months, but it was hard. However, I was able to get through it, and when I finished, I had confidence in my own abilities and felt that I would be able to make it in society. When you sell you get an image of yourself; you start seeing yourself selling well and people happy with what you are selling. That is really satisfying.

I went to Osaka sales office as a trainee employee in a real office at the end of the training period, and trained the sales women to begin to sell insurance, the new ones who came in. I didn't really want to be in sales. I didn't have any clear idea about what I did want to do. I told the company I would do anything. Afterwards, I was chosen as a teacher for the new trainees and I stayed there for three years. It was a period of three years where I was half teaching, half still learning. I had to follow their progress. Everyone had different dreams and hopes coming into the company. Then they meet the reality head on and there is often a big gap. We had to work really hard with them so they could learn to see what their strengths were, and come to see a way ahead for themselves in the working world.

Because of the teaching position, I had already been in the company for five years before I went to the Hiratsuka office to do my first real sales position. That was my first real experience in the outside world. There is stuff that you don't want to do but that you have to do in work – you can't get away with not doing it. By meeting those obligations head on I feel that I progressed as a working person. The sales ladies at the branches were junior to me in terms of work position, but senior in terms of life (older than me). But I had to teach them. You can't give them what you don't have yourself, so you have to try really hard alongside them. That experience taught me how to make progress in work. I feel the company brought me up. I had good working relations. I was lucky and I think I got off to a good start in the company. I think the work that I did was good. Work had a lot of depth – I felt always that I was doing something with meaning. I think that everyone had concerns and was worried from time to time. But we were all in it together so I think we were able to borrow from each other's strengths.

The work of a sales office branch head has a certain amount of influence with it from the very beginning. It is interesting work in that you can get information and feedback in terms of results and you can actually see how much you can realise in your work. When your work goes well because of what you have achieved personally it is really interesting and satisfying … My company gave me positions like that where I could see that very quickly. This is not anyone else's work but mine.

Because I feel that way, I can face my work with an attitude of challenge. If there is something going wrong in my work, I don't want to give the problem over to anyone else either. I want to fix it myself within the bounds of my own work. Yes, this is my very own work. I am not doing work like accounting or such that deals mainly with figures. I am working with people. That has its own interesting points and challenges. It is my own work 100 per cent. I go off to work and arrive at eight in the morning. Saturday is really a holiday but we go if we want to, it is our choice. Well, in practice, I am almost always at work on Saturday. It is best if you can do all your work between Monday and Friday, but I don't always have the ability to do that. What I haven't got done then I have to do on Saturday. Work carries on at its own pace. It is non-stop, it is really tiring (*shindoi*). I don't think there is anyone who says that their work is really easy. But you can't think about that because there is no way to swallow that and live with it if you have no choice but to carry on anyway.

Am I working hard for the company or for the people I work with? Hmmmm, that is hard to say. It is for yourself as well, of course. It is for the people you meet; it is also for the people that you are indebted to. This is the road I chose fourteen years ago. It was my decision, and I want to follow through on it, to go straight down that same road. I got this job with a pure heart and it was a clear decision that I made. I want to keep that feeling of purity. What would have to happen to change that feeling? I can't imagine anything that would change that feeling. It is important that I think of the company as my own company, and that I strictly fulfil my role within it. If you don't do that the company can't function (*mawaranai*). Our results are not so good now. It is very hard, but the organisation has changed slowly toward the way that I would like it to be. That is satisfying, in the same way that it is satisfying when

I have been able to change my sales office a little toward the direction that I have been asked to by the head office.

When I look at my juniors sometimes I see that some of them are trying really hard but that some of them are stuck (*ikizumaru*). They have to find their own solutions. Some are doing well for their generation. Our job is just to help them bring out their strengths. If they can't find their strengths and use them, the working world will be hard on them.

If you talk about how the environment is now, there is no end to that question. Our fathers went to war. If you compare the present situation to that, we are in an environment that it is still possible for us to make our way through. It is more difficult for us to sell insurance now, it is true; but it is not a problem so large that we can't deal with it. If you search always for the causes of the present situation, there are lots of things that you can't change. It is better to look only for the things that you can change and deal with those one by one first. It is most important to decide how you are going to live day by day right now. As a member of society your role becomes determined. Mine is in insurance sales. Some of my colleagues are in finance. I don't know what their everyday work is like. I don't know what their chances are like for changing jobs or whether mine will change after ten years or so.

Among the changing standards it is hard to say where the company will be in terms of life employment. There is a lot of restructuring. I just want to have a strong self and that is my protection against insecurity. If you let yourself go (*burete shimau*) you will waver and be weak. You can't be influenced by everything happening around you – your concentration will go. You need to keep a firm view on what you have decided to do and do it.

In the end, what happens within your own sphere of influence is your own problem. Blaming other people is a universal human trait but it comes to no good. You have to look for the blame inside yourself. There are a lot of things in the world that you can't change, but as far as work goes there are a lot of things that you can do something about. I have good colleagues and good staff. I need to fight for them as well. I want also to keep on growing myself. Sometimes large companies don't go well. Do we really know why that is? No. People just talk about it in vague terms. That vagueness is lethal. Against vagueness you can do nothing – you can't act to dispel the fears. A blank statement, like 'management is not doing well' – does that mean that all of the company is going badly? Not necessarily. There may be damaged parts, certainly, but not all of it. How will it recover? Through strong human will and effort; the efforts of people in the actual workplace. People who are anxious about the economy and say that insurance companies are 'in danger' often don't know why they are anxious. We ask them exactly what they are concerned about and then we tell them the exact facts about their concerns to set them straight. These are the bad places and these are the good places, we are trying to improve year by year, these are our plans. And then we ask them to watch us and see how we do (*wareware o mite kudasai*).

Every day I say optimistic things to customers. I have to be optimistic too. Well, sometimes it is really hard to do that (*shindoi*). I have been able to do the last fifteen years because I have this kind of optimistic attitude. Housewives turn up to work here and they are anxious because they haven't worked for a long time perhaps, and they don't know if they can do the work. I have to tell them how to do it. I have to encourage them to have a mindset that wants to take on challenges; to energise themselves, to have a forward-looking attitude. I think my wife is a little anxious about the company, because of all the rumours and the media, but she sees that I am working as usual and she leaves it up to me as to what I want to do. There are a lot of different areas inside the company that I don't know about it and there are a lot of other companies that I don't about either. You can easily think that other worlds are better than yours. I want to get my satisfaction from what I am doing now. If there was something I had really wanted to do I would have done it rather than getting into C-Life in the first place. There are a lot of rooms here, rooms I have never been in, rooms that I don't know whether I will like. I made this decision – I will keep to it.

If I couldn't keep on going in the company that would be OK too, if I wasn't useful in the company any more. That would be a decision I would have to make then. But I have confidence that I won't be told to quit, because I have done so much so far in the company. I feel a personal responsibility towards the work that I have done to date. When people say they want to do a certain kind of work, it is often the case that it is not that they really want to do that work, but that they just want to run away from what they are doing now. In that case, it is not a positive thing; it is a negative thing. If the company told me that it doesn't need me I could get an insurance bag and go out and sell. I would just pick up and do something else. I would do the same if I decided myself that I wasn't doing well in this industry. But I wouldn't change in a hurry. I would have a good think about the situation and make sure that there wasn't something I could do in my present job to enable me to do it better before I took the step of changing jobs.

Years ago we didn't think that anyone would quit. We all started with the same kind of feelings towards the company. But people change. At first it was a big shock for me that my colleagues quit. I have never really thought about changing my job. I want to carry on to the very end of this road; the road that I have decided upon. I don't know about the future – in this age a lot of things happen and you don't really know. In five years or ten years, society will change again. Even among those changes I still want to believe in myself. There are a lot of things I have done in fifteen years here. I want to treasure those experiences. If someone asked me my advice about moving to another company, I would ask them why they think that way and why they have made that decision, and then I can only try to understand what they have told me (*wakatte ageru*). There is nothing more that I can do. In the beginning I would have said, 'Stay – let's go for it together!' But now we are all middle-aged, we have families and children; it is not just us anymore alone with our own decisions. I think I would listen to them objectively. But I don't think that anyone would come to me looking for actual advice. I think they would be more likely to come to tell me what they had decided after they had already made the decision.

At first I really wanted to keep on working with all the *doki* that I started out with. But on the way I began to think that if they had found something else that they really wanted to do then maybe they should do that. When someone changes work other people can say all kinds of things to him, but in the end he is the only one that really knows why he has made that decision. You don't really know his *honne* (real feelings) in a case like that. It is no use saying, 'Why have you gone and done that?' You don't know the real story. Even if you hear rumours beforehand it is only when you see the official company roster of job changes (*jirei*) that you really know what has happened. It is not necessary to ask people why they have quit … that is their decision and in the end you have to accept it.

I became management last year – it was early. Not all of us (the *doki*) made it but some of us did. It is a very delicate topic, whether people become managers or not. It is all about what you have done with your own life during the last fifteen years. I can't make any statement about this, knowing that my own *doki* will see what I say. But I think that you need to ask yourself if you really did 100 per cent on the way to this point if you haven't become management. And often it will turn out to be the case that you really didn't put in 100 per cent. The company is going to go on changing and you have to think about what kind of position you want to have inside that changing company. You have to look at the reality of where you are now. So it really is your own responsibility. If you are told by someone else that they don't need you, then that can't be helped. You have to ask yourself what you can do by yourself right now to help that situation. I think everyone that has been restructured is thinking seriously about things. You have to have a firm self. If you don't it will be hard for you (*kibishii*). You have to have a clear view of yourself and a clear view of society. You need to ask yourself how many points you would get if you were giving yourself marks.

It doesn't matter what age we are in – *doki* are *doki*. We have fun together, we don't really think about the big issues. Everyone puts on a good face when they see each other (*minna au to ii kao o suru to*). They may be thinking about big issues and big problems behind the scenes. We talk about the company sometimes – we exchange information. But we think about positive forward-looking things, not about complicated issues. It is just a *dokikai* (*doki* party), after all. We don't talk about changing jobs at all, although we talk about it after the fact, after someone has made a decision.

In the company you have dreams and objectives. It is when they come true that you feel satisfied (*jikkan dekita toki ureshikatta*). My dreams now – I have a lot of dreams. I want the customers to understand what we are doing, to understand the importance of insurance. I want to increase that understanding. I have all kinds of objectives; long-term, short-term. I want to fulfil these one by one. My objective as a salaryman is to be someone useful to society. Compared to fifteen years ago, I think I have increasingly questioned what my responsibilities are. The level of responsibility that I have and my standards have changed. I have many colleagues and I now have a family. I think the influence that my decisions have is larger now than before and I want to continue to become someone who has a large sphere of influence. For myself, I don't feel that I am at my goal yet. I have fifteen years of assets in terms of the experience I have got in the company, but I would like to carry that on and use that to the limits that I can within this company.

Working life is not about whether you are suited to a certain type of work; it is about whether you are satisfied or not with what you are doing. That is my *honne* (real feeling). I ask myself: do you want to be a person who is able or incapable (*Dekinai jibun de ii no? Dekiru jibun de ii no?*)? Do you want to be dragging your feet or to be forward-looking (*Maemuki no jibun de itai? Ushiromuki de itai no?*)? I ask myself that question regularly and make the decision to be positive and to renew my efforts. I make that decision afresh in each small case and make the situation clear for myself. Life in the working world is hard and you need to assign clear reasoning to your decisions (*jibun de riyuuzuke o shite*) and go on from there. This is very simple. I don't make things any more complicated than that.

Family is very important to me. I got married on the understanding that I am working at this company, and on this salary. I told my wife before we were married that I would have to work all over the country and she married me on that understanding. So I think that I should keep on going on that basis even though sometimes it is unclear where my present situation will end up.

I like my company. We have great staff. My colleagues are really important to me. I can't even imagine what life would have been like in a different company. I don't know what other companies are like. I feel satisfied with my work and I make sure that I stay satisfied. I motivate myself all the time. I am not content with where I have got to yet. I don't think all the time about the meaning of my work; if you did before you know it it would be lunch time, and then dinner time! But I do think about self. That has a lot of importance for me. In the end, I am ego through and through (*jiga no katamari*).

Comment

Osaki has found fulfilment inside the company by embracing the work, good and bad, and polishing his skill at performing it, step by step. By embracing the company work as his own he owns it psychologically. There is no divide between what the company wants and what he wants. Because it is his own work, he feels satisfaction in it. Fulfilling the company goals equals company man equals fulfilling his own goals (*jiko jitsugen*). He has removed the possibility of conflict. His work in the insurance company already has meaning for him. He doesn't think a lot about the other possible choices he might have had.

To do work well is to become a member of society. It is because each member fulfils their role that society can operate. In joining the company Osaki feels recognised as a member of society for the first time. He aims at feeling 'useful'.

He is not concerned about whether the work 'fits' his personality or not. He sees all jobs as containing work that is hard or not enjoyable to do. That kind of work must be met head on. Changing companies is seen as running away. He perceives only his present options; he is concerned with whether or not he can do what he is given. He defines a company man as someone who 'does as much as he can with the work in front of him'. Each worker must fulfil their role in the company for the company to function. He is not concerned with the big picture, only with what lies within his own sphere of influence. He doesn't recognise even the concept of job satisfaction. It is all about 'whether you become a person who can, or a person who can't'.

Osaki has limited views on the environment. The big picture is left to top management. He doesn't look at what he can't change, only at what is in front of him and at living day by day. His dreams and aims are all company-oriented and work-based. He wants to carry on the same road he has started until the end. He wants to keep progressing. Working his way up in the company means increasing his sphere of influence; this is also an aim.

Company loyalty is people-based. Osaki is working for the company because it 'brought me up' (*sodatete moratta*), 'for people that I am indebted to'. This included *doki*, who are all working for each other, according to Osaki. Osaki was at the middle of a conflict between *doki* who had quit the company – including Uesaka and Takemitsu – and those who remained. He refused to talk to the *doki* that had quit for around five years and was instrumental in making sure they were not invited to *doki* reunions. The reunions that took place during the filming of the documentary was the first time that Osaki really sat and talked to Uesaka and Takemitsu about quitting C-Life and about their present jobs. He had mellowed considerably from his earlier stance as the economy had worsened and more and more *doki* quit. Now he simply says it is an individual choice; there is nothing that he can say against it.

Osaki still has strong individual views. He says he can work hard because his work (in the sales branch) is 'nobody's work but mine'. He says that to have a strong self is to be a 'tight castle' not invaded by doubts. But ultimately, self-fulfilment for Osaki means fulfilling the company's (group) objectives in one's own sphere of influence.

Aoki

Aoki is a tall, ex-university volleyball player. He leads the *doki* of 1985 and the *doki* inside the company looked to him for direction when considering whether to appear on NHK or not. He took on the role of co-ordinating my programme with the *doki* and the company. The *doki* in the sales offices around the country look to him as the representative who is closest to the centre of the company, and therefore closest to the news, gossip and information. He is expected to go on advancing within the company and is adamant that he would never think of quitting.

> My work now is selling group insurance (to other companies) and doing business with other organisations; being the window between C-Life and other companies. I do all kinds of business and not just insurance sales; marketing of insurance to groups, planning, and so on. Every one of my *doki* thought they would work all of their life at C-Life when they joined. People talk about whether one works for a company or works at a job. I never had any doubt that I was working for this company, rather than just doing a job, so I never thought of quitting at all.
>
> Why did I choose this company? I was thinking of going into another company … I was going to go to a certain company in the media industry that had been the first company to accept me. I had talked to other companies as well but I was already mostly decided. But then I had an argument with a director at the company that had accepted me when I went for the final interview with them. After that, a senior from my volleyball club from my university who had joined C-Life a couple of years previously called me up when he heard about the incident. So I went to see him and ended up joining C-Life through him without thinking too much about it.
>
> I was a member of the official volleyball team at university. It was an official sports club (*taiikukai*) – a very strict and conservative organisation. But I don't think it is because of that that I was able to become a real company man. I think that what's more important than whether you belonged to a conservative organisation like a *taiikukai* or not is that whatever you do at university, you do it properly (*kichitto*) for four full years. I did volleyball, and I did it properly.
>
> When I first entered C-Life I knew nothing. I hadn't really thought about what I would do in the company or what it would be like. First I went to the training institute with all the rest of my *doki* and learnt the

basics of the company's work (*kiso*). Then, from the second year we were all divided up. I hadn't really come into this company of my own free choice; I was invited in (by the senior). At first I thought that I was making a sacrifice of my own life! But the work that I learnt to do in the beginning was really useful and I gained a good understanding of company life. I felt that I could really build something valuable on the basis of what I had gained in the training.

If you are doing a sport like volleyball, you might want do all the interesting positions in the volleyball team without training in each of the basic positions and really learning the game first. The company is the same as that; you need to graduate from the basics first. I was in Tokyo for seven years and then Nagoya for a few years; I always did the same kind of work (group insurance sales) in each of the places that I moved to. I only had one break from that work; a few years out of the head office as an outplacement employee at the Life Insurance Association Labour Union.

Directly after the training I was sent into the group sales department with four of my *doki* including Uesaka and Takemitsu (above). I thought it was normal just to be landed in a company, knowing nothing. Work was interesting although it was hard. Everything that I experienced in the company was a first-time experience so it was a challenge and interesting.

Whether you are suited to your work or not is a decision of the company; it is not something that I can offer an opinion about. I think I have worked hard at all the work that the company has given me; as hard as I could. Whether you are successful in a Japanese company or not is hard to determine. Everyone has different standards. But the important thing you need to do is to successfully (*kichitto*) do the work that is given to you, and to think about how you can improve that work or take it one step further. You also need decision-making powers and the ability to see things from different angles.

Work is not really about what you yourself really want to do, it is about how well you do the work that is given you. I think all the work is the same. All companies have management and accounting, and depending on where you go you find out eventually whether that work suits you or not. You need to just do what you are given to do well and absorb it properly (*kyushu shite*) and then go on to the next step. I think that is the same for all companies. I just happen to be in this particular company now but if I changed company I think it would be the same there as well. Is there really such a thing as work that suits you? Do people really work because they like it? I think that no matter which company I had entered, once I had started I would have kept on going with it. There were companies in the mass media industry that I could have got into. I think if I had joined them then I would have done that work just as well and in just the same manner as I am doing my work in C-Life.

It is like marriage in some ways. If you get married and find you don't like your wife you can't change her that easily either … Young people ask themselves often whether they are working for a company (*shusha*) or whether they are working for a job (*shushoku*). They need to think very carefully about that question and its implications. People don't write their type of work when they are asked to write on a form what kind of work they are doing; they write that they are a salaryman. Is that not true? Do you write 'accounting' or 'insurance' down to describe the type of work that you do? No, you write 'company man' (*kaishain*). So if you write 'company man' on a form to describe your work, then that is the most important description of your work; and that is the same for all companies. If people ask me what I do for work, I respond that I am a company man. Then if they continue and ask me which company, I might give the company name, and then I might mention the size of the company; whether it is large or medium or small. But I would only mention my section, or the type of work that I do, last of all. Young people might think this is old thinking. But I say that if a person makes a decision to go into a company, then they should do it properly (*kicchitto*), and work with all their might (*isshokenmei*) until the end. People who can do that can work anywhere; people who are unable to do that would be unable to move companies easily even if they wanted to.

I am really satisfied now in the company. Seven years ago I got married and I have two kids and I am living happily. I feel that I have done good work when our customers are happy. If you belong to a beer company and the company makes good beer you should be happy. I have always been in sales, so for me, if we have sold a good product and the customer is happy, I feel my satisfaction in that. I am in a good place to work; it is very 'at home' and very 'flat' (in terms of hierarchy). I can say my opinions and I can say what I think properly (*kichitto*) to my bosses and colleagues. Well, in terms of everyone's consciousness it is very flat, though not in actual terms of the hierarchy itself, or classes and ranks. But we can all talk to each other without any problems.

People all have their own dreams going into the company but they are generally different to reality. After you enter the company, you have to get a new understanding. Some people leave: that is their own reality; their own life. They make their own decisions, and for some of them they have been successful in that. I look at that and it motivates me to try hard to do what I have chosen to do well. I don't think that I could give advice to *doki* of mine who are wanting to quit. Everyone has their own life and their own life plan. If they have a solid base behind them of having done good work, I can only say, 'Well, try your best.' But if they don't have that solid base, I would say, 'Hey, wait a minute. What are you going to do without a good base on which to build?' I think it would be better if all the *doki* who had joined the company at the same time could have all kept on going together, but everyone has their own life, and their own life vision. They have their wives and other people to think about. If people came to me for advice it is most likely that they would have already thought about the issue for a long time themselves, so I would try to be positive and forward looking and encourage them in the decision they had already made.

The difference between Uesaka and me is that he had something else that he really wanted to do. He really wanted to go to mass media, and that is why he quit. But for me, I think that in a really large company, in just three or four years in the company, you can't really see what the company is really like. If you don't do the work for quite a long time you don't really get a true vision of what the company is really like. I think you have to see how much you can really do (*konasu*) in the company in terms of actual work before you can decide anything about moving. I think that Takemitsu and Uesaka had something else they wanted to do in their hearts. Then, one day, they suddenly had a chance to do it and they were able to grasp that chance because they were young and unattached. If you ask the people who change companies if they really had something they wanted to do I am not sure that they could always answer that they did. In response to a person who insists that they would quit if the company doesn't change, I would ask them why they couldn't stay in the company and change the company. I don't think C-Life is at its best now. No company ever really is. There are always improvements to be made, there are always things to change. We always have to be thinking of that, especially in the present situation of the Japanese economy. We need to do a lot of thinking about that and to do it quickly.

I will stay in this company. Here, I can do the work that I want to do; the work that is given to me to do. I never thought I wanted to quit at the same time as Uesaka and Takemitsu. I had just started to be able to do interesting work. So I didn't want to do anything like quitting. For me that was never a choice. I really feel that it is my company. Even after you have been at university for four years you feel it is your university and that loyalty remains all your life. It is like that with the company, but I have been in the company for much longer than the four years I was at university.

I became a manager last April (section chief, which is the first level of management); just a year ago. Becoming section chief makes a big difference to one's attitude. In my case, I still have the same work – but my consciousness has changed. To be a manager: what does that mean? You have to think of leadership in connection with management, but what is leadership? Leadership comes hand in hand with a management position. You need to make sure that you are a true leader as well. You need to have decision-making powers, and to be an example for your staff. You need to be able to advance straight towards an objective and pull your team along with you; to give good directions. You can't just charge along by yourself; you must make sure that everyone is right along there with you. Company objectives become more detailed as you go along. You have to make them clear for your juniors. There is no company without any objectives. You have to know what the company's objectives are and make sure to build your own objectives around those. That is what being a company man is all about. Well, if you have your own business you would think like that. My father has a medium-sized company and I have thought about joining him in doing that from time to time – better to be the chicken's beak than the cow's tail – but there are risks in both staying in C-Life or leaving. If I had a chance of moving and it was clear that everyone concerned would benefit from that then I might make that decision.

I don't think that my feelings for the company have changed much. My passion for the company and for my work comes from the fact that it is my company. I want it to be better and for everyone involved to be happy. I want to change it towards that direction. When did I start thinking that way? After I had learned about how the company works: after ten years. Then you know the work, you know which direction you and the company are headed and you get a better idea of that. Normal salarymen have to be in the company for that long in order to be able to see all the different corners of the company and to really understand it. You really get a whole new view when you pass around the 30-year-old mark. Work in the real sense of work all starts then; you can do work with depth. Once you move up to positions with management responsibility (*shusa*), you get a new view. When you move higher, your boundaries expand, as does the type of work that you are able to do.

Has the restructuring changed everyone's consciousness about work? Well, what is the meaning of restructuring? Our company has a hundred-year history. We have to move to keep up with the age. It is part of that flow. The Japanese economy is changing – all the companies are changing and everyone is restructuring so there are big changes happening. If you don't keep up with those changes you can't maintain your position as a major company. That must be the base issue at the bottom of the company's policies on restructuring. I don't think that can be helped. You hear about pay cuts and people being laid off, and most people equate that with restructuring. But restructuring is not just about those things. Restructuring is about people discussing the relevant issues and coming to decisions about what they are going to do in the future; coming to good decisions.

The restructuring of 800 people is therefore a vital step on the way to making C-Life into a better company. If the company has decided it needs to do that, then that is the way that it is. I think it will allow the company to remain in business and to become a better company. Companies do change, and that is the way that things are. Well, I am just one manager, so I can't speak for the company about the overall plan. But I do think that we have to do things at speed; I have a feeling that speed is really necessary now. We have to develop things with the appropriate timing. If it is done too slowly or in too relaxed a manner, it won't be good enough. I always need to be in an exciting company. I want to always be able to keep on helping to change the company so that work stays exciting. I intend to change the company and to stay here until the end. I will remain and change it into a better company. It is quite a Japanese way of thinking. But American companies also change. They also respond to the times and restructure. Wanting to remain and change the company into a better company is not actually that Japanese an idea at all if you think about it; it is actually quite American.

I don't feel insecure now at all. If I were laid off then I would realise that something was at odds between my thinking and the company's thinking. And I would sit down and discuss it with the company. It is not possible that the company would just tell me I am expected to leave without any discussion at all. I would try to find a solution. I would ask what I would need to do in order for the company to want to keep me. I would always want to make absolutely sure that I am a person that is very necessary to the company. But everyone thinks that, don't they? I would want to discuss the issue with the company and assess what exactly my value is. It is possible for there to be a gap between the abilities you perceive in yourself and the abilities perceived by the company. You have to make sure that such gaps don't open up in the first place and that there are no misconceptions. If there is such a gap, then that can't be helped; you have to recognise the fact that that has happened and admit to it (*mitomeru*).

I think I have seen both good times and bad times in this company. I have to continue to expand on the good times and on my strengths. I have to think of what it is that is required of me as management. It is hard for companies to know when to expand and when to protect themselves and consolidate. You can't just be continually in attack mode. You can't just protect continually either. Where is the balance? That is a question for top management. When do you take a step back, and concentrate on protecting your castle?

What expectations do I have of the company (*kitai suru*)? I want people inside and outside the company to be happy. I don't want it to be a company where only the staff are happy; I want the customers to be happy as well. I don't really have a feeling that I am paying back debts (*ongaeshi*) to the company, but I do recognise that in the first year of our training the company really put a lot of effort into each one of us; the company really treated us as important assets (*taisetsu ni shite kureta*).

What kind of salaryman do I want to be? This is just my opinion but I would like the company to be a happy company, as well as all the staff and customers. What do we have to do to achieve that? I would like to be working towards making that a reality, and I would like for both sides – company and customers – to recognise my efforts towards making that happen. If everyone is happy, that will make me happy as well. If everyone is unhappy, how can I be happy and satisfied in the company? The first prerequisite must be that we are working towards people's happiness. We have to create a company that is making efforts towards that. If we can't do that then we need to know why we can't and try to change that.

At any rate, it is my hope that I might be able to become such an ideal salaryman. There is Japanese term -'*shachiku'* – combining the two characters of 'company' and 'domestic animals'. It is often used jokingly to denote hard-working company men. But what does that mean? Company employees in the time of the post-war growth era were called *moretsu shain* (fierce or passionately loyal company men). But I don't think that our age is at all as extreme as it used to be. I think that if an employee just worked all the time now then their families would panic about it! It is not the same as it used to be; employees don't sacrifice their families like they used to. Now people have a better balance in their lives.

I haven't really thought about what the company means to me. I am there for about ten hours a day; it is a large existence to me; about the same weight as my family. I probably should put more weight on my family but it is hard to do that. In practice, for me, work and the family have about the same weight. Although, the respective weight of my private life has got bigger through time since when I was a bachelor, of course. I don't think my consciousness of the company has changed. I like the company. If I didn't like it I wouldn't be able to do this. Yes, I guess I really love it.

Comment

For Aoki, whether work fits one's personality or not is not important. Growth in personality comes from polishing your ability to do what you are given. This is reminiscent of the traditional martial arts philosophy where talent and aptitude are almost completely disregarded, and the primary emphasis is on submitting to a teacher and mastering a discipline through perseverance. Aoki comes from a traditional sports background, which is more common in C-Life than in other major companies. In traditional university sports clubs, one works one's way up from being a first year 'slave' to a fourth year 'god'. The strict hierarchy and discipline have little to do with ability; if a first year has more ability than his seniors he had better be especially humble and obedient or risk being bullying. The clubs have much in common with the company and Aoki didn't feel that he had got into an unfamiliar environment at all when he entered the company dormitory. He had already experienced working his way up through junior high school, high school and university sports teams. He already knew the right attitude to have towards his seniors and what the rules are. He knows by experience that if he puts up with the hard times at the beginning then he will have an easier time later. He is used to being landed in a situation, knowing nothing and leaving everything up to his seniors.

Growth of the company as a whole and of the individual is the same for Aoki. Perfection is attained by hard work and perseverance. There is no conflict between the company on the one hand and the individual on the other, as there is for Uesaka.

Aoki, like Osaki, doesn't recognise the concept of job satisfaction stemming from doing a job that suits one's personality. It is not about being 'suited' to your work; whether you are suited or not is a decision of the company, according to Aoki. You need to be able to do what is given to you and to take it one step further. Work that 'suits' you doesn't even exist, according to Aoki. People don't work because they like it at all. Work is about absorbing what you are taught and advancing. Individual objectives should be built around those of the company. It is only ten years after you join the company that you can even see what it is all about. Loyalty is built up over those years. The company becomes 'yours' through time.

Any company would be the same for Aoki. So it is better to continue with the company that you have joined, to continue together with the *doki* that you have joined with. The company is like a family; it has looked after its employees and the best choice is to stay and change the company if the company is doing badly.

Like Osaki, Aoki downplays the dire financial situation of the company. It is just one moment in history. Financial health can be recovered. Saving the company is about everyone changing the company together. Aoki is absolutely confident that he would not be asked to leave the company. To make sure that you can stay is to make sure that you are a person necessary to the company, the first duty of an employee. In answer to Uehara and Takemitsu's stance of quitting because the company would not change, Aoki insists that employees should stay and change the company.

Aoki's idea of leadership is to take the work that is given to you and to take it further than expectations. A leader should be an example to the team and should advance straight towards his objectives, pulling his team along behind him and making sure that all are still together.

Aoki is the leader of the *doki* of the 1985 year. From the start of filming, he took on the task of co-ordinating between the PR department and NHK. The *doki* inside the company agreed to co-operate with the film only after Aoki did. Aoki is the *doki* that Hara (next) says is the sole remaining candidate for president of the company among that year's intake.

Hara

Hara is a good-looking man with the appearance of a 'Keio boy' – well-off, elegant and confident. He was a star employee in C-Life from his first year, where he scored one of the highest performances in training. A returnee school child, he speaks fairly fluent English but nevertheless describes himself as very Japanese. He has been careful to keep his international side hidden and play the role of a model employee. He joined the prestigious international department straight out of training, and the company invested in him by sending him to the New York office for four years. His resignation was apparently a surprise to his seniors, and a blow to the company.

I interviewed him in his twenty-first-storey office in his new company. From his west-facing office and spacious desk he has a view overlooking the whole of Tokyo Bay. It is a very different atmosphere from the crowded and ugly main office of C-Life with its metallic desks in hierarchical rows.

> My company, Global Wrap, does wrap accounts that are given over to sales companies to sell for us. I do the marketing plans and planning for them. I look at portfolio strategy, which is our selling point for our funds, and train the sales staff. The company is composed half of American and half of Japanese capital. The American half is owned by one of the largest American finance companies, which took over half of the company a couple of years ago. I have been here for a year and three months since I quit C-Life.
>
> There are a number of reasons I changed company. I am often asked if I got tired of C-Life but that was not it. I wanted change. I was very comfortable at C-Life. I did investment all the time there, which is what I wanted to do from the beginning. I think everyone wanted to go into the international department when they got into life insurance in the bubble. I was lucky to do investment all the time I was there. I mainly handled foreign bonds. If you are in a Japanese company you can see your future; ten years ahead, fifteen years ahead. You can see it all. In some ways that is not interesting. I would rather have change in my life considering that I have only one life.
>
> There was a special reason I got into C-Life. I was in Keio University cafeteria one day with my university *doki* Sonoda – we were from the same class at Keio. We were talking about which company we would try to join, and talking about different insurance companies. We were overheard by the personnel manager of C-Life who was there to visit the head of Keio University in order to ask him to introduce some good students to him. We were asked on the spot by the personnel manager to come together – both of us – and see C-Life. We said we would go. We were interviewed by a number of officials at C-Life. We got letters from important people in the company and were invited out to dinner. Because they seemed so earnest about wooing us into the company we

thought we should go and work there. Well, it's a delicate subject, but we were told that we would be hired on the understanding that we would be regarded as elite management candidates in the company. At the time we believed it. Even if it wasn't true it was good to hear it. We didn't get any special treatment from the beginning and we knew that we were not likely to get any, but we thought that being hired in that manner was an auspicious beginning to work.

I wanted to be in insurance because I wanted to go overseas. My father was in a trading company and initially I wanted to do that kind of work, but trading companies were not showing a lot of growth at the time. Life in a trading company is OK for the businessman but it is very hard for the family and my father advised me to choose another industry. So I thought about how else I could get to go overseas. I thought that banks would be OK as well but it wasn't possible to do new or innovative work at banks because most were already well established overseas. I thought there would be good chances to go overseas with life insurance companies. And I thought that I would have an especially good chance to go because I was a returnee schoolchild and I spoke better English than other kids at the time. In all honesty, it was quite hard to get a job when I was looking. I went to a lot of companies and I didn't get offers from many of them. I didn't have that many chances. And as I had a special relation with C-Life because of the personnel manager, I thought it was a lucky chance. It is better to be the chicken's beak than the cow's tail (a big fish in a small pond).

So it was a shock for the company that I quit, especially for some of my *doki*. I was always joking to one of them (Aoki) that if I got to be president I would make him vice-president. So now he is the sole candidate! My *sempai* were surprised that I quit. I am a very typical salaryman in many ways and I never disliked Japanese company life. They must have thought that I was a model Japanese employee and that I was quite easy for the company to make use of. They must have been expecting me to be there all my life. When I left, I think they wondered why I had chosen to leave then. But they were able to understand my reasons after I explained.

I wanted change, but with change comes risk. Newspapers often talk about this, how Japan won't grow until they can learn to accept risk. I think that is very true. If you don't take risks you don't get returns. In C-Life, life was stable but I knew exactly what the future would bring. I could only get limited returns there (*rakudai na return shika dekinai*), and I mean that not only in terms of money. As long as my family didn't meet with hardship my wife was OK about me moving company, so I decided to move. I didn't change because C-Life couldn't use my skills anymore. I think they stretched me to my limits in the time that I was there. But I wanted change. It was hard for me to do the kind of investment that I really wanted to do, in the style that I wanted. Japanese companies don't take many risks. And because of their asset problems they were not able to take risks. Even with investment specialists on board they couldn't do a really good job of investing. Although, having said that, it might have been partially my fault that I wasn't able to do the type of investing that I wanted to do … I could have made better plans and thus succeeded in convincing my bosses (*settoku sasete*) to do things differently from how they were done at the time….

The way in which people are quitting the company now has changed a lot from earlier. I quit in December 1998. I think people are still quitting in increasing numbers, and that is a trend across the whole country. There is increased competition now, and people need to fortify themselves (*chikara o tsukeru*) to prepare for that. Many people are quitting for much the same reasons that I did. There is an age limit in practice for people who want to change companies: after 37 or 38 it is impossible – so there are many people who are realising that now is their last chance. Some people say they want to stay and change the company, but others quit because the company is slow to change. When a recruitment magazine interviewed me a couple of years after I joined C-Life, they asked me which of those two choices I would choose. It was for an article for new graduates looking for jobs, and I had to tell the new graduates about my experiences of company life. I told them that I wasn't planning to be in the same company all my life, that I was planning to continue to elevate myself in my career (*jibun o kojo saseru*). I said that if I thought I couldn't grow any more in C-Life I would quit without hesitation (*sassato*). I really believed that even then. It just happens that that is the way it really turned out. I guess I had had that thought in the back of my mind all of the time that I was working. But I think that the trigger to change came from my American experience.

What made the difference for me between taking that step and not taking it? It is having skills that you can use anywhere. You have to have English, or investment specialist experience, or computer skills; skills that you can use at any kind of company. I had these skills so it was possible for me to move. That was at the root of it. Life-time employment in Japan is now changing to an American-style system. When you change jobs your awareness of things changes. I became sharply aware that I was now on the labour market. I felt that this is the age of assigning a value to oneself (*jiko hyoka*), and that that is how things are going to be from now on. I saw myself as a kind of a commodity. How much was I worth? I would be valued just like a commodity. How would I respond to that? My price is ultimately the total sum of my experience and my skills. In order to raise that value I need to increase my skills accordingly. If you move jobs you have to take risks, so I am not that scared of risk any more. The products that we sell are all about risk and reward and we continually tell customers that in order to get rewards they have to take risks. That equation is at the back of all my thinking, I guess.

At first in C-Life I wanted to advance until I made it to president, and all the time that I was in the company I thought that that was what

I really wanted. That was true right up until when I quit. I didn't get sick of working at a Japanese company. But now the market has become global and the laws have changed dramatically. Japanese companies can't fumble around (*ochiochi shite irarenai*) anymore. My thinking changed a little then and I don't think that can be helped. If you dawdle (*nombiri suru*) you will lose. Personally I am still trying to increase my skills by taking exams. I am taking the CFA (Chartered Financial Accountant certificate). I have been studying for five years overall to date. I started in America and passed the first exam there. There are three levels but you can only take one per year. After I got the first, I got the second one three years later. I am taking the third now. I failed last year and this year is my second time around. If I get it, I will have passed the qualification at last and will be able to put the letters after my name. It doesn't change anything as far as my job status goes, but I have learned a lot of things that I can apply to my work, especially things to do with long-term portfolio diversification. That is what we are teaching our customers about. There are a lot of merits in knowing about that for our customers and doing the CFA has made me realise that. Long-term portfolio diversification is what our company's products are all about. Since I got into this company, all the study that I do for the CFA is directly related to the work that I am doing. I feel a lot of motivation (*yarigai*) in that; in knowing more about portfolio strategy and investment diversification.

I don't actually have that much confidence in myself, and that is why I am still studying; waking up at six in the morning. Even after I have been out drinking with business associates at night, I try to do even ten minutes or fifteen minutes after I go home. It has been harder to study after I got back to Japan. But I tried to do four hours a day for six months a year when I was overseas and sometimes ten hours a day at weekends. That became a habit. If I didn't do it I didn't feel right. So it hasn't been that hard to study; it has been fun.

If I said that the problems of the industry had nothing to do with my decision to change I would be lying. The industry is saturated now, but that was still only one reason in the decision. The main reason is that I wanted to experience a change. I didn't ask my *doki* what I should do, or ask for any kind of advice. I told a couple of them what I was thinking of though. I had an affection for C-Life and still do, but I have also been influenced by America. When companies restructure they fire people. They have to do what they have to do in order to survive, and that means cutting people. I didn't think that I would be cut from C-Life, but you can never be 100 per cent sure. I never thought that the company would protect me 100 per cent, so I don't think my loyalty was terribly strong. I could see that bad times were coming. If a foreign company became involved with C-Life in the form of a merger or takeover, then they would be likely to really cut staff drastically. Rather than being caught up in that I thought it would be better to go out while I still had a value.

People do ask me what it is like to work outside. They ask for advice (my ex-colleagues at C-Life). Whether they are thinking of quitting or not, they are still interested in what it is like to change and work elsewhere … younger people are especially interested. For people who are already 38 years old, it is hard to change. There are a lot who have already accepted the fact that they don't have any chance ever to change. But I think there are still people among my *doki* that want to change. I think that all my *doki* in C-Life are feeling a pressure to do something, and there are a lot of people trying to change, but so many people are trying at once that it is hard to get jobs. People who haven't got any certificates or skills are going to have a really hard time; that is the kind of world that it is. I expected things to become like this so I made sure to prepare ahead. But I don't think that many other people in Japan were able to see that it was going to turn out to be this kind of environment.

I was 'brought up' (*sodatete moratta*) by the company and they invested a lot of money in me. Supporting an employee living overseas costs twice as much money as one living in Japan. But I do believe that I earned that amount of money back for the company in terms of investment and in terms of what I contributed in training my juniors. I don't think they can say that I robbed them.

I was at the New York office from 1994 to 1998 and I became aware of the good points of American business practices then. When I came back to Japan in March 1998, I didn't want to change companies straight away. I wanted to use my American experience and apply it in C-Life for a while. But I wanted also eventually to move to a company with American blood in it.

Even though I am Japanese the people around me in America – well, you can't generalise too much – but they all seemed to me to have long-term goals, and I thought that was great. I wanted to have medium- and long-term goals like so many of them did, and I wanted especially to become independent, to have my own company. The influence of that wish was big. I wanted and still want to be able to use my investment experience and the experience I am getting at my present company to make my own company in the future.

I like American management and business practices because Americans are professionals. The first condition of being a business professional is to produce what you are costing, or ideally, above what you are costing. You can call yourself a specialist in a Japanese company but not a professional. It doesn't matter how much you work, you just get an average bonus; and until lately no matter how little you worked you could still stay inside the company without getting fired. American companies think about management a lot more; if you make a mistake you get fired. Your performance is related to your pay. That is the attraction of their style.

My pay didn't change that much when I moved, but in terms of potential it has changed a lot. Investment wrapping is a new kind of venture, so it depends on what we do here as to whether we get a lot of business and bonuses. It depends on our performance how big we get. So we have motivation (*yarigai*). We have been doing well and our distributors have worked hard for us, although I don't get direct results as I am not in sales, so I don't have exact figures for myself. But I am very fulfilled now. My company has thirty people. C-Life had 3,000. We are a hundredth the size but I feel our performance is really good.

We have a very flat organisation. The president, vice-president, and then everyone else is the same.

This company is joint Japanese and international money so it is not like a normal very dry *gaishikei* (foreign capital company). It has Japanese thinking and Japanese manners work here. It is not like Goldman Sachs or Morgan Stanley – they sound very harsh environments to work in. In some ways they seem to be worse than Japanese companies in terms of flattering the boss or in the importance of the boss's opinion for promotion and bonuses. Bosses have a lot of influence, and it's not as objective as the Japanese personnel system. Four years of New York life may seem as if it changed me, but it hasn't really. I have an American dressing but inside I am still just Japanese salad! I think it is OK to be like that. I am traditional Japanese. We don't have life-time employment here. It is in between wet and dry.

I don't know what I will do in the future in the long term. I would like to be independent but I don't know whether that would be when I am 60 or some time in the next ten years. At the moment I want to get more skills, more knowledge, and to learn more. In this company I have that opportunity. In C-Life, I hadn't the opportunity to really talk with the sales staff. In this company I can see what happens in other areas of the company and plan new products and think about the big picture. I sit in meetings with the parent company (in English), and I maintain relations with the fund managers in the companies that we use. I can do all kinds of different work here, I can increase my knowledge and skills.

Is it OK for lifetime employment to disappear? As far as my own feelings go I don't like the thought of having to continually compete (*gisugisu suru*). But in the market system, you can't have a world where no-one has to compete and everyone has it easy either. If Japan tried to do that they would lose against the world. People will always go where the products are cheaper and better, and the companies that are producing those products will be the ones that survive. What will happen to those employees and families that are in the companies that are not competitive? They will be unemployed if we are going to compete in a free market outside Japan.

Americans often talk about life-long learning: to study all of your life. I want to continue to do that until I die. And there are also those who want to have a happy retirement at 40 or 45 and live in Hawaii or Florida or Texas or California. They have had dreams like that since their 20s or 30s. I would like to retire like that too. I would like to save money so that I can work without feeling hounded by work (*oitsumerareru*). So eventually I would like to have my own company, or to be at the top of some organisation. My *honne* (real feeling) is that I don't want to be employed at all. I think that in *tatemae* (on the surface) work is about self-realisation (*jiko jitsugen*). But in practice it is about money: the more pay the better. I have no complaints if I get a lot!

I think that companies need to evaluate people correctly, and compensate correctly. That is the first condition for employment. In my company now we have good human relations. In the best kind of company you need self-realisation (*jiko jitsugen*) as well as money. No amount of money makes up for not having self-realisation. Those are the conditions for a good company. In professional baseball they are real pros. If they don't hit the ball they don't get paid; they get fired. It is a dry world. I don't really like that. But in a dry world because you are not secure and are on edge (*kinchokan ga aru*) you do good work, you always try hard. I wrote a paper on that a while ago, that in Japan in order to drive people what you need is incentive, motivation. What is that? In the case of American companies it is money; bonuses, stock options, stock holdings. If the company does well you do well too. There is a different reality in the relations between you and the company. Because there are so many companies like that the American economy is strong – it is a world of professionals. Japan too will become a world where companies and humans are connected by money.

Older companies looked after employees and employees signed over their lives and well-being to the companies. Is it now the end of that kind of age? Headlines in magazines now often read: 'The search for the Japanese age (*mosaku*)'; 'American management is everything'; 'The end of wet style'. I don't think it is really possible for companies to look after everyone. It isn't a system where people work their best. If they can work in a company all their lives they will be too relaxed; they lose their strength. And the company's strength diminishes and it slows down, and they lose competitive power. If that happens the company goes under and says to the employees we thought we would protect you but sorry we can't after all.

Comment

Hara is very realistic about the age, and non-emotional about the role of the company towards the employee. He believes that the new Japan is approaching the 'dry' character of American business. For Hara, work is a separate part of life that is measurable in terms of risk and money. Company is a means to an end. He believes that Japan will turn to the same management style as America before long: 'Japan too will become a world where companies and humans are connected by money.'

His attention is focused on the changes in the overall environment and his own position in relation to those changes. He is constantly measuring his own worth in that changing environment. Career is something that is aggressively made, not passively attained, as Ogihara believes. Work is the means; at present self-fulfilment (*jiko jitsugen*) equals money and his (Hara's) net worth. But the end is to be free of work for money. It is in work for its own sake, and not for money.

Hara criticises Japanese management for its failure to breed competitive people. He became frustrated with the lack of calculated strategies to elicit higher returns and the lack of risk management. He thought that the company's response to the recession was slow and inadequate. He was given the opportunity to study advanced investment strategies in the USA but was not allowed to implement what he had learned.

Hara has taken two of the three exams required for the American Financial Analyst qualification. Passing this exam elevates his value in the foreign company market but makes no difference to his salary or position in C-Life.

He wants to work in a 'dry' world where performance is directly related to pay, where his own value as an employee is directly related to the experience and skills that he has. His motivation derives from advancing himself by acquiring further skills and thus greater value as an employee. In C-Life he quit at the point he thought he was no longer able to elevate himself in the company.

However, contrary to some, who idealise American management as the opposite of all that they dislike about Japanese management, Hara is realistic about American management. He doesn't want a totally American environment to work in and realises that such a world is too extreme for him. He has chosen to work in the Japanese subsidiary of a foreign securities company; an environment where the work content is largely Americanised but where company–employee relations are less 'dry' than would be normal in a wholly American securities company.

Matsumoto

Matsumoto was interviewed last on the documentary. He is a rather typical Japanese employee; very good-natured, hard-working and serious. He was very likeable in the interview and we thought that he would get a lot of sympathy from the audience, many of whom we expected to be facing the same dilemmas as Matsumoto. He was still inside C-Life but had reasons to be extremely critical of the company. He welcomed the opportunity to air his grievances and spoke frankly on the programme about his feelings towards C-Life.

> I have been in the Kagoshima office of the company for two years now. It is different in the provinces. Time goes more slowly. Every day now I wake, eat and go to the company. It takes less time to get to the office here – just ten minutes. Before, in Tokyo, it took one hour or an hour and a half. I go by car now. It is much better and not as much of a waste of time. It is easier to live in the provinces.
>
> It is hard to say if I am suited to my work or not. My results are OK. I think I do the best I can. This year I am really satisfied with what I have done. I have had my best results so far. I am doing insurance sales to companies at the moment. I like that work and would like to go on doing that, although the company may have other ideas. We have to look at insurance policies and plans for different companies, and if you think of good ideas for them they will take out your insurance. It feels good if they like the plan that you do and take out insurance with you.
>
> While I was applying to C-Life, I got a number of offers from manufacturing companies as well. I didn't really know how it would be in the finance industry. I couldn't really imagine it. I thought that I would learn the rules and the business of the company when I got into C-Life. But instead it was sales training from the beginning. 'Go door to door and get sales. Don't come back until you have done it.' It was that kind of world. A few years passed all at once. Before I knew it I could do the work. It was really tough but I know that I could work anywhere after that experience.
>
> I didn't mind being in sales immediately after the training. I thought it would be good to start in the hardest area. Everyone was dispersed all across the country. I was more worried that I might have to split up with my girlfriend! I wanted to be able to travel around the country and have interesting experiences. But the first four years were far tougher than I had ever dreamed. Sapporo was especially tough. I only collapsed once or twice, but that's because I was young. I remember thinking that if I had had to keep this going for years I would have died. From ten at night we went out to sell because that was when customers came home. I remember waiting for one customer from eight at night until one in the morning when he came home. He said, my company is tough, but yours is worse, and he got insurance on the spot! I remember waiting in my car for one customer and by the time he got home my car was tens of centimetres deep in snow. I gave my boss a letter of resignation the next morning. But he told me that night that he had lost it and wouldn't accept my resignation. I sent in my letter of resignation three times, although I hadn't actually found another job. One time the wife of my boss turned up and said, 'My

husband came home yesterday and cried, because he said that he had said something terrible to a junior and regretted it.' I was stopped by strategies like these a couple of times.

As I started to really work I was given more responsibility. My thinking towards the company changed and my liking for the company grew. I started to realise that my efforts were helping the company to grow. I wonder if it is like this, that love for the company grows over the years. At first I wondered why I had to work for the company like this. But as time went on I was surprised to find that, although I didn't think I was, I really am a company man after all. Now no-one knows whether it was good or bad that I stayed. That was at the time of the bubble and I could probably have moved. But who knows what would have happened? I am satisfied now with this company, I guess. I think that I am lucky. I have had a number of arguments with my bosses but I have been able to come this far anyway. It is quite possible I will be transferred in March, although I haven't heard anything yet. The company is having a big restructuring, I think the available posts and the content of work will change a lot. We can't imagine how things will be, as we used to.

It is sad that so many *doki* have left the company! Some people are glad that they have left. But the ones who are left behind think they have run out on us (*nigeyagatta*). It is hard to tell people to stay. Work is really quite tough. If you don't like it or if you are kind-hearted and not suited to tough competition then I don't think that it can be helped if you want to leave. Some of us quit during the training, others after it. Some of us were so shocked by the training that they quit then. They didn't really know what to expect in the company. Sometimes they told me that they were thinking about it. Different people have asked my advice about changing jobs. I said that it was their decision. It can't be helped that they want to do that. Changing jobs is a kind of gamble. There are risks in going and also risks in staying. It is hard to know what will happen until you are there.

I didn't really think much about whether I would be in the company all my life. Some people thought that they would stop at some time and move somewhere else. But it was very vague. No-one really knew what they would do. What we used to talk about as theory – changing jobs – has now become a reality. And I have a strong realisation now that I may not be able to be in the company until I retire. Even two years ago I hadn't yet become conscious of that. I am half in shock although the other half thinks that there are other opportunities out there. It is not all negative. But I never thought that I would actually act on my desire to change work. We talk about it now at home – how much savings we have; where we would live, Kagoshima, Tokyo; how much we need until our kids grow up. I wonder if staying in the company is also a risk – greater than I can handle. I need to think about the merits for me, for the company, think about the possibility of being restructured which is very realistic now. And think about having to make it alone. There are a lot of factors involved – my effort, the results of the company. Just for me to work hard is no longer enough. It used to be enough in the past. You put money in the bank and it grew. But now it is different.

Through the media now I have realised that when people get to 50 or so companies do horrible things to them. And I thought that sooner or later that would happen at my company as well. But I didn't think that it would come to us at the age of 38 or so, so I guess this age is unlucky – this age and the bubble age. But 40- and 50-year-olds are unlucky now too, in a different sense. It is unlucky, but if you think of nothing but that you just lose out. You need to try to think more positively.

Management has to be dry sometimes. They have responsibility to customers and responsibility to staff. And also to the FSA. You have to think of the importance you give to each if you are management. The company can't really fire people – they can just ask them to quit. But some people don't want to do that. They have kids or they can't move, so they take a pay cut and stay on. They take a big cut, apparently; but that can't be helped. Everyone is taking that quite coolly (*reisei*).

Japan may get more depressed or it may recover. If you have skills of your own you can think then when it happens. Life's fortunes go up and down like the stock market. It may change so that the company is asking people to stay next. At the moment it is the hardest time to change. Why sell your stocks when the price is at the lowest? If I can stay in the company I will. I wonder if I would really get merit from moving. I can't really see exactly what they would be. If we fall to a certain level I think we will begin to gather strength again. Our *doki* have a lot of strong people. It is hard to say this at the moment as the most talented are leaving. We feel jealous of the ones that have left – they have gone to greener turf. It looks like they are going to a new world. But whether those are the most talented or not is hard to say.

What is a pro? Some of us have skills in the company, like finance. But normal salesmen don't have special skills. It is hard to call them pros. In terms of certificates they have nothing, there are no tests that they would do well at. But we are good at suggesting plans for companies and dealing with customers. A pro is someone who can come up with the sales that the company has asked for on sales projections. That is what a sales pro is.

So I am concerned that I have no real skills. If something happened and I was kicked out of the company how would I sell myself? Why would a company want me? I would have to sell myself to the lowest bidder and it is hard to think about that. Well, certificates are not everything either – they don't exactly translate into skills. I am not making any special preparations in case I have to change job – if you don't have a fire you don't usually prepare to put it out. I think that I would act only when it actually happened.

Last year I made a big mistake and was sent to Kagoshima in disgrace. I did something that was OK according to internal company rules, but not according to the finance authorities. (In fact, someone else made a mistake and Matsumoto agreed to take the responsibility for it.) My rank was reduced because of that mistake that I made. My pay went down. It was very unfair. I don't really know why that happened to me and why they don't understand it. I was so angry I thought I would quit. I couldn't sleep. I would go out at night and walk for five hours until I exhausted myself enough to sleep. C-Life told me that after the FSA caught us they would blame it on me, and afterwards they would quietly resuscitate me. They may still be considering that…

At that time, I began to think about what exactly I had expected of this company. Was it strange of me to have expected too much of the company? Was that at the root of my being so disappointed? I think all my *doki* are in shock now. They love the company but they have been disappointed. Ultimately, people work in return for wages. If they had kept it that kind of simple exchange they wouldn't have been so devastated. Their wives wouldn't be wondering if their husbands were going to be OK or not. If you think of things more simply, they become clearer.

I have taken what the company dished out in silence. I am still taking it, and that stance is what is hard. But now I have become very cool and objective. If my superior's orders are unrealistic in any way I now say no clearly. I have developed an ability to say no. Before now I would try and do whatever I was asked, and I would regard the time and energy I wasted on proving that many tasks were impossible as a waste of my own time. But now I don't do that. If I think the task is impossible from the beginning then I turn it down straight off. My work has become less hard (*kurushii*) as a result.

Because I am in Kagoshima now, work has a smaller weight in my life. I can go out more easily into the countryside or out with people for meals. Because the future is so unclear I want to enjoy myself more now. Well, I work properly as well, but I think about my family and how we can enjoy ourselves. We can never get this time back to ourselves if we don't use it. In the future I don't want to look back and think I worked this hard and this is what happened. I would rather think that I had had a good time regardless of what happened. I have learned to think this way. I would like to be able to do my work with a comfortable margin and do it well. But work is not the only thing left any more. Still, in order to live a really fulfilling life I wonder if working the way that I am now is going to really be enough. You can take two stances here: a passive stance where you wait and see what happens, or an aggressive stance where you get out and actually change jobs.

If I had to change jobs I wonder if I would change immediately. I have worked for nearly fifteen years and I will work for many more before I retire. I wonder if I might not take a year or two off and travel overseas with my family. Or build a mountain hut to live in or do something that I have always wanted to do.

Because I still have work I am still loyal. I still want to work for the company. But that is not all there is to life. I see things much more objectively now (*reisei na me de*). There isn't enough leeway now for the company to really look after employees in the way that they used to. While Japanese companies were making profits they could do that, but it is no longer possible. There is competition and deregulation. I think that employees were really *amae* (optimistic, indulgent) toward the company. The company also was *amae* to employees (presuming on their good will), asking them to do things that were not in their contract or working more than they should have been expected to. Now employees can no longer *amaeru* toward (presume upon) the company, the company shouldn't *amaeru* towards employees. I think work is becoming more Western, both sides are work pros.

Doki do sometimes become senior and junior at work because of promotions, but we are still *doki*. There is something called luck in career paths. But now because the posts are disappearing it is hard to say what the difference is between the ones who go up and the ones who don't – it is just luck. A person's mentor could die and he be left without strong support in the company.

All the *doki* have a different life now – a different lifestyle – we talk about general things, and not especially about work. If you give people an especially difficult training, it is like people who have been to war together – all we fought together and became strong. In the Second World War there were people from the cities and people who had never left their villages before, all fighting in the same unit together. We were like that and became very very close.

I could quite probably be moved this time around (in the annual promotions). But I want to do as much as I can in my next post too. If it was a really impossible situation I would think about what to do then; either to quit or to continue to try my best. Whether you get a good assignment order (*jirei*) or not is an issue that comes up each year since I got into the company. Each time it happens, everyone has to decide whether they will take the order or whether they will quit, so the current restructuring is not really the first time we have to make that kind of decision. We have always had to move a lot…

In the past I did really hard work. Was that a waste? What was it? I don't think it was a waste. I think that I did my best. Even when I got demoted … I didn't really question that or think that it shouldn't have been that way. At each point in time – even when I worked so hard I didn't think anyone could have worked harder – I think it was OK like that. That is what I decided to do at the time – although sometimes I wanted to say if you think someone else can work harder get them to come in! I will probably regret having been demoted all my life, though.

Other people who work a normal nine to five life can go to their company and not be able to understand why some people work all day and night and go on Saturdays as well. But I can understand clients like this because I have the experience.

Having worked that hard I can live anywhere. It is a kind of satisfaction, a sad satisfaction perhaps; but you can say that it was a war and I did my best in it. It is a kind of satisfaction. Sometimes I look back and wonder if what I have done has been OK or whether I am just justifying after the fact. But sometimes you have to do that. You can't make everything into the fault of other people, or you can't even start to live.

It is a bit like the question whether it is easier to commit suicide or to die! The company is still a pyramid in the end and the posts get fewer. If a person has given everything to the company and still gets cut when they are close to the top it must be an even greater shock. I have known men like that who barely know their family because they have worked so hard. But then when they are laid off by the company the wife who has only married someone with the potential to become a company president divorces him.

I feel really easy (*raku*) in my heart (*kimochi*) now that I have accepted my situation. The directors now want the same attitude from employees that they always have (wet), but their treatment of the employees has become dry. The company's situation is like a boat with a faulty engine that has met with a typhoon. It is hard for it to avoid restructuring. The people who are asked to quit now will probably have something happen to them in the future if they don't quit as they are asked to. Japanese companies have 'window-sitters' (*madogiwazoku*) behind the scenes.

I am still a couple of years behind where I should have been because of my demotion and I don't think that I will be able to recoup that and I recognise that. Well, I think that there are a lot of tearful salarymen behind the company orders. If you think about it too much you will become neurotic. So I don't really think about it that much. This has made me stronger.

Comment

Outside circumstances forced Matsumoto to face the dilemma of whether or not to accept the company's goals as his. He has resolved his dilemma temporarily by loosening the emotional ties that attach him to the company itself and strengthening the ties that attach him to what he finds fulfilling; the type of work that he does and his personal life of hobbies and family.

As an individual he is the most caught between the ideals of the older generation and the younger. He started his career as an average employee, working hard within the structure of the company. His own beliefs have not led him into conflict with the company; but because of the economic downturn and the company's restructuring programme he has been demoted and not resuscitated.

He has never had the clear goals of some of the others. He thought that he would find his path in the company but wasn't sure what it was that he really wanted to do. Once in the company, his loyalty grew through the years that he has struggled with the severe training and harsh workload of the early years. He finds a sense of satisfaction in the relations that he has with other company employees and with those he supervises. He shows us album after album made for him by branch employees when he departed the branch. The albums are full of group photos and letters of gratitude. He derives his satisfaction from the 'number of tears when I leave'.

He compares his disillusionment with the company's values as an unrequited love affair. He realises that the only thing that working to extremes has achieved for him is the 'sad satisfaction' that having worked that hard, he is able to do anything now. After the initial shock and disappointment at the company's treatment of him, he realises that he has been at fault too for being unrealistic about the company's policies towards its workers during the crisis it is facing: 'I realised companies do horrible things to people'. Once he has pulled away emotionally from the company, and accepted a new relationship, he feels relief.

Loyalty has grown with the responsibility that the company has given him and as he realises the direct results that his efforts make for the company. He is surprised to find after the early years that he is a dedicated company man after all.

Matsumoto is still coming to terms with the possibility that he may not be able to remain inside C-Life. Now that this is a real possibility he has begun to think about options. But he is also paralysed by his lack of options and skills that would get him a job elsewhere in the job market. He has resolved his emotional dilemma by pulling away from the company, and imposing limits on how far he is prepared to go to do his job: 'If a boss gave me an unreasonable task I would refuse to do it'. Nonetheless he clings to the company while he still can.

Summary

Like most people, these Japanese company men are all, in their various ways, engaged in the search for fulfilment or realisation. And, perhaps in contrast to the 'group' generation above them, they are all interested in *jiko jitsugen* (self-realisation) – in fulfilling themselves through work. There are a number of themes that run through the stories of these different types, both uniting and dividing them as a generation, which I take up one by one.

Self is a key issue for the generation. It is one characteristic separating them from the generation above them, the '*kyujinrui*' or old generation. But the *doki* are divided in whether they perceive self-realisation as obtainable inside the company environment or through a search for an environment that fits them. This generation is diverse in the approaches it used to attain realisation. They can polish their characters inside the company environment and learn to fit the company. Alternatively, they can move from company to company until they find a fit. Or they can develop their abilities until they are skilled enough to fit into many different companies. These latter two types both call themselves individualist.

My *doki* mostly seem to have got into the company without thinking seriously about what they wanted to do in terms of work content, without a real image of what work would be like. Like most of the *doki*, Uesaka and Takemitsu, for example, talk of a big gap between the hazy dreams about working that they had as students and the reality that hits them once inside the company. On the company's side, conversely, the descriptions of what new employees will actually do in the company seem to have been left rather vague. Many *doki* told me that the first month's training was a shock, or that they perceived a big gap between their ideas about work and the reality of the company. Osaki, who was a trainer for the new employees, said that his main work was closing this gap between perception and reality. Uesaka says that he was conscious of this gap just one month into the company. He felt the need to combine work and his interests. Work in C-Life was not able to stimulate his imagination. Nor did it fit his personality.

This is, I think, the first generation that began not only to think about the work–personality fit, but actually to act on that by changing jobs. Part of the personality fit is to do with how much they can conceal their real self and play a role (*tatemae*) in the job. Sales-related jobs are very *tatemae*-oriented; so are traditional Japanese companies. Takemitsu, especially, felt uncomfortable in an environment where he could not express himself or show his real self (*honne*). This vocabulary is the vocabulary of individualism and that is the key point by which their generation differed from the group-oriented *kyujinrui* generation above them. Their dream is to be 'businessmen'; instead Takemitsu says he felt like a salaryman. To stay in the company is to 'kill themselves' or to sacrifice their individuality. When they feel a mismatch between themselves and the company they face the choice of changing themselves to fit the company or changing the company to fit them. They choose the former. Work, for both of them, must be something that relates on one hand to their individuality, and on the other hand, relates them to the wider society. Work is equal to hobbies. Work is not a part that is separate or detached from the other parts of their lives.

Yet while both Uesaka and Takemitsu felt a mismatch between their own individuality and the company, they did not act on this. They did not conceive going anywhere else but another large Japanese company. While they value work that fits their personality they don't conceive work outside of the normal environment of the company. This sums up the dilemma of the generation: how far can they subscribe to individualism in the Japanese company environment? Matsumoto says: 'Everyone wants to believe in themselves but they don't actually have the confidence to do that yet'. His question, 'What takes the place of that religion (groupism) for the older generation among our *doki*?' sums up the sense of confusion.

From this pattern of the earlier quitters, ten years have seen a dramatic change in attitudes to work, and also in the worsening position of C-Life.

One important thing in looking at these case studies is to realise that, for these employees, money was not the highest priority. They were competing for a range of benefits. These include prestige among one's generation in terms of the values of one's generation; status within the company hierarchy; a sense of self-realisation; a sense of growing achievement or maturity in one's job. It can be seen that these *doki* are not at all uniform but have a range of goals, and a range of strategies that they use to achieve these goals. The economic situation had a huge influence on both the goals and the strategies needed to achieve them.

In the next chapter I use what we have seen here, as well as the material presented in the earlier fieldwork chapters, as the basis of a detailed discussion of the nature of strategising amongst individuals and groups.

7 Ideology and economic strategising

In the last four chapters, we have seen how people are reacting to the changing conditions at C-Life. In chapter 6, in particular, we focused on a variety of individuals, all drawn from the same year-group, who profess markedly different attitudes towards their role in the company, who have different goals in life and different ways of trying to achieve those goals.

In this chapter, I focus on these issues in more depth, drawing together the different themes of the fieldwork chapters and analysing them with reference to the theoretical concerns introduced in chapter 1. This analysis paves the way for the next chapter, where I illustrate my theoretical conclusions with an account of the filming I carried out at the company and how everybody involved used it to try to achieve their various goals. This is 'strategising', and it lies at the heart of my analysis in this chapter.

Successful strategising, as I found it at C-Life, involves understanding, using and manipulating the ideology of the company. Indeed, the issues of ideology and strategising are very closely intertwined – a fact that we shall see illustrated throughout the rest of this book. I therefore begin this chapter with a look at the nature of ideology, arguing that its role in strategising is closely linked to its own complex nature.

The discussion therefore revolves around an analysis of the different types or levels of ideology and the way in which these interact. This conceptual framework is built and evaluated on the basis of not only the C-Life fieldwork but also other, more general, anthropological accounts of ideology.

I begin, then, by considering the nature of ideology. I look at the different ways in which it has been understood by anthropologists, concluding that it is essential to appreciate the different levels at which ideology functions. I therefore present a schema to separate the different layers of ideology and make some preliminary remarks concerning how they relate with each other and with practice.

With this in place, I consider the objectivity of ideology, before moving on to a discussion of what happens when the different levels of ideology come into conflict. I use the insights gleaned here to propose a way of understanding how *honne* and *tatemae* – reality and appearance, an ever-present feature of Japanese society – functions: in particular, why people seem to use it differently at different times.

I then move on to relate this material on ideology to strategising, the second focus of this chapter. I describe what I mean by 'strategising' before discussing the ways in which ideology is used in strategising. After this I turn to the equally central issue of consciousness and its role in strategising, focusing on a case study of consciousness in C-Life. I conclude with a look at how to be good at strategising.

What is an ideology?

First, it is necessary to define the term 'ideology', which has been used mainly in two ways in anthropology. The first is as the system of social and moral ideas of a group of people. Dumont (1986: 9) defines ideology as 'a system of ideas and values current in a given social milieu'. Geertz (1973: 22) defines ideology as 'maps of problematic social realities and matrices for the creation of social conscience'. This usage is close to the concept of 'culture'. Ideology is a system of ideas that are dominant in a society, although not necessarily shared by all members of the society; every member of the society has a hand in its making and maintenance.

The second sense in which ideology has been used is in a Marxist sense. The term sought to explain how the capitalist system exploits people by transferring the rewards of the toil of the labourers to the capitalist minority. Ideology in this scenario is a representation of the situation to the workers that makes it seem reasonable, so that it is accepted and taken for granted by both the labourers and the capitalists. Ideology thus serves to legitimate the process of exploitation by hiding reality.

How have anthropologists regarded ideology in the past? This is part of the wider issue of the nature of culture. The view that culture is a shared system of beliefs alone was current in anthropology for a long time, and characterised both functionalist and structuralist thought. According to theorists of these schools, a culture alters and progresses, but always moves towards a consistent, shared, harmonious whole. Culture is therefore something real, outside people, and objectified in that society's artefacts and institutions. Geertz, for example, sees culture as a system of historically transmitted symbols. The behaviour that we see comes from symbolic constructs, which are shared, maintained and perpetuated by a society. Concepts in the individual mind are shaped by these social concepts. So behaviour is a public manifestation of these concepts, not something inherent in the individual. It is only by participating in culture that the individual becomes a social being.

Ideas about culture in anthropology became more refined in the 1960s and culture began to be seen not as a bounded system belonging to 'a' society, but as symbolic meanings and mental representations shared by a number of different individuals. Humans were no longer thought to 'have' distinct cultures, but to live 'culturally'. In other words, culture was seen as a process rather than a 'thing'. We interpret and create meanings for ourselves – albeit shaped partly by an available repertoire of ideas. What we know is what we make ourselves and use in the cultural realm. Each element of our knowledge is a small theory in itself (Goodman 1978).

It seems, then, that the word 'ideology' – like 'social constructs' – has been used to denote a number of different things. This can be seen from the fact that it is often opposed to different concepts: to practice, to the private opinion of an individual or to the truth. To add to the confusion, some authors use it interchangeably with 'socio-cultural construct' or 'culture'. In this chapter, I sometimes oppose it to practice; but sometimes, too, I have found it necessary to oppose public ideology – in the sense of a shared system of cultural symbols – to individual, private meaning. These different usages have vastly different implications for any discussion of ideology. We must therefore devote some time to untangling the different threads that mean 'ideology' to different people.

This task is of particular importance to a study of Japan such as the one outlined here. Terms such as *omote* and *ura* (front and back region), *uchi/soto* (inside and outside) and *honne/tatemae* are central to Japanese life. These words are most often translated into English as 'ideology' and 'practice'. Yet which sense of the word 'ideology' are we translating it into? If we do not define precisely what we mean, we risk importing the indeterminate nature of the word into our account of this central Japanese concept.

Ways of viewing ideology

In this section, I consider some of the ways in which ideology has been treated in anthropological literature. I work on the principle that each different approach has valuable insights to offer us, although, without an adequate appreciation of the different levels at which ideology functions, none provides a complete account. My aim throughout this is to ground the theory in actuality, so throughout the discussion I test the accounts both of others and my own by reference to examples from C-Life. I begin with the relatively straightforward view of ideology as a system of shared beliefs or norms that characterise a society.

Shared norms

Geertz (1973) describes culture as a system of historically transmitted symbols, shaped by social and cultural institutions but created and transferred by the mind. This was certainly true in some ways at C-Life. The majority opinion of what was going on was, by definition, a shared system of beliefs. It meant that the majority of C-Life people subscribed, to some extent, to that view. But they did not believe equally, or believe exactly the same thing.

For example, the ideology of the *doki* as 'very close' was avidly believed. In normal situations most employees never had to question it. So it was a strong element of the company's dominant ideology. But it was also strongly manipulated by the company during the training period. There were clear agendas for all involved: for the company to manipulate the constructs, for the trainers to instil the constructs, and ultimately for the employees to subscribe to them. Almost all of the trainees' time was spent together, selling was arranged so they had to work together, and they were physically living together as well. By being close, they learnt to feel close. And there were significant social, financial and career rewards for being close over their entire careers. So this ideology was actively promoted by many people. Only occasionally when conducting my fieldwork did I hear someone say that perhaps *doki* are not so close after all. There were a few people who recognised the discrepancy and adjusted their individual meaning accordingly.

As an ideology that expressed a certain degree of shared belief, beliefs such as this were immensely powerful. They were cited as the reason people stayed with the company, the reason that the company existed, the reason that people worked such long hours. For some employees, it served as justification for why they stayed with the company despite their dislike of the work.

However, not only did individuals share the symbols in different ways and to different degrees, they were aware to differing degrees of the existence of the symbols, and aware to different degrees of what their own stance was towards company ideology. There was certainly a motley range of individuals that arrived at the C-Life dormitory to be trained, even though a much more uniform group left the training centre nine months later. So, while the *constructs* that we live by may be actualised in public in a communal way, it does not follow that the *meanings* by which we live are actualised in a communal way. The ideology is actualised in public but the individual retains their own private interpretations of the shared constructs and practice. In other words, we cannot assume that individual meaning – a person's own view of the situation – will conform to the dominant ideology. It was very clear in my fieldwork that different individuals – despite their thinking being formed and channelled in culturally appropriate directions by participating in Japanese and company culture – were ultimately free to form their own interpretation and meaning from this experience. In Simmel's (1971) terminology, the form may remain the same, but the content can differ.

The claim that ideology is a shared system of beliefs is, then, true at some levels, but it does not capture the level of individual meaning. We must distinguish between the dominant ideology – the society's set of majority beliefs – and what the individual believes. And we have seen that a dominant ideology may not simply be believed, but may be actively promoted. It may become an official picture or story.

To the extent to which ideology can be thought of as a system of shared norms, however, it is reasonable to ask next how it functions: what is the point of having such a system? One interesting answer is to focus on the way in which ideology is a means of communication within a society, as a system of shared concepts. I look at this idea next.

Shared concepts

Many theorists treat ideology as a means of shared communication. Victor Turner, for example, regarded social symbols as devices that condense the most central ideas of a society. In symbols, the concepts of all the members of that society are compressed together and expressed. Garfinkel (1972) states that shared norms allow people to interpret conversation as meaningful and orderly. Common social structure allows members to understand conversation, and this understanding replicates social structure. But there is room left for an independent individual: interpretations of the meaning of the shared norm will not necessarily be the same for all members of the group. Moerman (1988) concludes that conversations derive from and replicate common worlds of sense, orientation and experience: matter-of-fact assumptions known by 'anyone in their right minds'.

Geertz (1973) uses the notion of common sense to describe common shared notions. He defines these as matter-of-fact assumptions – an ordered body of considered thought, a cultural system of learnt symbols. Examples of such symbol-systems may be religion, politics, common sense, and so on. Symbols are vehicles for concepts. In this view, culture is the sum of these symbol-systems by which people make sense of the world. Members of the same culture share its symbol-systems, and there is constant exchange of symbols. But these exchanges are inherently ambiguous, so the receiver must actively interpret the symbols as well as passively receive them. The content differs from one society to another, but the style, way of knowing, attitude to life and tone in which wisdom is expressed, may be universal.

The importance of common sense and shared norms is shown by the fact that, whenever they are transgressed, even in minor ways, it can be very unsettling. At one time, for example, when I was working at C-Life, the international section planned to go on a drinking session after work. We had arranged to go to a bar a short train-ride away. We all prepared to leave work together to go to the station when one colleague said that he would meet us there. This was very strange as it implied that he would take a separate route to walk by himself to the station, even though we were all leaving from the same place and going to the same destination. He may have had some perfectly good reason for taking the detour, but if so he did not give it – he simply announced that he was going a different way, and left. Small examples of non-conformity like this were very serious in the eyes of the other employees. That incident was talked about at length and an accumulation of such incidents led to the employee being talked of as rather weird.

So, common sense is a short-cut to communication with others. The interpretations of each person may be very different, but they must have some common expectation of predictability so that that each person finds interaction with the other understandable and meaningful. These shared social constructs are what Simmel (1971) called forms, as opposed to content, which is individual meaning. One respondent told me that employees in C-Life had been able to relate 'normally' to me because I had been in Japan from a relatively young age – so that I understood the shared forms (of Japan, Japanese-ness). And so, as far as C-Life's shared forms went, I was a 'blank sheet' and could thus learn the forms easily. To belong to Japanese society, then, is to share and be able to use a fund of forms. And equally, to belong to C-Life was to share a knowledge of the normal use and proper practice of its fund of forms.

Simmel says that individuals use forms to gain meaning and significance in their own lives – and, furthermore, they use the forms that are available to them, that already exist, that they are familiar with. We could see this most clearly in the training. Almost all of the employees – to different degrees – struggled with the harsh training, trying to make sense of it, trying to understand their place in it, how they would live their lives now as members of society – their new role for which they did not know the rules or implications. The forms that they used to assign meaning to this experience were invariably Japanese forms that they had used in other contexts or had seen in the media – forms that were familiar. In this way, they turned the harsh experience of training into a feat of endurance, a battle which they would fight through, using metaphors that one sees in countless Japanese TV dramas. Many of the employees talked of reaching a point at some time in the training at which they came to a realisation of what their new role was to be. For some this came when they sold their first policies and felt that they had been trusted and recognised as 'members of society' – another frequently used symbolic expression. With this came a feeling of gratitude to the company and an acceptance of their role, together with a desire to fulfil the duties of that role. To assign meaning to their harsh experience, therefore, the employees grasped at socially acceptable ideologies in order to understand their situations. They reconciled their individual meanings or beliefs (the content) with the group ideology and company ideology about what an individual should be – the individual role. It must be noted, however, that the particular forms that the employees made use of to assign meaning to their situations were different according to each individual. Some failed to assign an appropriate meaning to the situation, and quit as a result.

Sometimes, when the individual clashed with external circumstances or ideology, they adjusted their own individual meaning to conform to the new circumstances or to the group ideologies around them. In this way, some of them became even more firmly committed to the actions that they were undertaking. They became even more strongly convinced that they continued working as they did out of a sense of loyalty to the company. Examples of this phenomenon could be seen among the salesmen, who had to sell insurance to people who would challenge them on the basis of media reports that C-Life was doing badly and might be unable to pay out insurance. The salesmen had to cope with the jarring discrepancies between their actions – selling insurance – together with their self-image as honest men, and the new information that they were constantly presented with. They had to adjust their personal outlooks to take all this into account.

Most employees seemed to feel sorry for the salesmen. When I asked them what they thought of the salesmen maintaining to the last their loyalty to the company, they were very uncomfortable – especially those who thought that the company was in a seriously bad way. They hesitated a lot, struggling to explain why they were like that. They concluded that the salesmen had no choice but to believe in what they did. If they were spouting the company ideology every day to customers and selling company policies, they had no choice but to believe what they said. As they told the same story over and over again, they came to believe it, according to my respondents. The metaphors that the salesmen used and that they professed to believe were images of all pulling together, *doki* supporting each other until the last, battling together to save the company, putting 100 per cent effort in to protect the policy-holders.

So, individual meanings are based on individuals' experience and outlook on the world, coupled with collective forms that provide a structure, or readily available explanations, and influence the outlook of the individual. The metaphors that I have described above were culturally appropriate, understandable metaphors that were common currency in other realms of Japanese life as well as in C-Life.

In the light of what we have seen so far, then, it seems that dominant ideology plays an important role in maintaining the cohesiveness of a society. I now focus on one particularly interesting way in which some writers have described this role: that of maintaining reality for the members of the society.

Reality maintenance

Schneider (1976) describes culture as the representation of reality for a particular society. Thus, different members of a society will have similar outlooks on the world. By attaining a representation of reality in culture, the individual is provided with logical explanations for action. This view does not, however, take into account any behaviour that is not in line with culture: it focuses on ideology and ignores practice. Conflict between the two is ignored or dismissed. However, the idea of ideology as reality maintenance is not unfruitful, especially if we combine it with the insight that different individuals may interpret the same ideology in different ways.

The fact that the dominant ideology functioned as reality maintenance for employees in C-Life is reflected in the distress experienced when it began to clash with personal interpretations of the situation and could therefore no longer fulfil this role. Individuals experienced a lot of inner turmoil when they found that they were unhappy with the ideology and were beginning to rebel and plan an unusual move, such as quitting their jobs. This was particularly true for those who quit the company at an early stage. In retrospect, their moves were part of a large social movement with increasing numbers of young people making the decision to move out of their companies. But this was not at all apparent to them at the time. Their struggle was an individual struggle, as their individual ideas and sense of satisfaction and motivation became increasingly in conflict with the ideology around them. Each of them had to question whether their ideas were deviant or abnormal. For some of them it took months or even years of struggle before they summoned up the courage to quit. Others were never able to make that move.

Indeed, dominant ideology does not just provide oneself with logic and rationale in one's world-view and actions; by subscribing to it, individuals reassure others that they are normal. This is reflected in my fieldwork concerning 'foreign-ness': anyone who deviated from the norm was considered 'un-Japanese'. In this sense, it is common adherence to the ideology that provided the assurance to others that you were on the same team, that the cultural norms that one lived by were normal. In a sense, it was mutual assurance.

So far in this section, then, we have focused on the social role of ideology: the extent to which dominant ideology can be considered shared norms or a shared system of concepts like a language, and the way in which it works as reality maintenance. Central to all of these areas is the way in which ideology features in social interaction. If, as we have seen, ideology can be thought of as a form of reality maintenance, and if it can even help people to communicate, then how is it communicated itself, in daily life and conversation?

Interaction

This topic is particularly important given the centrality of interaction to social life in general. Indeed, Simmel (1971: 24) claims that interaction is the stuff of which society itself is made: 'It is evident that that which constitutes society … is identical with … interaction' (see also Sapir 1956). This insight is now recognised by many anthropologists, and the concept of discourse is becoming more central, changing many of the ways people think about the anthropological process.

We have seen that it is essential to the normal functioning of society that people adhere to the same norms, to at least some extent. Yet we have also seen how individuals' own views may differ from each other and from the dominant ideology. Conversation provides a forum wherein, using the same societal forms, different individual views may converge. In interaction, socio-cultural reality is constituted and reconstituted. Failure to interact successfully may indicate a pathological condition of some kind (Bateson et al. 1974) – we have already seen the consequences of upsetting the predictability of everyday interaction. These considerations are connected to the insight that communities can be understood in relational terms (Cohen 1985). But to understand what socio-cultural realities are inhabited when, and by whom – to get the meaning for the individual from the interaction – a micro-social analysis of both situation and context is necessary (Rapport 1993). These considerations suggest that we need to examine the social role of conversation more closely, particularly with reference to social structures and their relation to the individual.

What, then, is the purpose of conversation? It is in conversation that individuals' views are brought out and clarified. This exchange that takes place in conversation creates social reality (Baumann and Sherzer 1974, Bruner 1983). Berger and Luckmann (1966) focus on the ongoing, communal nature of the construction of social reality: it works by a process of interaction between different members of society. In this view conversation has the vital function of maintaining reality. As conversation progresses, the individual confirms and strengthens his reality and the consistency of his own world. Moerman (1988) argues that, in talking, people experience and create their roles and personalities: talking to someone else is thus an exercise in developing oneself. Victor Turner, indeed, sees life as an intrinsically dialectical process. Berger and Luckmann go further (1969) to describe conversation as the tool of world-making. It is the means by which individual perceptions are brought out, compared, sorted and ultimately ordered by existing social structures into new ones. So conversation, in creating and maintaining social structures, constrains itself by setting the agenda for subsequent conversation.

It is certainly true that it is in conversation that world-creation occurs. We can frame this in the terminology I am developing by saying that it is in sharing their different personal viewpoints through the common forms of conversation that individuals create the dominant ideology of the group. We see this in C-Life when we talked in groups about things that touched the lives of all the employees deeply, but that they rarely discussed or put into words – like the meaning of *doki*. They were extremely interested in what others had to say and welcomed other people clarifying their own thoughts for them. As we discussed the topic, its meaning was clarified anew by each participant. Thus, they each shared their individual viewpoint with the group, thereby affecting the dominant ideology, at least of that small group.

But, because of the role of individual interpretation, sometimes it further polarised opinions. Discourse is a very complex phenomenon that does not necessarily determine meaning without the interpretative work of the listener. Individuals make personal meaning from their own perspectives on life (Sapir 1956). In this way, conversation can sometimes have the effect of increasing differences between the participants, not bringing them closer together. In C-Life, in a group discussion with seniors and juniors, the conversation would sometimes give rise to a greater *tatemae* agreement, but greater real opposition below the surface. So it could sometimes widen the gap between *honne* and *tatemae*.

Devereux (1978) points out that individuals need not be in agreement when they begin interacting, and at the end of the interaction their ideas may not be any closer. Like Simmel, Devereux sees that individuality and collectivity are conjoined and the development of the two takes place through tensions of opposition. When employees were discussing the issues between them, one could see their common definition moving closer as they opposed opinion to opinion and came to a closer understanding. This was most often seen in *doki*, although the exact opposite also happened: a heated discussion where both sides failed completely to reunite opinions and ended up more polarised than ever.

It is on this basis that Rapport and Overing (2000) have argued against interaction as reality maintenance, pointing out that it is difficult to say that the contours of reality are being maintained when two people do not agree. But we can say they are sharing mutually understandable conventions of how social interaction should be, maintaining the rules of the game, sharing social forms, although their interpretation of the content itself is different. Maintaining the formal designation is important. Even if the content of the interaction is meaningless, there is a meaning in two individuals coming together and meeting and sharing language and social behaviour. In fact, the meeting itself may convey many messages, quite apart from the content of what is said. Bourdieu emphasises the role of body language in communication.

So it is important to distinguish between the forms of conversation – which ensure its predictability – and different people's interpretations of what is said. Indeed, the processes of social interaction do not always run perfectly smoothly. Simmel (1971) shows that, in sharing exchange, individuals use common forms of language, behaviour, and so on, but in the end their interpretation of what has taken place is individual. There is an inherent duality because the individual is in contrast with society. Similarly, Hymes (1973) points out that we cannot conclude from an orderly conversation between people to what extent they share the same world view.

Bakhtin (1981) argues that people can maintain their individuality because they engage in habitual social interaction; communally accepted ways of interaction exist because of continuing individual traits. Garfinkel (1972) also sees conversation as having an essentially conservative role, as maintaining the order of everyday life and ensuring that social norms are reasonable, predictable and relatively stable. Indeed, conversation, like ideology itself, can function as a defining characteristic of the group.

We should therefore think of conversation, and the symbols it defines, as intrinsically variable. Socio-cultural structures emerge from communication but are always changing. Sometimes these forms will be predictable and interpreted from the individual's existing menu of types and behaviours, but there is always new material to be interpreted and classified.

This is related to modern views of language in general. According to Bakhtin and others, language is fragmentary and continually redefined. It is interesting to note that this worked in the same way in C-Life for socio-cultural constructs. '*Kaisha ningen*' (company man) is a prime example of a word that was once a symbol of an admirable hard-working company employee, but now denotes a non-thinking automaton, a company-owned employee. It is usually a rather derogatory term. Yet, at the same time, one may hear older members of the company say, 'Well, we were all *kaisha ningen*, so that is the way it was'. In such a context it is much less judgmental.

Conversation must be understood in conjunction with other sources and transmitters of ideology. In C-Life, for example, there were few common assumptions or interpretations about restructuring. They had to be created. There was no real agreement either. The media were terribly important in providing the material which the C-Life members sifted through in their minds to arrive at their own images and interpretations of what was happening to them. Media images of previous restructurings, other companies and people, were foremost in their minds when they were asked questions about matters with which they had no direct experience.

So the influences on ideology are continually changing. The outside environment significantly alters circumstances so that individual actors have to redefine reality. What is the relation of circumstances changing and the background knowledge? In C-Life, environmental change was the most instrumental of all the factors in changing the attitudes of the employees. The media also played an important role in providing information that countered the company's ideology.

However, when we look at what actually made people decide to quit C-Life, it was invariably personal experience – such as a close acquaintance who had quit, or a head-hunter calling to find new personnel for one company or another. The media made new ideas available to C-Life employees, but it was personal and direct knowledge of these new ideas happening in practice that drove home the fact that it was possible, not for someone else, but for them also.

Throughout this section, I have focused on the nature and role of dominant ideology. But, in so doing, I have constantly been referring to the level of individual meaning, and clarifying the relation between that level and the dominant ideology. In the final part of this section, then, I discuss this relation in more detail. I begin with the straightforward and popular view that ideology simply is the total of all the individual viewpoints.

The sum total of the individuals' beliefs

From the preceding sections, it should be clear that it is inadequate to characterise ideology as the sum total of everyone's beliefs. This fails to take into account the possibility of discrepancies between the dominant ideology and different individuals' own beliefs. Nevertheless, it is valuable to consider the ways in which the individual beliefs of many members of a society may influence or determine dominant ideology, even if they are not identical with it.

Earlier in this section we have seen how 'forms' may persist in a society if they are useful to its members. In this way, dominant ideology may consist of concepts or ideas that are common to many people, just like language. But forms are not constant. They change, just as language changes, and if they fall into disuse they may disappear entirely. I would suggest that this happens when individual beliefs conflict with collective forms. For example, the ideology of the soldier or the pawn battling his way forward move by move across a chessboard is no longer a metaphor that young employees in C-Life want to adopt. It conflicts with other ideologies that they pick up from the media, such as negative images of salarymen. This happened all through my fieldwork as the individual strategies and positions of C-Life employees were altered by pay cuts, being demoted or transferred. The ideology of loyalty to the company became increasingly unrealistic, bearing little relation to people's lives. There came a point when the individuals involved could no longer justify working hard for increasingly less pay by appeal to loyalty to the company. With this conflict and the resulting psychological turmoil, they came to new individual conclusions. This is the paradox of culture where individual creativity is continually threatened by the forms it has produced and must produce new ones to express itself.

So the distinction between the dominant ideology and individual meaning helps us to understand the dynamics of change in ideology, and this is one reason why it is overly simplistic to think of (dominant) ideology simply as the sum of all individual viewpoints. So to what extent is dominant ideology constituted by numerous individual beliefs, and to what extent must individual beliefs change before we can detect a shift in dominant ideology?

Four years after I started work at C-Life came a year in which many of my *doki* quit the company. In retrospect this could be seen as part of an increasing trend whereby growing numbers of company employees all over Japan were quitting their companies and changing jobs. It was the first period in which employees were changing from one large company to another. The reality is that this was becoming a sizeable trend in society. However, at the time, the employees involved in the change could not see that. They were not in a position to see everyone's beliefs or actions. All they could see was the dominant ideology, which held that their actions were extremely unusual. At the time that I was in the company, two years before these events, they would have told me that Japanese employees don't quit their companies. So they went through great turmoil in deciding to quit. One employee took a year to make the decision. It was only in retrospect that they could see that many others had been going through the same thing. The great pressure felt by the employees struggling to make the decision to quit was the pressure of majority opinion. This was, in part, an illusion, as we can see in retrospect that the early quitters were part of a new trend in Japanese society: as they themselves were the new reality. Thus, not only is it inaccurate to say that ideology is what everyone believes, because there will always be dissenting voices; it is also the case that no-one can know precisely what everybody believes.

The important issue is what we are influenced by; what we have to define our ideology. In the case of the quitters, the dominant ideology represented what the majority of the people believed at that time, and what the majority of people had actually done until that time. In practice the majority was now moving away from that ideology, because a large trend shift was occurring. But because it was only later that people realised this, it was only later that the dominant ideology could change to take this shift into account.

In other words, there is a time-lag, as the dominant ideology takes time to 'catch up' with reality. This explains why it can be that ideology can constrain people even when it is out of synch with what is actually happening. And it shows that methodological individualism, which claims that individuals are constrained by nothing more than the desires and intentions, loyalties and behaviour, including behaviour with unintended results, of other people, is mistaken. No individual can know the sum total of what is happening now. It is not what is actually happening that constrains him, but the ideology current at that time, and this is inevitably out of date. So the early quitters had come to the conclusion – individually and separately – that work did not mean everything in life, that it was not worth sacrificing oneself for the sake of the company. They had come to these conclusions in reaction to the dominant ideology at the time. Perhaps they had a sense that it was out of date, that it no longer fitted with other elements of society or of their lives. But they suffered indecision in private as they rebelled against the majority (even as they were becoming a new majority).

The dominant ideology, then, is not the sum of all the happenings. It may not even be a pure majority. If we allow for a time-lag between dominant ideology and practice, or even between dominant ideology and individuals' viewpoints, then we can explain how it can constrain more than just the minority who don't subscribe to it. In times of rapid or radical change, there must be situations where the majority of people no longer subscribe to what has until that point been the dominant ideology – and when this has reached a crisis point, change happens.

In C-Life, for example, the company ideology – the official ideal promulgated by the company – held that training should be conducted according to certain rules. But things went wrong one year when an individual trainer, given power by the company, interpreted those rules in rather an extreme way, even by C-Life's normal standards, and took them beyond what the new trainees would tolerate. Many trainees quit en masse. The company ideology itself was out of date with the young people's expectations, which were also influenced by the atmosphere of their generation, such as what their friends were doing in other companies; and by the mass media, which has gradually introduced different ideas of working.

So company policy may lag behind individuals' expectations or views. And moreover, even without taking this time factor into account, different individuals may have differing interpretations of the same situation. It is certainly true – *à la* Geertz (1973) – that the conscious imposition of meaning on life is the primary condition of human existence and also its purpose. In C-Life, to become human was to become individual; but it was to become individual within the context of existing cultural patterns – historically created systems of meaning. With the help of these, the employees interpreted and gave meaning to their lives. However, even different individuals within the same society may have different backgrounds, which channel their interpretations in different ways. This means that the same situation could be interpreted in radically different ways by different people, with contrasting results.

For example, the C-Life employees thrown into training had to handle a reality that was sharply different from what they had expected. They had to assess their lives and find new meaning in that situation. Some employees rejected the C-Life ideology in favour of their individual selves and left the training. But there were also those who adjusted their individual ideas and expectations to meet the expectations of C-Life. Both groups borrowed from the available cultural models, or rejected those models absolutely. Those who stayed in C-Life explained that they stayed because they felt they could become '*hitorimae*': socially recognised adults in the context of the company. Those who quit did so for exactly the opposite reason: because they felt that they could not become fully-fledged adults or individuals in the context of the company. Thus, the same socio-cultural construct influences the actions of both of these individuals. But their individual interpretations are different: one is in line with the company ideology and one is opposed to it.

In some sense, then, we are at the mercy of social phenomena – not because they have an internal dynamic of their own, but because it takes time for a new dominant ideology to take shape out of the viewpoints and decisions of individuals. We are all, in a sense, at the mercy of impersonal forces as they have left the hands of the people who made them. In the above example, the dominant ideology was what pressured the employees to stay in their companies and conform to the ideal of a Japanese worker. It was through the dominant ideology that the weight of a seemingly impersonal 'society' shaped their actions and limited and channelled their thought and their decisions. C-Life people very often spoke of 'society' (*seken*), as in 'the pressures of society' or 'not going against the eyes of society'. When they did so, '*seken*' had the sense of an impersonal force that constrains and controls their lives. This was so whether they were submitting to it or rebelling against it.

The struggle between the meaning that the individual assigns to his current life and the company ideology was always present in C-Life. This was most obvious in situations such as the training, where the individuals involved had to reconcile a very large gap between their individual expectations and company ideology. Often, after much thought and agonising, these employees would become resigned to their position and accept it. This is an example of behaviour being influenced – and, ultimately, determined – by socio-cultural constructs. During C-Life training, employees were faced with a situation that was very harsh and highly disagreeable. But they were also influenced by the ideology that the individual matures through association with a group, that hardship and perseverance leads to spiritual growth or that they should repay debts to their parents by gaining stable employment. In many cases, these socio-cultural constructs and the company ideology were one and the same, and the training bosses would manipulate these ideas to persuade employees to stay. Often, employees would mull the issue over and then make a conscious decision to conform. Once decided, they would then put their very best efforts into wholly conforming. This may seem quite alien to Western readers. But, during the mulling over process, the employees were thinking of their choices and what would happen to them. They were thinking of the alternatives, which were often not very promising; of the effect on their families; of parental opposition; of the courage and determination that would be necessary if they were to quit. They had to take into account the ostracism and bullying they would almost certainly have to negotiate when transferring to another large company; the almost certain drop in pay, benefits, prestige and status if they transferred to a smaller company. On a psychological level, to be eternally dissatisfied with one's position but remain inside it is not seen as a sustainable prospect. They did not want to not be 'ordinary' or to be at odds with others around them. Having summed up all of the choices, they then put their whole determination into following the choice that they have made.

In this section, we have assessed some of the different ways of understanding ideology that have been suggested by various authors, and we have built upon their insights to build up a picture of what ideology is and how it works. In the next section I systematise this picture, to suggest a schema of the different levels of ideology. This provides the conceptual framework for the rest of the chapter.

Levels of ideology – a model

I suggest that there are several kinds of ideology, which I describe here briefly and apply throughout the rest of this chapter. By thus providing illustrations of the different levels of ideology, I hope to demonstrate that this schema is a useful one in analysing the nature of ideology.

- *Ideal ideology*
  This is the ideal view of a society. In the case of C-Life, this is the image of the Japanese company that an employee might have portrayed to a

foreigner new to Japan. It is the image that is portrayed in some of the *nihonjinron* literature which was mentioned in chapter 5. Such an image may bear little relation to reality. Indeed, it may be that no-one actually believes it to be true; but it is nevertheless significant as a determining factor in people's behaviour. People may represent reality as the ideal even if they know that it does not reflect the current state of affairs. If the ideal is presented to someone from outside the society, and the individual who is presenting the ideal knows that it does not match reality, then the ideal may correspond to *tatemae* and the individual's own beliefs (see below) to *honne*.

- *Dominant ideology*
  This is the set of majority beliefs of a society. Thus, the dominant ideology of Japan is what most Japanese believe; and the dominant ideology of C-Life is what most of the company employees believe. In other words, dominant ideologies may exist at different levels, from nations right down to couples; they could 'nest' within each other. This point is important to my discussion below of how *honne* and *tatemae* work in different situations. This is not to say, of course, that it is easy to determine what the dominant ideology is. In particular, it should not be confused with reality (see below).
- *Group ideology*
  I assume that groups within societies, like societies as a whole, have ideal ideologies. Thus, any group ideology is a subset of the ideology of the culture of which it is a part, that may or may not be in perfect accordance with it. Group ideology, however, is intimately connected with the agenda of the group. Thus, it may be ideology in the manipulated sense, where ideology is created in accordance with, and with the intention of promoting, the group's agenda. In the context of C-Life, I speak of the 'company agenda': an ideology promoted by management with certain aims, such as ensuring the loyalty and industriousness of its workforce. It is clear that group ideology, like ideal ideology, is an important determinant of behaviour; the difference is that ideal ideology is not presented as an accurate description of the current situation, whereas group ideology is. Thus, for example, the management of C-Life expected the information that it distributed to its salesmen to be passed on to their anxious customers as an accurate description of what was actually happening at the company.
- *Individual meaning*
  This is the meaning that the individual attributes to a certain situation, that comes ultimately from his own inviolable self. This may be strongly influenced by the dominant ideology. For most members of a group, their individual meaning will be much the same as the dominant ideology – otherwise the latter would not be dominant; but it does not follow that any individual will be in accord with the dominant ideology

on every subject. There may be individuals who disagree with the dominant ideology on many matters.

The relationships between these different levels may be highly complex. For example, an individual may believe that most people believe x, but be mistaken. Thus, there can be an erroneous individual interpretation of dominant ideology. Indeed, it could be that most people believe that most people believe x, but be mistaken, in which case the dominant ideology itself will be wrong about itself. There may be an ideal to which everyone aspires but which most people do not believe actually reflects reality: thus, ideal ideology and dominant ideology may be at odds. Again, a group's leaders may promulgate an ideology to pursue the group's own agenda, but fail to get most people to believe it – so the dominant ideology and the group ideology may diverge. On the other hand, of course, some of them may agree.

Note that this is quite apart from the question of the relation of ideology to practice: these are all different levels of ideology. There are thus four different kinds of ideology. The first three of these function at the level of the group, the fourth at the level of the individual. Corresponding to this, I distinguish two levels of reality, or practice.

- *The actual situation*
  This is the total sum of the decisions and actions of all the individuals. The actual situation, or reality, cannot be known to any individual at any time, except perhaps in retrospect. The ideology that he is influenced by in his everyday dealings is the dominant ideology (see above). It is important not to get confused by the fact that the individual may well believe the dominant ideology to be the reality. The individual may believe that everyone does x, whereas there are people unknown to him who do not do x. Thus, the individual at any one time has access only to the dominant ideology. So the reality is never truly accessible to any individual, except perhaps in retrospect. This is why, as will be explained later, the dominant ideology can never be the sum total of individual actions.
- *Individual practice*
  Finally, we need to recognise the realm of individual practice, as opposed to any ideology; the actions of many individuals are the reality of what has occurred or the practice of a group, as opposed to their group ideology.

With this schema in place, we are now in a position to consider a number of issues connected to the nature and function of ideology: the objectivity of ideology, its role in conflict, the way it changes and its role as narrative and myth. I begin with a discussion of the objectivity of ideology: in what way, if any, can we talk of ideology as existing 'out there'?

The objectivity of ideology

One of the most important issues of the society versus individual priority debate is whether ideologies or social structures can take on an independent character; whether they can exist independently of the forces that created or maintain them. Blau (1967) speaks of social structures in terms of 'emergent' entities, which exert independent influence of their own. I consider this interesting idea to be very insightful; in particular, it accords with the emphasis I have placed in this chapter on the 'time-lag' between reality and the different levels of ideology. In particular, it helps us understand the role writing may have in conserving ideology.

Anthropologists have treated writing in a number of ways. It is an objectification of speech, or a fixing of discourse, which can be preserved to translate anew at a later date (Ricoeur 1981). By doing so, it increases the scope of available knowledge. This can have two effects: it provides greater scope for innovation – and, paradoxically, it also brings about standardisation and conservation of past ideology. In this view, writing is an objectification but relies on fresh interpretation. Street (1984) points out that social institutions can use writing to structure ideological reality.

Because of the relative permanence of the written word, a bridge is formed between the past and the present. Writing allows the ideas of the past to continue to exert influence now. At the same time, of course, the present exercises considerable control over the past, or rather, what is currently believed about the past. For example, Bohannon (1952) shows that ancestors are not remembered unless they have relevance to the present situation. Thus, the past can act as the legitimisation of the present, and the present therefore has an interest in controlling the image of the past. There is a complex relationship between the two.

In fact, writing is one of the most important ways in which ideology is transmitted. In C-Life, the company ideology was transmitted in various ways: through rituals, speeches, morning radio talks and videos; but the bulk of it was disseminated through manuals, educative materials, memorandums, rules and other written material. The speeches, radio talks and weekly videos that were sent from the education section to the branch offices around the country were all immediate information, absorbed and then discarded. Some of the written information, particularly memos, functioned like this also; but some had a more lasting effect. The latter included histories of C-Life – brought to life each year in the annual report, or educational materials such as the brochures that were disseminated to university careers offices for people wanting to join C-Life. All of the written information was dated to some extent, and therefore represented views that quickly became discrepant with the general ideology of the company as well as with the reality.

We have seen how the company ideology (the group ideology) is not the same thing as the dominant ideology (what most people believe). Because it represented the strategy of the company as an organisation, the company ideology was necessarily rosy. It emphasised harmony and the positive values of how the company should ideally be. This meant that it was quite different from both reality and the dominant ideology. Again, because the company ideology was created by a large group of people, the views expressed were generalised, or smoothed out, so that they represented the true view of none of the individuals who created it. This vagueness had a positive function, since it ensured that the ideology would be useful in a large number of situations. The company ideology lost its influence, however, as it became more distant from both reality and the dominant ideology. The harsher the economic conditions became, the less the employees trusted the company information and the more they turned to alternative sources of information.

The important point here is that these written forms of ideology remained even as the world changed around them – and they continued to exert some influence. Thus, writing can play a vital role in restricting the flexibility of ideology and its ability to change and adapt. It allows the ideology of the past to affect the ideology of the present. However, ideology is always different from reality. And this means that there is always the possibility of conflict.

Ideology and conflict

In this section I look at what happens when ideology conflicts with reality, or when different levels of ideology conflict with each other.

There is now general recognition that conflict must be taken seriously. In fact, the recognition that inconsistency can exist in thought patterns is not new. Malinowski (1948) recognised that logical contradictions can exist when beliefs are opposed to them. We must take care not to rearrange in logic patterns and thought patterns of the West and deconstruct what was in order and logical in another society. In this work, I have sought to avoid this where possible by quoting from interviews with my respondents. But the problem remains – are the interviews real? Is the behaviour real?

Wallace (1964) terms orderly relations that occur in a stable socio-cultural system 'equivalence structures': sets of behavioural expectancies. 'Democratic violence' refers to people allowing each other to interpret in different ways, while coming up with their own individual (unexpressed and possibly violent) interpretations underneath. It enables individual creativity to live beneath an ambiguous surface of social-structural calm and within a form of behavioural norms which individuals continue to share. Mutual expectations of social interaction let them orient themselves to each other in interaction without the sharp differences in individual opinion disrupting the surface of the interaction.

Ideological conflict is an especially important topic in the context of Japan since, as we shall see, it helps us to understand the vexed issue of *honne* and *tatemae* a little more clearly. I begin with an important issue in understanding psychological conflict, that of dissonance.

Dissonance

The concept of dissonance is taken from social psychology and is based on the assumption that humans do not hold inconsistent beliefs and actions, at least not happily. Where beliefs become inconsistent with each other or with action, then a new belief will be added to mediate between the two, or beliefs will be changed to become compatible. For example, after a trip to the USA an employee may believe that Japanese management is inefficient. But he also believes that he is intelligent and motivated. He is working for an inefficient company. In this case he is not likely to devalue himself; his options are to quit the company, or he can reconcile himself to the fact that Japanese companies aren't so bad after all. Or he can bring a time factor in to resolve the equation. He can say that he is intelligent, Japanese management is bad, he works for an inefficient company, but he is going to quit as soon as he can.

The desire to minimise dissonance means that a new environment can alter a person's beliefs. At the training centre, the new employees carried out rituals, sang company songs and sold life insurance from morning to night. As they acted they began to shift their beliefs in the direction of their actions. For those who were unable to shift their beliefs in this way, the psychological discomfort caused by dissonance grew and grew until they quit the company to resolve it. Successfully fitting in to a society, then, can involve changing one's beliefs to the extent that they fit into the parameters of actions acceptable to that society. A striking example is provided by Evans-Pritchard (1976: 244), writing about his fieldwork among the Azande:

> In my own culture … I rejected, and reject, Zande notions of witchcraft … In their culture, or in the set of ideas I then lived in, I accepted them; in a kind of way I believed them … If one must act as though one believed, one ends in believing, or half-believing as one acts.

Even more interesting things happen when one level of ideology clashes not with practice but with another level of ideology.

Ideologies at odds

The possibility of ideologies clashing is important because, as we have already suggested and will see later in more depth, it is in this way that ideology changes. For example, M, one of my *doki*, made a mistake in his work and was transferred to a posting in a remote part of Japan, where he felt isolated and abandoned. He had believed (at the level of individual meaning) in the company ideology that the company would look after him for the duration of his working life. But he became aware of an increasingly large gap between the dominant ideology (the nation as expressed particularly in the media) and the company ideology. In retrospect he could see that, although he believed two years ago, say, that life insurance companies would not go under, he could see now that they did in fact go bankrupt. Extrapolating from this experience, he came to believe that Japanese companies would no longer look after their employees. He believed that he was intelligent, yet he was giving all of his time to a company which he no longer believed would look after him for life. He experienced severe dissonance, almost suffering a breakdown, for months on end. In the end, he resolved it by deciding firmly that he would go on working for the company but he would regard his work on strictly contractual terms and that he would give only as much work as his salary deserved and do no more. Thus, his individual meaning had changed, and with it his practice. As economic conditions worsen, we can imagine the same thing happening to many people; eventually, the dominant ideology will have changed. And, even later, the ideal ideology may change too, to become more plausible.

That is what may happen when individual belief clashes with the dominant or ideal ideology. But the dominant and ideal ideologies may also clash with each other. Companies may have ideologies that are opposed to national dominant ideology, for example, the radically Western-style maverick software companies springing up in Japan. Note that the company ideology may be opposed to the dominant ideology of companies in Japan or that of employees of all companies, and it may be an ideal ideology – an example held up of the way that things 'should' be. The ideal ideology of companies, such as that expressed in the *nihonjinron* literature, may be radically opposed to reality. Individual employees within a company may be radically opposed to the dominant ideology of that company. Returnee schoolchildren may on the individual level be strikingly different in their thinking to the dominant ideology of Japan.

These observations shed light on the problem encountered by Bourdieu in his Moroccan fieldwork. Bourdieu's informants consistently told him that they always married their cross-cousins, whilst his statistics informed him that this was not true at all. In this case, 'we always marry our cross-cousins' was clearly the dominant ideology. Informants may subscribe to the dominant ideology without being aware of the reality. The ideology takes time to catch up with the ever-changing reality, and if reality is changing quickly then there may be a sizeable gap between them. It is not normally necessary to be conscious of reality, or to investigate if there is a gap between ideology and practice unless there are particular circumstances, such as change of some kind or a personal agenda. One can imagine that if a young man had wanted to marry someone who was not a cross-cousin, it would have taken him little time to find examples of others not marrying their cross-cousins to support his case. He might then become aware for the first time of the gap between ideology and practice and rebel against those who maintained that ideology was reality. This individual rebellion could be a one-off exception, but many simultaneous individual rebellions could lead to the dominant ideology changing.

Honne *and* tatemae

With these points in place, it is easier to see the shifting and often confusing way that *honne* and *tatemae* work. This can be especially puzzling to a foreigner, who may be unable to understand why the Japanese appear to say different things about the same subject under different circumstances. Are they being dishonest?

In fact, as I argued in my first book, *Inside the Japanese Company*, the reason for the confusion is that a Japanese person will sometimes talk *tatemae* and sometimes give their *honne* opinion, depending on whether the person they are talking to is a member of their own group or not. So, for example, if two C-Life employees are discussing the company's prospects together, they will probably speak *honne*. But if they were to discuss the same subject with an outsider, they are likely to talk *tatemae*.

The complicating factor is that any single individual will be a member of many different groups, from – at the widest extreme – the group of all humanity, down to the group of their own families, or even just themselves. So the C-Life man who presents a *tatemae* account of his company to a member of a rival life insurer will, when the subject moves on to the wider fortunes of the life insurance industry as a whole, shift to giving his *honne* opinion. His interlocutor has changed from being an outsider to being an insider, because the context has shifted.

In the terminology I have been developing, we can express this idea by saying that an individual belongs to a number of groups. Each of those groups has its own dominant ideology and also its own ideal ideology. Plus, of course, there will be the individual's own take on the group, as well as the reality and the individual's own actions. Thus, for any given group that the individual belongs to there is a wide range of opinions he can express regarding it, corresponding to these different levels of ideology. And he may express one kind of ideology regarding one group, and another kind regarding another.

By thinking in terms of the levels of ideology that I have suggested, then, we can shed some light on what is, to the foreigner, an especially confusing aspect of Japanese society. It certainly helps to explain the difficulty faced by outside researchers: any attempt to establish what is going on in a group by asking members of that group is likely to yield only the group ideology – *tatemae*.

Although I had the advantage of having been an employee myself, and was therefore not really an outsider, I still had to deal with these issues when studying C-Life – a fact that I illustrate further in chapter 8. It was impossible to judge from the actions of the employees what their real stance was on any issue, unless you looked at how they had voted with their feet – whether they had stayed or not stayed in C-Life. Alternatively one could ask them and hope that they would give their true opinion, their *honne*.

The fact that they might be willing to do this reflects another thread in the perplexing tapestry of *honne/tatemae* – the fact that people have agendas to promote. For example, employees might be unlikely to express *honne* if they thought that their seniors would not approve and it might hamper their career. But if they were satisfied that what they said would not be broadcast, they might have no objection to stating their individual opinions.

Of course, at any one time most employees did have one agenda or another. Who doesn't have an agenda of making themselves look good when they are talking to someone about their career choices? I had to judge constantly whether the employees were speaking *honne* or not, and always asked others whether they thought that someone else had been speaking *honne* when he said this or that. This kind of fieldwork may sound very imprecise and judgmental; but then it is no more than we all do every day when we are talking to people in any kind of situation. We are always judging whether they are speaking from their hearts, whether they have a hidden agenda, whether they are united with someone else, and so on. In particular, we learn to decide whether people are giving their personal viewpoint or the dominant ideology. By talking to many people, we gradually form a picture of what the dominant ideology is. In the next two chapters, I explore these issues further.

This point reminds us that the dominant ideology may, to a certain extent, be ambiguous. There was certainly not total agreement over it in C-Life. Not everybody could point out what the norms were, or even who was being ostracised. But asking enough people led to the emergence of a majority opinion, in which most people believed the same things and on which most people were agreed on who was inside or outside certain groups. Extremely vague in principle, it worked in practice. Most of the people, most of the time, could not outline the general ideology of the group in perfect agreement with others, but they had a good enough working knowledge of it. When I say good enough, I mean good enough not to cause problems for the individual – clashes, ostracism, disagreements with key people – or to interfere with the ongoing work of advancing their personal agenda.

So, ideology, and its expression by individuals, is a very messy business. There is not only the simple distinction between *honne* and *tatemae*, but the seriously complicating matter of personal agendas. And this leads us directly on to the subject of strategising, and the role that ideology plays in this central feature of company life.

Strategies

Throughout this book, we have been studying the changing economic conditions at C-Life, and the reactions of its employees to them. How is the subject of strategising particularly relevant to this? In fact, these changing conditions made strategising all the more important. In better times, the ideal relation of employees to the company was one of 'give-and-take'. This contract was largely unconscious until it came to be questioned as uncertainty in the outside environment increased. As the company lost the ability to assure employees that it would fulfil its side of the bargain – life-time employment and seniority promotion – the employees lost their loyalty and motivation to work in fairly direct proportion. This was impressed upon me again and again in my fieldwork. There were many employees who had no illusions about what was happening in C-Life, and no special feelings of loyalty to the company, but who remained in the company. This was because they believed they would still get their pay, or because they thought that the risks of going outweighed the risks of staying, or because they had no particularly attractive options – and for some, they had no other real options at all.

What is strategising?

Strategising, then, is a central theme to have come out of the fieldwork presented in this book. What do I mean by this term?

The notion of company strategy has been an extremely important theme in management studies in recent years. Mintzberg, Ahlstrand and Lampel (1998), who have surveyed the vast field of writing on strategy, divide the different ways management experts have dealt with the topic into three basic stances. The first type looks at strategy as prescriptive, looking at how the theorists think that organisations *should* strategise. The second stance is descriptive, seeking to explain how organisations actually go about planning and executing their development. A third alternative they suggest is to look at strategy as a process of transformation. Thus they comment, 'if organizations settle into stable states, then strategy making has to describe the leap from one state to another' (1988: 7).

However, this discussion of strategy is primarily a discussion of how strategy is achieved for the company as a whole, and is a different topic to the kind of strategising I deal with here. My focus is not on the organisation as a whole but on the individuals within it, and how they go about following their own, personal agendas; and it is solely descriptive. So by 'strategising' here I mean a group of related issues: essentially, what people are trying to get out of life (the 'goods' that they play for) and the different methods they use to try to get them.

These issues have received relatively little attention in the context of the Japanese company. An exception is Wong (1999), who has looked at accounting for the motivation of workers in Japanese companies. He argues that much of it is connected to relationships of power within the company. Different workers react in different ways to the power that the company has over them: they may adapt to it, become ambitious to gain it for themselves or rebel against it. These different approaches represent different strategies. For example, an ambitious employee may adopt a strategy of buckling down and conforming to the model of a successful and loyal worker, whilst a rebellious one might become confrontational when given a demanding task to do.

Here, however, I want to look at how employees play for a wide variety of goals in the company, and how they adopt a wide range of strategies to do so. What sort of things are they playing for, and why do they do so in such different ways? Why are some individuals successful and others less so? The issues that these questions raise are particularly associated with the work of Pierre Bourdieu.

Bourdieu, as we saw in chapter 1, argues that people compete for scarce goods and make strategies around obtaining them. He therefore believes that individual strategy is crucial in looking at the economy. But in contrast to Marxist economics, he recognises that the scarce goods – the 'capital' – that people compete for include not just material, but social and symbolic goods that are valued in a particular society. He can therefore talk of 'symbolic' goods as well as 'material' ones.

In looking at C-Life, therefore, we have to look at the kinds of goods that were valuable in the company and for which the employees were competing. Status was of prime importance in C-Life. The next most commonly cited goal was money. How does this fit in with the company's ideology of hard-working employees driven by loyalty to their company? The C-Life employees stated their motives differently in different circumstances. Those who were speaking more honestly and had no particular agenda attached to proclaiming their loyalty to the company were more prone to say: 'We work hard to get status!' – 'And because we want money!'

I am not arguing that some people had agendas and some did not. As we see in the next chapter, everyone involved in the filming of C-Life certainly had some kind of agenda – including the anthropologist. But some people had specific agendas that were advanced by proclaiming their loyalty to the company. For some, the programme that I was making was a remarkably good vehicle with which to broadcast their loyalty. These were the employees still inside C-Life, those whose bosses had introduced me to them, those who had bosses who were also involved in the programme, those who knew that the PR department was involved, and so on. It was mainly the middle-aged and younger members of the company who had agendas towards proclaiming loyalty to the company. The older members mostly had little to gain from proclaiming such an ideology.

For Bourdieu, capital includes symbolic capital: status, prestige and authority, all the goods that are sought after in a particular social formation. For the C-Life employees, becoming a department head inside a major company was still a high-priority goal. But the risks associated with obtaining that goal had increased dramatically. For most employees, however, despite the increased risks, the risk of moving was still greater than the risk of staying. Indeed, for many, particularly those over 40, moving was an impossibility unless they already had solid assets in the form of transferable skills. It was very clear that all of the C-Life employees were constantly weighing up the risks of going versus the risks of staying. Those inside who were able to do something about acquiring skills were busy doing so.

Together, these different decisions taken by different individuals affect the social system. Barth (1959, 1966) has said that normative systems exist as a result of the decisions that are made by individual actors making strategic decisions that maximise their individual interests. It is a picture of feedback and flow where structure is an arrangement of the outcome of a number of decisions, which then serve as directional factors for future decisions. This is just what was occurring in C-Life. But it is not possible for this flow to be instantaneous – there has to be a time-lag for communication to flow from one party to another. This was clearly so in my C-Life fieldwork. The employees had been thrown into unimaginable confusion by the recession, and the threat of restructuring. There was immediate pressure from continually decreasing wages threatening their ability to sustain themselves economically. Yet they had been greatly influenced by an ideology that said that they would be in the same company for life. This ideology was impressed upon them very strongly at the training centre, where they came to accept – to varying degrees – their new roles in the company. Having been through this initiation it acted, as they put it, like a new religion or cult on them, so it was hard for them to readjust their ideas to the economic reality.

The result was that many people had a strikingly limited appreciation of what was happening overall. I was struck constantly by the feeling that, in Peacock's metaphor, I was a spectator at the cinema, able to empathise with the characters but also having an overview of the total plot, which the individual characters had only to a limited degree. I am not arguing by any means that I was the only one with an overview, nor that I could see my own position clearly when I was in the company. All of the characters in C-Life, including myself, had a limited understanding of their own situations at the time. But they had to gather new information and interpret it in an ongoing process. It took time to change their ideas. The time factor of the whole process was crucial. Bailey (1971) has said that social structure equals the 'current rules of the game'. I agree that individuals make their choices according to such rules and that those choices, as a total, influence the making of future rules. However, social structure in C-Life reflected old information, which had to be overthrown before a new social order could be created.

Overseas, as we have seen, the C-Life employees found themselves opened up to new ways of thinking. Goodman (1978) has said that our knowledge – each fact – is a small theory in itself. The C-Life employees overseas had a new range of theories to test and digest. In some cases, like J, this meant changing an entire paradigm of beliefs, resulting in an unsustainable mismatch with C-Life's socio-cultural constructs.

New facts in C-Life remained plural and conflicting until they finally solidified into common opinion. The uncontested knowledge slowly solidified its way into company narrative, into 'fact', into new forms of ideology. When new facts dramatically conflicted with the ideology to date, then that too underwent a period of consolidation as the ideology changed to accommodate the new fact.

According to Ingold (1986) and Weiner (1991), our constructs are uncertain and ever-changing and we live within an ever-changing world of socio-cultural exchange. In C-Life this was precisely the case. New information and new circumstances led to change. One example was the notorious occasion when fourteen trainees all quit together in response to the increasingly harsh regime at the training centre. This cumulative action by those employees served to change the company ideology and stance. The training itself was dramatically changed the following year: both shortened and made milder.

To interpret the world, therefore, is also to construct it. Individuals are the initiating energy. The individual has the responsibility for determining his own meanings; to maintain habits or to break anew. It was when their individual strategic interests came into direct conflict with ideology that C-Life employees were forced to change their individual views, and this pressure, built up by many individuals over a period of time, resulted in changes in ideology.

These considerations suggest that a solid understanding of strategising and the processes which drive it is essential to a wider account of phenomena such as social structure and ideology, and the ways in which they change. I build on this claim in the next section, on strategising in the workplace. First, however, I flesh out our account of how strategising actually went on in the 'game' that is C-Life. We need to know something of how people used the 'rules' of this game.

The rules of the game

On the basis of the fieldwork material presented in the body of this book, and the analysis offered so far in this chapter, we may say that, at C-Life, there was a definite game to be played, with definite stakes. Everyone was competing earnestly in this game on the basis of rules that they thought that they had worked out. All the time there were coalitions forming and being abandoned, as people worked out joint strategies in the game. The coalitions of seniors and juniors in cliques or factions were long-term coalitions in this same game. All the employees thought that they were making the best decisions at the time in terms of their strategies to get ahead. But, in reality, no-one actually knew the rules perfectly. The rules could never be known because they depended on a fluctuating and amorphous ideology made by humans with sharply different characters and ideas themselves.

As we have seen throughout the fieldwork chapters, some employees were very good at this game. These people were generally characterised by a certain amount of detachment. They could take or leave whatever was served up without getting too entangled or fixed on one stance. They could deal with the inherent uncertainties of a very human game with human idiosyncrasies continually and inexplicably changing the shape of the results.

If this sounds like a cloak-and-dagger operation of great intrigue, that is because it was. I think that in C-Life – or any large Japanese company like it – intrigue is rife and permeates the whole organisation because of the long-term nature of the social relations involved. The situation is exacerbated by the murky atmosphere of the company, the two-sided character of the *honne* and *tatemae* unclearness about who stands where, who believes what, whether that action was real or the motives different. The vocabulary of opaqueness permeated the company, and included such words as *moya moya* (unclear), *zuru zuru* (to drag on), *nanto naku* (somehow). When to use *tatemae* and when to use *honne* was an important tool in feeling one's way in the murky politics of C-Life.

Were the rules of the game a kind of ideology in themselves? It seems reasonable to describe them as part of the ideology: the generally accepted norms, the accepted standards of behaviour. Anyone who failed to observe these norms was likely to be ostracised for not maintaining the current social rules. This, then, requires that the beliefs which compose the ideology include beliefs about behaviour, about the way individuals should act. The rules were not necessarily the same as the company ideology, that is, the 'official' ideology promoted by C-Life itself. Adhering to company ideology alone was not a winning strategy but a naïve stand that could end in trouble. One example of this is the star employee – U – who was praised constantly to me by employees and bosses alike, although he quit the company shortly after filming. When he was mentioned at one *dokikai* (*doki* party), my *doki* recalled when U had been invited to a wedding by another *doki* but had been late for the wedding because he had been doing overtime at work. The *doki* were sharply critical of this action, saying that letting work get in the way of an important occasion for a friend was bad. Thus, by causing bad feeling among his *doki*, and thereby lowering the esteem in which he was held, U slipped up.

This is a case where duty (*giri*) conflicted directly with *ninjo* (human feeling) – or company ideology of sacrificing oneself for the company conflicted with what most people believed was in fact appropriate behaviour. This dichotomy of feelings belonging to the realm of *soto* (outside) and those belonging to the realm of *uchi* (inside) are the basic human dilemma that lies at the base of an enormous amount of novels, plays, songs and failed human relationships. According to the *doki*, U should not, in this circumstance, have prioritised *giri* over *ninjo*. His *doki* were not interested in why U had done it. At the same time, they may have had personal agendas of being as critical as possible of U since he was so massively successful otherwise. But what is clear here is that simply following company ideology is not always the best way to advance one's agenda. Company ideology and a *tatemae* stance that maintains this is important at times, for one must be seen to be toeing the company line, but at other times following that same agenda will get one into trouble, as it did U. The relative importance of annoying one's *doki* like this in favour of pleasing one's bosses must, of course, be taken into account. At the very end of a career in the Japanese life-time employment system it is only one's *doki* who remain – apart from one's juniors, there is no-one else. And promotion depends very much on a general evaluation of one's character from everybody. By acting as he did, U distanced himself from his *doki*. He appeared somehow untrustworthy, bringing his character into question. People wondered if he really had any affection for his *doki*. And by extension, they wondered how trustworthy he could be. This balancing of *giri* (duty) and *ninjo* (human feeling) is important in the company, as it is in almost every sphere of life at C-Life.

The example shows not only how company ideology (sacrifice everything for the company) may conflict with the ideology of one's peers (remain close to one's *doki*), but also how company ideology, if it is to be effective, cannot become too discrepant with other norms. If the company had praised U for missing his friend's wedding, this would not have been popular with the employees. Thus, company literature did stress the importance of good personal relations between *doki*, and general comradeship in general in the company.

In view of all this, we may safely say that a winning strategy involves sensitivity to *honne* and *tatemae* and consciousness of the rules themselves, inasmuch as that is possible. An ability to be sensitive to what the current rules of the game were at any given moment was one of the greatest bonus cards of all in C-Life. But the rules of the game were social rules. If one divulged one's strategy in the wrong way, one risked breaking the rules of society and suffering as a result. In other words, almost everyone was strategising – but one of the most important skills of strategising was not to be seen to be doing it. Following a strategy openly would invite ostracism and enmity from those around who are competing for the same goals.

This suggests that, to play the game effectively, it is crucial to know what one is doing, for otherwise one could not conceal it when necessary. In other words, consciousness is a central factor in the game. We shall be seeing this important fact throughout the current chapter.

Strategy and the manipulation of ideology

In this section, I bring together our discussions of ideology and strategy by considering one of the most interesting ways in which agents construct strategies to pursue their goals: by manipulating what other people believe. This serves not only to deepen our understanding of strategising, but also to show how such an understanding is essential to a wider account of social phenomena – in this case, the way ideology is formed and used.

Is it possible for agents to pursue their goals by manipulating people's beliefs? As we saw in chapter 1, Bourdieu suggests this when he says that symbolic capital is not always recognised as a convertible source of power. The process of conversion may be 'masked'. This is a very interesting issue that has also been raised in the work of Althusser, and in the Japan literature by Allison. Some anthropologists have followed a Marxist line and argue that the ruling class may use symbolic systems to create a false consciousness in other classes. How does this apply to C-Life? Did the company purposefully manipulate cultural meanings in order to promote their own agenda?

Allison is an interesting example of this approach in the Japan literature. In an article describing how ordinary mothers in Japanese homes spend an enormous amount of effort – an average of forty minutes each morning – on making their children's lunches for school, she follows the idea that lunch is significant as a cultural meaningful practice invested with a gendered state ideology. According to Allison, the practice of making the lunch in a certain culturally accepted way is overseen by the authorities of nursery school institutions, which are linked to and monitored by the state. The producer of the lunch box is constructed as a woman and mother through the practice of making the lunch. The concept of ideological state apparatus comes from Althusser (1971), who argues that there are two major structures of power in modern capitalist societies: repressive state apparatuses or institutions such as the law or police that operate through the threat of force, and a second structure of power that operates through ideology including education and the media. The second category is disguised and screened, but is far-reaching in its power to coerce people into seeing the world in a certain way.

I consider this to be interesting and generally true. But I would add to it by saying that we must also take into account the individual's very active role in maintaining the ideology. I believe that Allison's example could have made more of the degree to which mothers participate in, and endorse, the ideology of lunch-making and what their motivations are for doing so. Ideology is a social construct, existing in a complex relationship with the beliefs and practices of each individual. It is not a ready-made package handed down by the state and adhered to by mothers. Mothers rank themselves in the contest of lunch-making. They create and recreate the ideology themselves by participating in it. This is not to say that group ideology (at the kindergarten) does not makes use of already existing social models and ideologies. In this example, I would argue that the status of the mother is judged partly by other mothers on how well they fulfil a sign of 'motherhood', namely, making the lunch in the 'correct' way.

What this means for our account of strategising is that it is not possible to think of one group of people (consciously) following their strategies by manipulating the (unconscious) ideology of everyone else. Reality is not as simple as this. Certainly, in C-Life, an ethos and an ideology already existed when new employees came into the company. In that sense, the ideology came before them and would exist after they left. But it was the product of all of the participants in it. It was not solely the product of top management, and top management lacked the sole power to manipulate it. Top management could, of course, create the company ideology, but only one kind of group ideology; they were unable to manipulate the overall worldview of employees or what they actually believed as individuals.

The key point here is the extent to which each and every party participating in the culture is making use of the ideology in order to advance their own interests. Mothers also subscribe to the lunchbox ideology because it has immediate tangible benefits for them in relation to the groups that they care most about: gaining status in the eyes of their peers, being praised for being 'good' mothers in the 'eyes of society'. As Bourdieu argues, the value of any cultural notion is not its meaningfulness or its usefulness, but the social distinction embedded in such meaning or use – that is, the effects of the cultural products on the social positions of the producers.

In C-Life, similarly, it was not a simple matter of one party – management – creating and manipulating ideology for their own agenda. Top management were certainly creating and manipulating ideology, but then so were all of the members of the company, at different times, to different degrees and in different ways. A one-way arrangement whereby the top management was conscious of ideology as ideology and the rest of the employees were mainly hoodwinked was simply not the case at C-Life. There is, in any case, no very clear line between top management and the rest of the workforce. Indeed, in the case of the bankruptcies of large companies such as Nissan Life, or indeed C-Life, the directors themselves didn't even know about the bankruptcy more than a day before it happened.

The complex way in which different people try to influence the behaviour of others through manipulating ideology is illustrated well by the training centre, where employees spent their first year at C-Life. There, the trainers would coerce the trainees to work hard and stick at it by using ideology that they were already familiar with from home and school. They would say things like: you can't let your parents down; you must repay your parents; you are now a society man and must stand on your own two feet; your *doki* are depending on you; walking out would be an admission of defeat; why not succeed a little and then decide what to do when you have something to be proud of; and so on. That this was not simply a case of those in charge manipulating those beneath them can be seen from the fact that the trainees used similar techniques on each other. They frequently appealed to an 'all together' ideology. A – who skipped selling for the first few months, being particularly unmotivated – was caught in this way. The pressure on him from *doki* increased greatly as the training went on. He says that he had to conform in the end, as he became unable to cause them trouble any longer. Of course, the training was carefully arranged from the start to harness this pressure on trainees. Teams were set up so that everyone had to compete against each other in groups. Failure to sell thus resulted in pressure – not from the trainers, but from the other members of the group. It was peer pressure that exhorted them to sell.

The situation becomes still more complex when one takes account of the fact that people in C-Life were also interacting with outsiders. Above C-Life, for example, there were other parties trying to manipulate ideology for their agendas at the expense of C-Life itself. One notable example occurred when C-Life's situation began to look more desperate. The authorities – the Ministry of Finance and the life insurance industry authority – increasingly put pressure on C-Life's main bank to support the company. The rationale, of course, was worded in terms of the fact that fellow businesses should help each other. C-Life also pressured the main bank with the same powerful ideology. When the bank eventually decided that it would not help, it was one of the first examples of a main bank pulling out its support for a struggling company in its business group of related companies (*keiretsu*). This, of course, will provide an example and rationale for other main banks to do the same in similar cases in the future, and so will have a significant impact on changing that way that *keiretsu* support each other, ultimately weakening the *keiretsu* system.

The generally accepted ideology of work life, then, was something that was built up and maintained by all of the participants. Ogasawara (1998) remarks in her study that the supposedly powerless office ladies in the office were quite active in seizing ways to show their displeasure. In C-Life, although secretaries have not been the focus of my study, I can say that they certainly sabotaged the work of bosses whom they disliked. However, employees did not simply sabotage unpopular individuals' work to bring those individuals down; they aimed to enhance their own standing. In other words, it was part of their individual strategies, designed to maximise their share of the symbolic good of status.

Having established the nature and role of strategising, I turn now to a central issue: the role of consciousness in strategising.

Strategising and consciousness

In what we have seen so far, consciousness has emerged as a crucial element in strategising. I have suggested that an ability to recognise the rules of the game, and to be able deliberately to conceal the fact that one is playing it, are extremely valuable routes to success. In this section, I consider the nature and role of consciousness in greater depth.

Consciousness in society

First, what do we mean by 'consciousness', a word with a wide range of meanings? Here, I take it to mean, essentially, an ability to recognise the underlying social structure beneath one's actions. Some anthropologists seem to deny that their subjects really can do this. It is on this basis, for example, that many have criticised Bourdieu's account of strategising, particularly the emphasis he places on 'habitus'. By use of this concept – 'internalised schemes which having been constituted in the course of collective history, are acquired in the course of individual history' – he seeks to explain why humans seem to act automatically in line with their cultures. Bourdieu seems to believe that these internalised schemes are unconscious.

This theory rings true when one considers how the Japanese, and indeed people from any society, are socialised into certain types of behaviours as children. But one problem with the concept of habitus is that there is no room for the possibility of acquiring social competency in another culture in adulthood. Yet we know that people change their ideas and their behaviour, after they live overseas for example.

Others have sought to modify this viewpoint, taking into account the reality of unconscious determining but keeping in sight the ability of agents to be aware of what is going on and to influence it. For example, Rapport and Overing (2000) point out that consciousness is a matter of degree, a continuum, rather than a binary opposition between the conscious and the unconscious. Social competence involves a certain degree of unconsciousness of one's actions, since they come naturally to one. This, then, is habitus, and it is in this way that social structures come into being which determine social practice.

In fact, the importance of an agent's awareness of his situation is now recognised by many anthropologists. As Giddens (1984) puts it, all social actors can be social scientists. All actors are able to reflect on their social realm, interpret it and act on it. Because we are all conscious, we must be constantly analysing the world and ourselves.

All natives, then, must be able to explain their own social practices; they are not limited within their own linguistic social and cultural categories from moving beyond that to discourse with other peoples. It is ridiculous, as well as arrogant and patronising, to imagine that anthropologists are conscious scientists collecting objective data, while their subjects are living unconsciously inside their cultural practices. Indeed, there are valuable points to be drawn from considering the self-consciousness of agents.

Some theorists, for example, consider the consequences of agents' consciousness of their social worlds. This consciousness of the 'game' can allow actors to detach themselves from it. Irony is an example of this detachment from the world and consideration of other possibilities. People are able to realise that social rules are not always right, and that there is some other reality behind the social rules. Irony explores other possibilities apart from the immediately apparent, thereby allowing people to question their values and to begin to reinterpret them. Appadurai (1991) suggests that people can see their lives as an ironic compromise between what they can imagine could happen and what social life will allow to happen.

Alternatively, tension between the individual and structures can be creative. The individual can 'take a step back' from the world, and change the structures from which he has stepped back. This involves a moment of 'conversion.' Fernandez (1995) argues that conversion can be said to originate from a meaning deficit and a search for new values. The converted individual changes his ideas, becomes detached and can look back at the point from which he came.

A similar role can be played by shame. Shaming serves to make behaviour that has been automatic suddenly bare. The individual has to think about things that he has not thought about before, and put things into a new context. 'It was then that I realised that I was in a one-sided love affair with the company!' declared M, whose eyes were opened by the fact that the company had unexpectedly demoted him.

The particular relevance of the topic of consciousness to Japanese anthropology is that without it we cannot appreciate the full complexity of *honne* and *tatemae*, or practice and ideology. Indeed, without an appreciation of the varying degrees of consciousness possessed by different individuals, it is impossible to talk of *honne* and *tatemae*. These modes of thought and behaviour – which are such ingrained concepts in Japan and so crucial to Japanese society – are not possible without a distinct individual self which can move consciously between two ways of interacting with others. As Rosenberger (1992) has noted, the Japanese in general lay great emphasis on coming to understand the distinction between *ura* and *omote* ('back region' and 'front region', in the terminology of Goffman), *honne* and *tatemae*. Indeed, coming to know the crucial distinction between *honne* and *tatemae* is the mark of maturity. Most relevant to our concerns here, it is essential to successful strategising. Knowing the difference between the *honne* and *tatemae*, and when to use each, allows an individual to follow his strategies without detection. Following a strategy openly would, in many cases, invite ostracism and enmity from those around who are competing for the same goals.

This point suggests a further, and very important, one – not everyone is conscious to the same degree. This was quite apparent to me as I conducted my fieldwork. Some employees in the company were extraordinarily good at knowing what was going on and predicting what would happen. They were very adept at managing politically and socially – which meant more or less that they had a talent for managing *honne* and *tatemae* situations. Analysing the company and their surroundings like a lay scientist was more than a hobby, it was something that imbued their lives and within which atmosphere they lived their lives. All the employees were lay social scientists in this manner to a greater degree than I have seen in non-Japanese companies, although I believe that all of us are in a sense lay social scientists. Again, I think this is because of the intensity of the human relations in C-Life which were longer term, more inescapable and where promotion was directly related to how well you got on with others.

It is interesting, for example, to consider again the occasion when a group of employees, including myself, decided to go to a restaurant together. As we saw earlier (p.179), one member of the group announced that he was going to take a different route, even though he was leaving at the same time as us to go to the same place. The others considered this very strange. He may have had a perfectly good reason for wanting to take a different route, but the fact that he just did so without a word of explanation was extremely socially maladroit in C-Life. If that employee had been aware of the repercussions that this small action would have, no doubt he would have made the effort to walk to the station with everyone else, or explained why he wanted to go a different way. But he was not aware of this. In some sense, even I had more awareness of these kinds of social rules than he did, even though I was a foreigner in the company. This points to there being a spectrum of consciousness or awareness of what the appropriate social rules are.

Consciousness, then, plays an important role in the relation of individuals to society at large. And it is particularly important to strategising – especially in a context such as the Japanese company, where success in strategising depends to a large extent on the skilful use of *honne* and *tatemae*.

I now ground some of the points we have seen made in this chapter, particularly the crucial role played by consciousness in strategising, with a study of a conversation recorded during the last stage of my fieldwork. Here, the way in which different individuals are conscious to differing degrees should become plain.

Consciousness in C-Life: a study

The following conversation is illustrative of a number of individual employees and their thoughts on and approaches to the issue of consciousness. Two transferees are talking together about ostracism. Both were mid-career transferees into the international department at C-Life. H was very aware of 'the game', but left the company after being pressured out. W, by contrast, was rather naïve, but was well liked by the other employees. He was the only mid-career transferee to stay at C-Life until the end.

H: Yes, yes, yes, we have ostracism (*murahachibu*) in C-Life. He doesn't think that they do, but everyone knows there is ostracism.

W: My *doki* were very few. There were only thirteen of us.

H: But if they were asked who they would sacrifice first then you would be the one hunted down. You would be the one they would aim at. Because they have been in common ownership of the company – been a common body – for so long (*kyoyu shite iru kara*). If you think of the company as a village it is really easy to understand.

W: You don't have to think that deeply about things.

H actively analyses C-Life to establish the culture and how it works. He is – and wants to be – conscious of these rules. W, by contrast, doesn't want to think deeply about things. He simply aims to go on living his life as best as he can in C-Life without searching for the structural bones that lie beneath the surface. The conversation continues:

H: It is because individuals are not independent ... it is because individuals are not established as individuals. If they were established as individuals, they would be floating. It is because people in the company do not have established individuality.

In this statement, H suggests that the ability to fit into the company is diametrically opposed to individualism. To be an individual is incompatible with company life at C-Life. For H, to be individual is in itself enough to occasion one to be ejected from the village. He suggests that W is in this position:

H: He (W) has a very established sense of self (*kojin ga kakuritsu shite iru*) so he is really out of it – floating – in the company (*uite iru*). You can see that he is. He doesn't realise it himself but everyone thinks it in their heart. He is very un-Japanese (*nihonjin banare shite iru*).

To fit into the company is Japanese in itself; to fail to fit in is to be un-Japanese or literally to be drifting away from being Japanese. (Here we see how undesirable qualities are described as foreign, and 'Japanese-ness' is defined in opposition to them.) In this case, H claims that W is unaware that he is ostracised; unaware of a reality that everyone else knows. But there is more:

H: It is the impression of everybody that he is un-Japanese, well, in a good sense anyway. I think that everyone is envious of him. People can't take actions like him. For example, to go to the Ministry of Finance and raise his voice at them! There was a famous episode where he was stopped by one of the directors.

So to be un-Japanese is not necessarily a bad thing. One can be floating in a positive or a negative sense, on either side of a spectrum. But the fact remains that if one is not average, and Japanese, and within the accepted range, or within the 'eight-tenths of the village' as it is termed, one will still float.

Q: So W, what do you think of that?
W: I am a Japanese. I am 100 per cent Japanese.
Q: Do you think that you are a Westernised kind of Japanese?

W: Well, that might be true. I went to an American university and I lived in Madrid and Birmingham. I was in a foreign bank for a long time. So I have always done international work. I don't really have any consciousness about what part of me is domestic or Japanese or what part of me is Western. Sometimes I feel a contradiction but it is no benefit to think that hard about things. What is going to happen is going to happen. That is the reality of things. If you think that deeply about things you get tired!

H: But I just like to know the reality of things. I want to understand objectively the reality; what kind of position I'm in. You are not looking at that. You just go your own way (in English, 'go my way')! That in itself is already American or Western. To ponder deeply on things or to think on things like me, is so Japanese. Because I am conscious of things – because I am aware of things like that while I act – don't you think that's amazing? There is not that much difference between us about what we do but I am conscious about what happens and he is not conscious.

The very act of not being conscious is seen as un-Japanese, such is the importance of *tatemae/honne* and the ability to manipulate it. *Tatemae/honne* is a crucial concept in Japanese society, and one which employees devote much effort and energy into analysing and manipulating. To use *tatemae/honne* is in itself seen as Japanese. To fail to be conscious of this, or to 'go my way', is like a Westerner: un-Japanese.

W: I don't think it is necessary to be that conscious about villages and discrimination and such!

H: But you are being discriminated against!

T: Was he really? I worked with W. And I don't think that he really was. I don't think that anyone was looking at him in a different way.

H: In the international department they weren't, but in the domestic departments….

W: I don't get hooked on things like that (*kodawaranai*).

Who is right? W, who refuses to analyse his own position, or H who maintains he is ostracised, or T who looks from the side and thinks that W is not ostracised even though he often was? In fact, if majority opinion in C-Life is the reality, all three of them were ostracised in different ways. Taking the three one by one, T was ostracised, to a degree, for his affluent background and personal circumstances, although he could have compensated for his background had he been exceptionally talented or more socially aware. It is the very fact that he was not particularly aware of circumstances that makes him say that no-one looked at W in a different way. T is unaware of the fact that W was indeed looked at in a different way by most of the company, and neither is he aware that he himself had not fitted in terribly well with the company either, and is on the border of the 'eight-tenths of the village'. H, a transferee, was ostracised for being an outsider, and for not compensating for this by getting on well with others and maintaining the good social relations that might have allowed him to enter and stay within 'the village'. In the first period of restructuring in C-Life, he was pushed out. I was told very early on by the people around H that he was on his way out, at a time that H himself may not have been aware of it. W also suffered discrimination as an outsider and because of his personality quirks. The incident of him going and shouting at an official in the feared and revered Ministry of Finance is an extremely 'un-Japanese' action to take. However, as I have mentioned, he was sincere and very much liked personally and made a great deal of effort to fit in socially. He survived the first wave of restructuring, the only mid-career transferee to do so.

What, then, is the difference between W and H – one conscious and the other not? Despite being highly 'individual' in character, W was within the parameters of accepted norms about how an individual should be. Additionally, he was not seen to be strategising or to be dishonest (not expressing his *honne*). W never needed to be conscious or to work out what was happening, because he didn't sense that he was in conflict with C-Life society. H was certainly in conflict with it, so he had to know his enemy. But the issues are complex. H and W both entered C-Life at the same time, as mid-career transferees, and searched out their '*doki*' – people of their own age, who would have been their *doki* if they had always been at C-Life. Both received much the same cool reception. But each of these individuals interpreted their reception, and the blatant atmosphere of ostracism, in different ways, according to their different personalities and standpoints. H rejected the *doki* and persevered in the company without them, while W persevered in making contact with them. At the time of my third period of fieldwork, H had been pushed out of the company, whereas W was still inside and fitted in. In the end, H's personality perhaps made him unable to fit in: it was his awareness itself that made that impossible. In other words, once one is aware of discrimination, it becomes unbearable.

What this conversation illustrates is that consciousness is a central issue in successful strategising – but also that it is not the be-all and end-all. H was conscious of what was going on, but was notably less successful in the company than W, who actively rejected the importance of such social awareness. Being conscious is not in itself enough to ensure success.

Being good at strategising

It should be clear by now that keeping ahead of the company game was an intricate business, and it required great skill to play it well enough to come out ahead. As we have seen, this was in part because it was so hard to tell exactly what was going on. The murky character of reality in the company meant that nothing was really clear to anyone ever, even the most basic things like how well you were doing in the company, who liked you and who didn't, and so on. This very murkiness put enormous pressure on employees that were not able to handle that kind of atmosphere, while others – and those who were good at it – revelled in it. There were some such employees in C-Life who were extremely good at managing the Japanese company. It is in this sense that changing to another company would have meant that they lost the bulk of their accumulated assets: the in-depth knowledge of character, of who was doing well, of whom to get information from. In a sense they had a hundred pots on the boil: different human relations scenarios in the process of developing, and to leave would have meant losing that knowledge which ensured survival and promotion inside C-Life.

But none of the individuals had a complete view of where they were or how they were seen by others. In particular, most employees believed that they were still on the career ladder long after it was obvious to everyone else around them that they were not. But these same individuals could talk to me of the general rules by which the company ran even though they could not see their own position clearly inside that.

In such an environment, how could players ensure that they stayed ahead of the game? According to Bourdieu, they must possess a 'feel' for it, which implies a practical mastery of the logic of the game – what Giddens (1984) calls 'practical consciousness'. Such competence is shared unequally by the players and determines their mastery of the game in proportion to their competence.

To be competent is, in a sense, people's awareness of the game itself and how it works. The differences in competence between players in C-Life were obvious. Those with the skills of knowing how the game worked held a hugely valuable trump card. It must be noted that this was not the only criterion, however, as the example of the conversation between three employees discussed earlier in this chapter shows. H was conscious of one important rule – ostracism – and very conscious of how the rules work and what one must do in order to play the game in such a way as to be accepted by other members. He could not play the game successfully himself, however, and his very consciousness of the game and his own inability to play it made life in the company unbearable to him.

W, on the other hand, was not too conscious or too concerned with being conscious of the rules of the game. Yet he was honest and likeable and as a result was forgiven his trespasses against the norms. A third employee, T, was rather unconscious of the rules, but was able to remain in the company by virtue of his connections – until they ceased to be valid and he came to leave. Knowing the rules is not enough, either. If one knows the rules, one must keep that knowledge quiet – except perhaps among very close acquaintances – and use that information in a socially correct manner. The successful people in C-Life were the ones who knew when to act in a *tatemae* manner and when to reveal their *honne*. This in itself was possibly the most important rule of behaviour or skill in the company, and indeed, probably in any sphere of Japanese life.

Those who were 'good' at getting ahead were adept at manipulating ideology and practice. A really skilful player of the game would be able to use this distinction to their advantage, perhaps by doing something which went against what was acceptable but concealing the fact. For example, one employee, highly adept at playing the game, sometimes took less aware people – including W – to one side and gave them some help. He knew the right time to spout company ideology, the right time to laugh about the company ideology with his *doki* and the right time to help someone out who was struggling. It is notable that he did not tell anyone that at one time he was helping an unpopular department head, unless it was afterwards in terms of ridiculing the department head who had to have private lessons in company practices. Telling other people about it at the time would have made him seem to be sucking up to the boss and breaking ranks with the others who were united in demonstrating the department head's outsiderness.

Another example of using the *honne/tatemae* distinction to personal advantage can be found in relations between the *doki*. As can be seen in some of the comments quoted in chapter 6, employees would profess great loyalty to their *doki*, and claim close ties of friendship – even when, in fact, they rarely met. In fact, beneath this profession of closeness, there was great rivalry between *doki* as they jostled for the limited number of places available on the promotion ladder. They knew this even while they believed in the ideology of closeness, or wished to believe in it, or simply professed it. Whether they would admit this to each other or to outsiders depended very much on the agendas involved. *Doki* had a vested interest in maintaining good relations with each other. This was the key to their information network, so they needed to keep it open. They therefore had a big vested interest in professing their affection for each other as *doki* to each other. Drinking sessions like the *dokikai* were therefore in a sense rituals where that ideology was publicly expressed and maintained. Maintaining this sometimes *tatemae* appearance was thus part of their personal strategies. Here again we see how an understanding of strategising sheds light on the nature of ideology.

Bourdieu found that the subjects of his Moroccan fieldwork often marry people other than their cross-cousins. They insisted that they invariably do marry their cross-cousins, while the evidence showed that they don't always. Similarly, the *doki*, while professing closeness, were often not close. I don't think that the *doki* had really considered whether the statement 'the *doki* are very close' is true as a broad statement or not. It was much more common for them to make that statement simply when it served their purposes. There were plenty of times when they asserted it as part of a get-together, as part of drinking for the first time in a long time with other *doki*, but there were no occasions when they were forced to bring the subject out in the open and really think about it. The times when I made it an issue in an interview, many would admit that perhaps they weren't as close as they said they were, but most of the time there was no need to question the ideology so it went unchallenged. I think – apart from my questions – the only kind of time it was really challenged and brought out into the open was when a *doki* had transgressed the rules, as in the example above. Those occasions were fascinating as examples of ideology being spouted while reality was happening as well. At the *dokikai* there was an immediate separation into those still in the company and those not. Those who had not been promoted at the same rate as the others would not turn up. Much of the *dokikai* was spent gossiping about who had reached what position and speculating about the future of others. One *doki* told me that they only reason he turned up at the *dokikai* was because he didn't want to be the one being gossiped about! The ideology of *doki* was useful for everyone's agendas, even mine, and even while it didn't reflect the reality.

In sum, then, much of company life could be regarded as the outcome of individuals' strategising to achieve their personal goals. Again and again during my fieldwork it was revealed that no matter what the initial explanation, the real reasons for a person's actions were to do with his status, his career advancement, his job security. For example, consider the story of M, told in chapter 3. He and his colleagues were summoned to a basement room by the sales head, who showed them magazine articles about people being bullied until they quit their companies, told them that people with poor results would be asked to leave and left them to draw their own conclusions. We could interpret this sales head's behaviour as part of a strategy designed to avoid personal responsibility. He needed to get a certain number of people to resign, but it was in his interest not to be seen to be the one doing it, since that would make him appear responsible for much unhappiness.

Indeed, avoiding responsibility for potentially bad decisions seemed to be a common goal in company life. By avoiding responsibility, people could maximise their job security. As we shall see in the next chapter, I particularly found this to be the case in my dealings with various people in the company as I was making my two films there. As the following statement makes clear, underneath the initial explanation is invariably the issue of individual job security.

H: I think that the PR department is really troubled by the fact that you are making this programme. On the surface, they are not opposed. It will be probably be a really interesting thing if the programme gets aired in Japan. It is Y from the PR department that is handling it, isn't it? Well, he can't say anything other than that he won't oppose the programme. But if possible, he would rather that you didn't take it, probably. Well, a lot of things will come out in the programme. I guess in any company it would be the same thing. That is why he doesn't want you to take it. They don't think it is necessary for C-Life at all. Well, I think that what they are really thinking about is their own positions. Or

> if you say the opposite, if they say no, they are more frightened of the reaction. So rather than the company as a whole, they are concerned about their departments. Rather than their departments, they are concerned about their own individual positions.

This comment shows clearly the order of priority: the self, the department, then the company. We see this illustrated graphically in the next chapter, which outlines the strategising that occurred while I was filming at the company. In returning to C-Life as a former member of the company, I was drawn into the social space of the company and ended up being unable to avoid strategising and playing 'the game' along with the other players in the various fields. It seems, then, that the issue of strategising and the manipulation of ideology in pursuit of individual agendas have significance for the practice of anthropology as well as its subject, something I consider in chapter 9.

It is worthwhile noting that what we have seen in this section contrasts somewhat with much of the existing Japan literature. I am suggesting a rather individualistic account of Japanese society, where individuals follow their own strategies to achieve their own personal goals. My account suggests that very often the company's welfare was secondary to individualistic or even selfish strategising. The ideology of taking certain actions 'for the good of the company' may be used to justify them, but it does not follow that this is necessarily the real motivation for acting in that way.

In this chapter, then, we have seen that strategising can be viewed as a driving force behind much or even most of what went on in the company, to the extent that, more than is usual in much of the Japan literature, we can think of Japanese employees as acting primarily out of individualistic self-interest rather than a groupist desire to further the company's interests. In this analysis, we focused on the two central issues in the role of ideology and the importance of consciousness of the rules as a vital but unevenly distributed tool in the game of company life.

All of the points raised in this chapter were illustrated colourfully by one event: my filming of C-Life during the final stages of my fieldwork. Everybody connected with the film used it to pursue their own agendas, which varied greatly from person to person and group to group. In the next chapter, I describe the filming process in detail and examine the different ways in which people used it to pursue their own agendas.

8 Strategising during the filming of C-Life

In this study, I have presented the economic background to C-Life's difficulties, followed by four chapters of fieldwork at the company, describing those difficulties and the range of strategies developed by employees to deal with them. I then used this material as the basis of a discussion of ideology and practice, goods and strategy. But this is not the whole story. My fieldwork took several forms, culminating in a period of filming of various C-Life employees. This was in many ways the most revealing period of fieldwork, because of the way in which people reacted to the filming process. It proved to be a perfect example of the ways in which people strategise to achieve their goals: everybody involved in the filming – including me – was trying to use it to push their own agendas. In this chapter, I describe the process of making my film and show how it illustrated the theoretical conclusions presented in chapter 7.

Filming C-Life

Obtaining permission to film

Formal permission to make the programme had to be granted by C-Life's PR department. Both the head and the vice-head of this department were former members of the international division, and I had taught English to them both for the two-year period when I was employed in the company. I also had an initial introduction. My first approach was relatively formal: I went on company time to the PR department and explained that I was making a programme which NHK planned to show.

They seemed totally mystified by why anyone should want to film C-Life. What was interesting about normal C-Life employees? I think that, behind this apparent bewilderment, they were trying to get behind what I was telling them to my 'real' motives. They were sure that what we really wanted to do was an exposé of C-Life's inefficiencies and economic trauma. They said that would understand if that was what we wanted to do. But why would we want to film ordinary, uninteresting, company men? No amount of explanation that I was an anthropologist interested in looking at ordinary company men sufficed. At the same time, of course, I really was interested in C-Life's disastrous prospects, although I did not necessarily want to make an exposé of the type that would be highly damaging to the company.

Finally, the PR department asked me to put in a formal proposal outlining the benefits to C-Life of the programme. They implied throughout this first interview and the related phone calls that if I could write a proposal stressing enough benefits to C-Life, they might be able to push it through the board. I don't think they were taking the proposal terribly seriously; rather, they wanted to see whether the project was really being taken seriously by NHK. They probably suspected that the film was my own idea and wondered if NHK themselves were really committed to it. I thus wrote a formal proposal to C-Life stressing the proposed viewer ratings (several million) and the potential advantages the programme could have to C-Life as a relatively positive portrayal balancing the sharply negative reports in other media at that time. I emphasised in the proposal that I would write a fair account of employee stories without dwelling on the economic downturn or C-Life's current performance. This formal proposal went to the board of directors – the very top level – and was refused.

This was an important turning point in the programme's fortunes. Once it had met with this fate, the decision could not be reversed, and for the rest of the programme's duration we had to work around that refusal. If I had foreseen that that would happen I would have put a lot more groundwork into making sure the proposal would probably go through informally before I put the formal proposal forward.

At this stage, it became necessary to bring the significant weight of NHK to bear on the story. I got the 'desk' or producer in charge of the programme to come to C-Life for a meeting with the PR department. It was very unusual for NHK to take such a step in calling the producer out. I explained to the producer that C-Life needed to see that NHK was really serious about doing the programme. The line taken towards the C-Life side was to tell the PR section that NHK was certainly planning on doing the film and thus would appreciate as much co-operation as possible. This let the C-Life side know one important thing: that NHK was indeed planning to make the programme regardless of whether C-Life co-operated or not, and were not likely to back out.

After the all-important formal meeting between NHK, the PR section and me, I had a second meeting with the PR department after NHK had left. The PR section was obviously worried now that they realised the programme was going to happen. I assured them that I would do my very best to make sure that NHK did not make a programme that was too negative about C-Life. I stressed the fact that, as a former employee, I was sympathetic to C-Life. We discussed at great length the fact that NHK could, potentially, make a programme that was very damaging to C-Life. We went over the type of programme that could potentially be made. I explained that by far the most dangerous situation from C-Life's point of view – and what we really needed to worry about and avoid if possible – was the situation in which we did not obtain permission to film inside C-Life or the C-Life employees and could film only the people who had already quit or left C-Life. Doing this would mean that we would be taking only people with very negative viewpoints – those who had been bullied into leaving, those who had no faith left in Japanese companies, those who had left in disgust. We would also have no chance to take any of the loyal C-Life employees left inside the company with which to balance out the negative opinions.

I brought up a list of names of employees that we would 'be forced' to interview if we had no-one inside whom we could use. Hearing those names, the PR section employees recalled their histories and realised the gravity of the situation. When I had first contacted the PR section some six months earlier one of them had told me about a certain employee who was on his way out of the company. He was still clinging on, they said, but he was unlikely to be able to last much longer. That man's name was on the list. I explained that on those grounds, it was very much to C-Life's advantage to co-operate with the programme, since otherwise, even with the very best intentions, it would be difficult for me to prevent a negative programme from being made.

The PR section did appreciate that inside input was absolutely crucial in order to balance the programme and this, I think, made them much more co-operative. As we will see later, the PR section was already heavily implicated in the programme and its outcome on a level of personal responsibility, as their names were on the proposal that had gone up to the directors and been rejected. Because the programme was an NHK programme, the directors of the company – and the president – would certainly watch it, and any negative repercussions from it would certainly be matters for the PR department to deal with.

During the negotiations, strategies were in evidence every step of the way in everyone's behaviour. The primary agenda of the PR section was to not have to deal with repercussions or responsibility back-firing onto them. However, the programme was now at a stage where they realised that they could not stop it and had to deal with it. Now they had to figure out a new strategy. On the surface, of course, they were extremely co-operative with me on a personal level and told me that if it were purely a personal matter, they would not hesitate to help me make my programme.

At all times, therefore, I had to be very conscious of the hidden meaning behind each nuance. On the other hand, in trying to bring about what I wanted, I had to be very careful not to be seen to be forcing anyone's hand. I had to be very conscious of protecting the face of all concerned. In short, I needed to be conscious of the elements listed in Table 8.1 (see below).

On a formal level, the directors of C-Life had rejected the filming at a board-level meeting. On an informal level, the PR department, after meeting with NHK's representatives, wanted to co-operate, as did the people I wished to film. The PR department realised that the programme could be very negative if permission of some kind were not given. And, if such a PR disaster happened, the responsibility would quite clearly rest with the PR department. The PR department were thus now in a very difficult situation, and they began to concentrate their energies on finding the best way to extricate themselves from the dangerous position of responsibility in which they had been put – without, somehow, going directly against the formal decision of the board.

If we look at Table 8.1 we can see how decision-making and ideology and practice interconnect.

Table 8.1

	Omote (surface or formal arena)	*Ura (backstage or informal arena)*
Uchi (insiders)	No conflict should exist	Conflict does exist but is usually solved implicitly
Soto (outsiders)	No concession should be made	Negotiation is possible if neither party loses face and both can maintain integrity

Inside the group (*uchi*) no conflict is recognised on the surface. Of course it does exist, but it is resolved behind the scenes without ever surfacing to a formal, open level of resolution. Where there is a conflict with people outside the group (*soto*), on a formal level the two groups will not make any kind of compromise unless both are sure that they will not lose face by doing so.

In these terms, the C-Life board's formal decision was no, whilst NHK intended to go ahead. On a formal level, there was no going back on the board's decision and formal concession was impossible. We had to find another way whereby the programme could go ahead without the PR section having been seen to give permission (thus going against the directors) and where trouble could not reflect back on the PR section – remembering that this was always the primary concern of the PR section.

Within C-Life, there were differences of opinion. The board wanted things one way, but the PR department were now leaning the other way, towards allowing my programme to be filmed, and were thus now aligned together with the individuals who had given me permission to film them. Furthermore, as we will see, there was an ongoing feud within the PR department that I only found out about later. Formally, of course, none of this conflict was discussed at formal meetings with NHK. I was given the details of what was happening later in private meetings.

The final outcome was that between the PR section and myself, we agreed that I should do my very best to ensure a non-biased, fair programme to be shown on NHK that would not be unduly negative about C-Life. It was agreed that I should not film on company premises or during company time. In this way, I would follow the one unbreakable rule – the formal ruling of the directors against the programme.

On an informal level, however, the PR department gave me their word that they would not actively obstruct the NHK programme in any way and would do anything they could that did not expressly go against the above conditions. This informal permission was absolutely crucial. With that permission, the people I wanted to film inside the company were happy to go ahead and do the programme.

The filming

The first period of filming – filming all the international department members – took place from October 2000 to January 2001. The PR section seemed to be following what I was doing quite closely. Some of the people I wanted to interview would phone up the PR department of their own accord and tell them the time that they had scheduled.

Thus began several weeks of hide and seek as we scrabbled to reach employees of the company before the PR section did, as the PR department scrabbled to determine the content of what should be disclosed and as employees scrabbled to decide their strategies as to how best they could use the fact that we were filming to advance their own purposes.

I then set about filming my *doki* – the members of the year-group who we discussed in chapter 6. We had been told that we could interview the *doki* but were given no further limitations, apart from not filming on company grounds. The PR department seemed to be quite relaxed about these employees, not imagining that we would actually travel to film some of the more geographically remote and disgruntled ones.

Persuading the *doki* to be filmed was not a simple matter. It essentially meant putting in a lot of groundwork to renew acquaintances and build up a relationship. It depended primarily on getting the support of Aoki, the leader of that year-group. Without the permission of the *doki* leader, the others would not have co-operated. The ones in the sales offices didn't have the time or the knowledge of inner-head-office politics to make a decision on something as unusual as filming for NHK. They therefore left the decision entirely up to the *doki* head, so getting this permission was crucial.

I went first for advice to the *doki* I knew the best. He contacted Aoki for me and set up a meeting. I asked Aoki if he could gather together the *doki* for me so I could propose the film to them collectively while we were drinking. As with most things in Japan, a casual decision would be better made over drinks. We decided to term the gathering a normal '*dokikai*' (*doki* party) to stress the fact that I was a *doki* formerly in the company and, hopefully, to create the friendly atmosphere between *doki* that was there more often than not.

This *doki* meeting was absolutely crucial to the programme. Without the permission of Aoki and the goodwill of my former colleagues I would not be able to make the film. Aoki assured me that he would do his best to persuade the others. I told him that I would bring the NHK crew with me to the *dokikai*, but, as the others had not had a sit-down discussion about the film, I understood that it was likely that they would want to talk about it more before actually being filmed. So I said that I would bring the NHK director along just to introduce him to the *doki*, but not to actually film unless they gave us permission to do so.

I then explained this situation very carefully to my co-director: that the crew would come to the *dokikai* but that it was just an introduction and that it was unlikely that we would be able to film that night.

The *dokikai* went well at first. I think there was quite an element of nostalgia in the meeting – not necessarily because of me personally – but because the meeting reminded everyone of a past age when things had been a lot easier in the company. I think they also welcomed the chance to talk; about old and happier times, about where everyone had got to in their careers – which is an eternal source of gossip in the company at any time – and as a chance to sum up the flow of their lives, and of C-Life's fortunes.

I got to the *dokikai* early – I had asked the crew to come an hour later – and things were well underway with a party atmosphere by the time the NHK crew arrived. When they came I told them that there would definitely be no filming that night, as the *doki* had said they wanted to use the time that night to discuss it. I was going to have a difficult night persuading everyone to participate in the programme.

The co-director, however, disregarded my advice. When asked to introduce himself, he lurched into an impassioned plea to let him film that night, even though he had already been refused permission. This made for an extremely awkward situation. The co-director had put his foot in it badly by failing first to establish relations on an informal level before making a formal request.

It took until the early hours of the morning and several drinking establishments before the *doki* concluded that they would trust me to make the programme, provided that Aoki had decided that it was a good idea and would be in it himself. They agreed that the co-director's behaviour had been most inappropriate and that he should have just sat down, got to know them and discussed the programme casually over a drink. It was a prime example of polite, formal behaviour putting a spanner in the works when a casual approach would have worked.

At NHK the following day, I asked the 'desk' to make sure that the co-director understood that if he didn't follow my instincts in this programme then we were unlikely to get permission at all. He was duly told to be more delicate in his approach. I think this was a matter of a Japanese being unwilling to accept the judgment of a foreigner concerning a Japanese company, even when it was my programme, my company and my colleagues! To his credit, he realised his mistake and decided to follow my lead in judging which people were amenable to being filmed and which weren't. He apologised for his abruptness to the C-Life employees the next time they met and, once permission had been gained, things went much more smoothly. We could then go ahead and decide whom to film.

We telephoned all fifty of my *doki* to hear their stories and to start to get an idea of people whom we might film. We needed people who had interesting stories that also portrayed a piece of the larger story of what is happening inside Japanese companies today.

Whilst doing this, we found that Matsumoto, in Kagoshima, had an enormously interesting story of betrayal by the company and that he was more than willing to tell it. He relished the idea of airing his grievance to our 2.5 million strong audience, but also – and most crucially – to the directors and every top official in the company who he knew would watch the programme. So we had found someone whom we should interview immediately before anything happened to disrupt it. We made very sure he understood the full implications of what he was doing by making such a statement on national television and, assured that he did, we decided to fly to Kagoshima with the crew to film him first of all. I guessed – rightly – that the PR department would not be expecting us to go to the provinces and I wanted to make sure we were able to film without their having a sudden panic about the programme.

As it was, several weeks later the PR department did eventually get around to calling each and every one of the *doki* who were remaining in the company to give them the routine information that a film crew might ask if they wanted to participate in a documentary and that they had the OK to do so if they wished on a private level. When they got to Mastsumoto they discovered – to their great surprise and consternation – that we had already been there and filmed.

Honne/tatemae during filming

In conducting the fieldwork for this book, one recurring theme was when, and if, my respondents were talking *honne* and when were they taking a *tatemae* stance. In investigating *honne/tatemae* this is a crucial question, yet it could be very hard to answer. As I suggested in the last chapter, however, it is not impossible.

I decided at an early stage in the filming that I would just go ahead and film the employees who were still inside the company without thinking too much about how real the opinions were that I was getting and without digging too deeply. The employees who had left C-Life supported me in this decision. They warned me of their own accord that I was unlikely to get much *honne* from anyone inside the company, especially those in a delicate position. They encouraged me not to put any unfair pressure on them. Those inside the company were expected to state standard positions and the audience would know that they were taking a fairly standard company line partly because they were still in the company.

So I basically took the opinions of those inside the company at face value, expecting that I would be able to follow up on those opinions once their positions had changed – when they had left the company or when the company itself went under. And that, indeed, turned out to be the case. The insiders' opinions did change dramatically, as we shall see, once their position in the company had changed.

At the same time, I was surprised by the extent to which the C-Life employees did open up. This may have reflected the degree to which their faith in the company had already been shaken. It could also have reflected the extent to which these very stressed and worried employees needed to talk, and the absence of people to whom they could talk about the company.

As far as those outside the company were concerned, on the other hand, it was clear right from the start that they had nothing to hide and were giving their real opinions. They would bring up the topic of *honne/tatemae* themselves. They would say, for example, how they had had to maintain a *tatemae* stance when they were in the company, which they no longer had to do. This was invariably said with a feeling of real relief.

But having said this, I also got the feeling that there was a considerable degree of bitterness towards C-Life on the part of those employees who had been forced out of the company rather than leaving of their own accord. And there was also a lot of self-justification in their explanations. So it was still not entirely clear that they were giving an absolutely true view of the situation.

As a result, while we conducted the interviews we always kept in mind what the person's position was, what their agenda was, what they had to gain from associating with the camera crew and what kind of message they might want to convey to the audience. We also had to judge how aware they were of who would be watching the film. Some of them realised that the entire board of C-Life was likely to watch the programme; others hadn't considered this, although they had been told that it would be on NHK. Additionally, we had to judge who needed psychologically to inflate their position, or their importance, or to distort their stories.

I also asked a lot of questions about what they thought the stance of the others was. This was very illuminating, especially in cases where all of the participants agreed on a person's stance, while he insisted that he held a completely opposite position.

Timing was another important issue. The opinions of respondents varied dramatically according to when they had left the company. The earlier quitters had already been out of C-Life for ten years. They were very open about their reasons for quitting and their dislike of their previous jobs. They had nothing to gain from presenting a *tatemae* opinion and nothing to fear from a *honne* opinion – after ten years there was no fear of hurting any of the participants still in the company. A respondent such as J, on the other hand, had only just quit C-Life. He was particularly concerned about offending his *doki* who were still in the company, or as being seen to be thumbing his nose at former bosses who had given him chances and promotions in the company. When I worded questions directly on C-Life he was reluctant to answer, although he criticised Japanese management loud and long when questions were framed in a general way.

J had a dual and conflicting desire. He wanted to look good, to be seen to be lucky to have made a good job change, to be seen to be talented in the eyes of his new company which would also be seeing the programme. But he needed to remain diplomatic in terms of ties with his former colleagues that he still valued and would try his best to maintain.

I had to give a lot of thought to what kind of personal position each respondent was in. All people work, ultimately, to save their own self-esteem. I had to take this into account when evaluating their opinions. People like H, who had been pushed out of the company, were scathing about Japanese management and gleeful about the demise of C-Life. I had to take into account the self-satisfaction that H got from a feeling of revenge together with his obvious interest in having a forum to voice his dissatisfactions.

Others, like C, were in a terribly difficult position in some ways, having been at the forefront of investing at the time of the bubble when it had all begun to go wrong. When asked questions about Japanese management, these employees could have taken these questions as general, as specific to C-Life, or on a very personal level and become defensive about the level of their own responsibility.

Some respondents made it quite clear that they were speaking a *tatemae* position on camera. They interviewed along relatively neutral lines, close to company ideology. But when the interview finished they would talk in much more immediate emotional terms about how hard the situation was for them and how the uncertainty was tiring. D was one such example. In his interview he said that it was important for the sake of the company to go on striving with the utmost effort. He said that he believed the company could be saved and that he was selling insurance on that assumption.

After the interview, we went out again, just the two of us, to drink coffee. Although he didn't exactly reverse his opinion, he talked about how very difficult the situation was. He had three young children and large housing loans. The continual pay cuts had affected his family very much and he seemed exhausted with the continual effort of keeping up appearances and with the uncertainty. He was in one of the worst positions, I think, as he saw himself as having no real transferable skills beyond sales.

It was difficult to question these respondents about what they 'really' believed. And, in any case, I don't think that belief is always fixed, or that the respondents themselves really knew what to believe. I think, rather, that many of them were living with a feeling of continual dread and uncertainty with limited options. Clarity of belief often came only with the option to act. If an employee had options, then he summed up the situation in his mind in order to make a decision about it.

Sometimes, I felt that even though the employee might have accepted subconsciously that the company was likely to go under, they were reluctant to admit it at the conscious level. This was especially so for the salesmen, who were selling new policies every day and did not want to admit to themselves anything other than that the company would survive. To clarify the thought in their minds that the company would not survive would have been to think of themselves as crooks.

So, in sum, the factors of the particular agenda, the position in the company, the need to protect face, the need to protect self-esteem, the need not to hurt others and the need to justify after the fact, all came into a judgment about where a particular individual stood on the *honne/tatemae* line.

Strategising during filming

Since one of the aims of my anthropological documentary was to look at how people strategise in order to promote their agendas, it was fascinating to watch the negotiations of all the people involved in the filming. This was one incident among many in the lives of those involved, but to the anthropologist – myself – it was an opportunity to watch one single event and look at the motives and manipulations of all the participants around that event.

There were, as we shall see, various issues over which people were strategising.

Responsibility

During the negotiations with C-Life for permission to film, the issue everybody was most concerned about was responsibility.

When I first approached individuals to ask their permission I was quite surprised by how readily they agreed to be filmed. I think some of this was genuine kindness to a former colleague, and perhaps in some cases nostalgia. They were quite willing to film on their own time; as for filming inside the company, they asked me to contact the personnel department but gave me advice about the best way to do this. They were anxious to comply with official company policy, but apart from that they were most helpful. I found that being filmed had a big carry-over effect. If one person had been filmed, others became automatically more willing to be filmed themselves.

How, then, did different parties strategise during the filming?

Strategies – NHK

NHK's primary motive was to use my access to C-Life to get an interesting programme. But responsibility was also a big issue for NHK.

Almost a decade earlier, NHK had broadcast a documentary about a group of newly retired employees of C-Life. The company had co-operated with them in making this programme, although almost all the filming had been done at the respondents' homes and followed their lives after retirement. The film had featured the story of one respondent who had had a stroke shortly after he retired and C-Life had been upset as they thought it showed a negative image of the company. Thus, they were less keen than they might have been at the prospect of another programme being made.

Moreover, for NHK to gain access to employees at such a delicate moment in C-Life's history would, under normal circumstances, have been impossible. C-Life's president had not given interviews to any of the Japanese press for some time. The PR department explained to me that they were unable to give (Reuters) an interview without inviting all the Japanese press as well, since it would have been regarded as unfair to give access to just one company. All interviews, therefore, were invariably large formal press conferences. This was not necessarily the same for other large Japanese companies, but C-Life was a domestic company that had little experience of being in the media limelight.

So NHK wanted the access to C-Life, but they also wanted to absolve themselves of the responsibility if something went wrong. The best solution was to put me in the film itself, and to subtitle it as 'A foreign journalist looks at the Japanese company'. In this way, the documentary could be seen as 'my' views, rather than those of NHK.

Strategies – the PR department

The PR department was supposed to be my window into the company, and into the board of directors, for approaching them about gaining permission. But once permission was refused, and we had to proceed on an informal basis, the gatekeepers of the permission changed. To a certain extent, the PR department retained this role, since they could have decided to boycott the programme but chose not to do so. But once they decided not to obstruct me, I then had to get informal permission from the informal 'society' inside C-Life. In effect this meant senior people – as senior as possible in the case of my own programme. And for the programme for NHK, which focused on my *doki*, it meant the head of the *doki*, or Aoki, as I have already stated.

Many members of the company told me throughout the process that the people in the PR department didn't really care at all about whether my programme went ahead or not. They would have been quite co-operative with me because of our personal relations; but what they were most concerned about was their own positions. As we have seen, they were worried about who would take responsibility if the programme was negative. They knew that if it was an NHK programme, all the company directors would see it, so there was great potential for taking a lot of blame. So they were very careful to stick to the decisions that the directors themselves had made. In this way, anything that happened was the directors' decision, not theirs, and therefore not their responsibility.

Beyond that, they were all very co-operative. They would tell me to call them up and check facts and names if necessary, and they went to the lengths of looking up documents that I needed, such as past annual reports or photographs. We were unable to film any C-Life employees – whether in subsidiaries or not – inside their working environment. However, we were able to stretch the point and take still photographs of them at their desks. We did that with all of them. The employees let us do anything that the PR section hadn't specifically forbidden – I was surprised at how co-operative the employees were.

Strategies – the anthropologist

Of course, as an anthropologist with a doctorate to write and a film to be made, I too had a clear agenda. But additional agendas included not walking all over my former colleagues or misleading my audience, not dwelling to an unnecessary extent on the misfortunes of those involved and presenting an honest picture of events.

The bulk of my strategising occurred whilst negotiating permission to make the documentary. To do this, I had to align myself with first one party, then another, in the C-Life/NHK negotiations. I had to be seen to be protecting C-Life from NHK. I used the common Japanese journalist's line: if you weren't to co-operate it would be unfortunate as the programme/article might end up very one-sided (*ippo-teki ni narimasu yo*). This is often used as follows: a conflict is reported between two parties. The journalist calls up the first and asks for a comment, which is refused. The journalist implies that the other party has already given a comment, adding that without a comment from this side the article might end up rather one-sided. Once the comment is obtained, the journalist calls the other side and repeats the procedure, thus ensuring comments from both sides of the conflict.

In C-Life's case, of course, the argument was that if they did not co-operate the content of the programme would feature only the employees who had quit C-life, rather than those still inside who had more positive views of the company.

Contrary to what one might expect, even when the company began to realise the necessity of putting good people forward in order to protect the company, they did not ask anyone to go on the programme. It was left entirely to the individuals to decide whether or not they wanted to be involved, and the company put no pressure of any kind on them in a formal sense. In fact, in most cases in C-Life pressure was not formal at all, but informal, or at least delivered in an informal manner.

Strategies – the individual

As the filming continued, it was impossible not to get caught up in other people's agendas and strategies and be forced to act myself to protect my own agenda.

For example, I had rather frustrating and slow progress with the PR department until I realised what was going on behind the scenes. I was dealing primarily with two people. There was the department head, whom I'd taught English to previously; then there was the section chief, whom I'd also taught English to; so I knew both of them quite well. What I didn't know at the time was that they were on extremely bad terms with each other. It slowly dawned on me that whatever I told the section chief on the phone was not getting through to the head, but it took a long time to work this out. At our meetings, the head would be at a loss over what was going on, and obviously uncomfortable. Behaviour like that of the section chief is probably the most direct way to obstruct your supervisors if you don't like them – so that was obstructiveness in action.

At the same time, the section chief didn't tell me that he wasn't transmitting information to the head. So by acting in the middle, and obstructing both sides, he was putting himself in a more powerful position to manipulate information. The control of information is one of the most important sources of power in the Japanese company. So the section chief could transmit to me information that was favourable or not to the head's position.

It was only when I understood what was happening here that I could adjust my own strategy and make better progress.

Strategies – in sum

Who was the 'company' in the negotiations with C-Life? It might have been the directors who had ultimate responsibility for the company. I had no direct dealings with them, so I had no chance to see exactly what their agendas were. I think it would be safe to say that it is very unlikely that any of them had anything at all to gain from any kind of association with the programme. On the adverse side, however, they had an enormous amount to lose by approving a potential public relations catastrophe. In this matter, then, as in many matters in the Japanese company, the directors took the most conservative stand possible – they refused permission for the programme.

Everyone below director level had different agendas, as we have seen. It was a constant balancing between risk and reward in all decisions made.

All through the filming strategising was a constant motif, hand-in-hand with *honne/tatemae*. The participants all had times where they were playing a game, or putting on a front. This was most clearly evident in people such as Aoki, who led all the *doki* into the filming, but at the same time showed his bosses that he was the *doki* leader, that he was vocal in support of C-Life and standing up for company values.

Strategising was continually evident in formal meetings with the PR section. I would have a very serious and drawn-out meeting with them at lunchtime where the members of the PR section participated poker-faced in the meeting, stressing to me that they were loyal to C-Life and had to make sure that C-Life's reputation was not compromised. Yet they would call me at home later to ask me to correct their English resume as they were currently job-hunting in order to escape going down with C-Life! It was taken for granted, of course, that I would do them this favour and not talk to their bosses about it, and that they would help me to get permission for my film behind the scenes. This is the natural way that almost anything got done in C-Life; strategising was at the heart of all social action.

In this chapter, we have considered strategising, the manipulation of ideology and *honne* and *tatemae* not as abstract facts but within the concrete context of a narrative. Indeed, throughout this book I have focused on narratives at a number of different levels. In the next chapter, I offer some reflections on the role and importance of narrative in a company such as C-Life, its relations to ideology and strategising, and its methodological implications for a work such as the present study.

9 Narrative and myth

Throughout this book, there is a concentration on narrative. It has taken various forms: on one level there is the narrative of the decline of the Japanese economy and the increasingly desperate struggle of companies such as C-Life to stay viable. On another there is the narrative of C-Life and my involvement with it, first as an employee and then – in the final chapter – as a film-maker and anthropologist. There are the narratives I tell of individual employees I met during this process and finally, and very importantly, there are the narratives that they told me. All of these narratives are central to the descriptive and analytical material I have presented, and all of them can be – and have been – understood in very different ways. In this chapter I consider the role and importance of narrative in management and anthropology, with particular reference to some of the issues that have been raised in the preceding chapters. I also go on to look at the nature and role of myth, and how it relates to ideology; I focus in particular on the *nihonjinron* literature, and how looking at it as a myth itself can help us to understand it. The reflections I offer here are not intended to be an exhaustive survey of the subject, which is a very large and involved one: rather, my aim is to bring these issues to the fore and relate them to what we have already seen.

Management and the role of narrative

The role of stories and narrative has been very much to the fore of management literature in recent times. Why is this?

Czarniawska (1999) argues that management, as a social discipline, has lagged behind sociology and anthropology. It has adhered to Enlightenment scientific ideals which drew a sharp distinction between literary and scientific endeavours, placing narrative firmly on the side of the former. Science, after all, was supposed to be about measurement; and one can hardly measure a story. Today, however, many disciplines, from anthropology to theology, have become far more aware of the centrality of narrative to the ways that human beings communicate and codify knowledge. And management studies are now beginning to catch up with this, recognising the importance of considering how knowledge is transmitted through narrative.

Czarniawska (1997) suggests that narrative in organisational studies comes in three forms: research written in a narrative style; research that collects narrative stories; and research that conceptualises organisational life as story-making and organisation theory as story-reading. As I have suggested, the present work takes in all three of these approaches to varying degrees.

Story-telling, indeed, is the construction of meaning in organisations (Gabriel 1995, Yanow 1996). Czarniawska (1997: 14), following MacIntyre (1981), suggests that social life is itself a narrative, and that to understand any action we must place it in the context of a narrative:

> the common way of understanding human action is by placing it in a narrative, that is, a narrative of an individual history, which in turn must be placed in a narrative of social history or in a history of the narrative.

We are not, however, the sole authors of our narratives. In our interactions with others, positioning occurs (Davies and Harré 1991) whereby our positions are proposed, are accepted or rejected, and improve or deteriorate.

One of the most thoroughgoing studies of narrative in an organisational context is Gabriel (2000), who draws attention to the centrality of stories to organisational life in the fact that different individuals would tell the same story to him. He comments (p. 2) 'These stories acted as symbolic landmarks in the cultural life of organizations', and argues:

> stories open valuable windows into the emotional, political, and symbolic lives of orgaizations, offering researchers a powerful instrument for carrying out research. By collecting stories in different organizations, by listening and comparing different accounts, by investigating how narratives are constructed around specific events, by examining which events in an organization's history generate stories and which ones fail to do so, we gain access to deeper organizational realities, closely linked to their members' experiences. In this way, stories enable us to study organizational politics, culture, and change in uniquely illuminating ways, revealing how wider organizational issues are viewed, commented upon, and worked upon by their members.

However, we must be careful, as Boland and Tankasi (1991) have warned, not to regard these organisational narratives as petrified historic artefacts that can be collected like fossils. As Weick (1979) argues, we need to consider the politics, conflicting interests and conflicting interpretations in an unclear world. This is because a narrative exists not as an isolated entity in a vacuum, but as one element in a multifaceted world. And because it exists in a social world of interacting individuals, it makes sense only as it is interpreted. And, as we have already seen hinted at over the last two chapters, this raises a whole host of methodological issues.

Narrative

Narration is often identified as one of the most fundamental activities of society. It is the post-structuralist critic Barthes (1982) who describes humans as narrating animals. The essence of narrative, according to Kerby (1991), is the setting of a series of events into a meaningful sequence. Sequence, then, is at the heart of the meaning of any narrative. We can say, in fact, that narrative in this way performs a primary function of ideology: it classifies the world and sets it into a meaningful order. In narrative, time itself is made into a human construct, and thereby tamed. The C-Life employees were bombarded with narrative in all its forms: myth, stories, film, media, books, histories, dramas, television, comedy, newspapers, conversation. The amount of information on the economy and on industry is so vast in a developed economy such as Japan that employees had a wealth of information from which to make up their opinions. How does this situation relate to the different levels of ideology we have seen in this book?

The universal human desire to narrate (so argued by Bruner 1990) is intimately connected with human consciousness. Human consciousness of past, present and future are supposedly universal. Thus, we are all, as humans, part of an ongoing past, present and future. So we need to place ourselves within a narrative framework to order our consciousness of time. We are the characters in our own narration, and make up the narration around ourselves as we act through life. Through this exercise we attain meaning (Kerby 1991). Czarniawska (1999: 14) draws attention to the same point – narrative is a way of making sense through plot:

> The narrative mode of knowing consists of organising one's experience around the intentionality of human action. The *plot* is the basic means by which specific events, otherwise represented as lists or chronicles, are put into one meaningful whole.

Indeed, for Weick (1979), sense-making and plot-making are practically the same thing. His focus is on the interpretation of already existing stories rather than the creation of new ones, but he speaks nevertheless of the importance to this of sense-making. He suggests (pp. 60–61) that what is necessary in this endeavour is:

> something that preserves plausibility and coherence, something that is reasonable and memorable, something that embodies past experience and expectations, something that resonates with other people, something that can be constructed retrospectively but also can be used prospectively, something that captures both feeling and thought, something that allows for embellishment to fit current oddities, something that is fun to contrast. In short, what is necessary in sensemaking is a good story.

The C-Life employees all certainly showed a desire to place themselves into a narration by connecting what had happened – the rise of the bubble, the collapse of the bubble – to wider events of responsibility – the Anglo-Saxons' fault, the fault of the Bank of Japan for not moving at the right moment, the fault of the company for not having hedged its risks – in order to explain to themselves how they had arrived at the current point in time. The narration I heard in 2000 was clearly vastly different from what I was told at the time of the bubble, or even during my second bout of fieldwork in the early 1990s.

In a social sense, building narratives about our societies classifies the place of our society and creates solidarity with past members of the group (Toren 1993). It thus has great unifying power. Narrative is, however, not a purely group-based exercise. Within the conventional forms of narrative, we still garner an individual meaning that is different from that of others, just as in conversation. This is because narrative is commonly experienced in the form of *stories*, which are something more than pure narrative. Gabriel (2000: 239) defines them in this way:

> Stories are narratives with plots and characters, generating emotion in narrator and audience, through a poetic elaboration of symbolic material. This material may be a product of fantasy or experience, including an experience of earlier narratives. Story plots entail conflicts, predicaments, trials, coincidences, and crises that call for choices, decisions, actions, and interactions, whose actual outcomes are often at odds with the characters' intentions and purposes.

In other words, a story is a narrative that engages the teller or hearer in an emotional way. It demands and involves personal commitment on the part of those who come into contact with it. And this means that different individuals will react to it in different ways. The story that is heard in common reverberates against the experience and world-view of the individual. Equally, individual narrative is not solely individual. It is strongly influenced by cultural patterns of language, style, expression, and so on.

This emotional and personal involvement in stories, and the individual interpretations that it engenders, was evident at C-Life. The exchanging of stories allowed employees to understand, to have empathy for those who had done badly, to sympathise with each other. All of the C-Life people had a narrative to tell me about the bubble and what was happening to them now, whether it was the American conspiracy or the story of inevitable advancing globalisation. The same patterns occurred again and again in people's stories, yet just as I became resigned to hearing the same story again, an individual touch was added, so the tinge of the whole story altered according to that person's individual experience. As new events impacted on their experience, and new elements of knowledge came up, they reinterpreted their narrations to update them. The individual lives inside the text slightly altered the context of the narration, and that narration influenced their lives and the action that they would take in a circular motion.

The writing of the individual narrative is, then, created from a bricolage of cultural constructs, words, images, and so on common to society, but the narrative itself is the expression of the individual's view of the world. Narrative history is, in part, created by the self. And conversely, the self arises through its own narrating. Creating our own story creates our individuality, helps our lives attain meaning and coherence. Making one's narration is a kind of expression of consciousness.

Thus, we may say that the *nihonjinron* literature, inasmuch as it was a narrative told by the Japanese about themselves, acted to reinforce and structure Japanese people's view of the world and their place in it. In so doing, it helped to create their own self-consciousness and self-pride.

I could see this happening at a more immediate level with the narratives that the C-Life employees told of their own lives, and the way in which these narratives changed. I think that the very occasion of my reappearance in the company made the employees I interviewed conscious of the passage of time. If narrative history is in part created by the self, and that self also arises through its own narrating, the C-Life employees were replacing themselves in the context of their lives and of their work by their answers to my questions. Creating our own story creates our individuality, helps our lives attain meaning and coherence. Their individual narratives, were, however, influenced by cultural patterns of language, style, expression, and so on. Their narratives were clearly Japanese narratives told within the wider values of Japanese society. There were many common themes: the theme of continual achievement, of slow but steady progress to a certain goal, achievement within the context of a wider group (the company in this case), but there were also new themes: of individual satisfaction and finding work that motivated and fulfilled one.

They also had narratives to tell me about the changes in Japan, about the direction in which companies were going, about what would happen. Indeed, Gabriel (2000) identifies this concern with the interaction of the normal with the extraordinary as a common element of stories: they feature unusual events, giving insight into what lies behind the mundane world. In C-Life, one might say the situation was reversed: the company and its employees were going through a time of crisis, and so the need for explanation and rationalisation was stronger than ever before.

To take an example, I think that the attempt to see C-Life as being on a road to somewhere helped to dissipate the feeling that the future was completely unknown, although the view of the road that C-Life was headed down ranged considerably: from being on a precipice to being a slump on the way to recovery. Thus, the context does determine the narrative – but not totally. The C-Life *doki*, who were so uniform, with so uniform an experience in the company, still drew such different conclusions from it.

Another kind of narrative, rather different from stories, is myth. Gabriel (2000) draws a clear line between the two, suggesting that the kind of stories he collected from modern companies lacked the complexity and depth of myths. But here I suggest that myth can also be a useful tool for understanding company life, especially the role of ideology.

Myth

Myth in anthropology was originally seen as the sign of an irrational, primitive mind. 'Myth' has thus traditionally had quite negative connotations, as it has been opposed to rationality. There have, however, been various ways of evaluating myths. In the functionalist view, the value of myth to society is emphasised. For Durkheim, myth plays an important role in maintaining social unity. It tends to play a conservative role in reinforcing traditional social mores and beliefs. Myth is thus one part of the wider framework of social constructs that reinforce social structure. Malinowski (1948) argued that myth is not an explanation of the past; its worth is in its psychological and social value. This view locates myth within the social context, but still sees myth as little more than a pragmatic tool in maintaining society.

These points can be illustrated by considering how ideology functioned in C-Life –particularly company ideology, which certainly reinforced social cohesion and unity. It justified the existing, traditional order, and reminded C-Life of its identity. It was a public means of expressing and outlining social norms, and reinforced belief in those who already subscribed to them. In others, as I have argued above, if a divide was already there, it served to widen it still further. But beyond looking at the social use of ideology, we need to look at the content as well, since content determines how ideology is used. For example, an ideology of the company as family could be used (manipulated) by management to serve its own agenda of keeping people working hard but content, to provide them with a rationale for working hard. But that piece of ideology is powerful because it has deep resonances somewhere in the Japanese psyche. In this sense, the ideology works because it already has meaning for the participants. As we have seen, management cannot simply invent and install a new ideology. It is only after much thought and analysis that the C-Life people conclude that the family-like metaphors are reminiscent of the Japanese village. This is why it carries an air of nostalgia, of the way things should be, of a forgotten harmony (which never existed in a perfect form in the village either, of course).

So ideology must be seen within the social context: it is more than just a device to elicit a certain response. This is evident in the structualist approach to myth, which argues that the surface content lies above a deeper structure at a subconscious level, where the true meaning is to be found. In Lévi-Strauss' view, there is no place for a conscious user of the myth. The advantage of this approach was that it enabled anthropologists to assign a positive value to what they regarded as false beliefs. The difficulty in looking at other people's beliefs (that, according to Western science, are incorrect) is how we can constructively analyse beliefs that we hold to be false. The Lévi-Straussian solution to this is to separate it into two levels. The first – content – assumes the beliefs to be untrue. But the second – form – assumes that the laws of thought – that is, why they think, why they need to classify, to understand – are real and can be objectively known and have universal application.

It is now recognised that this view overemphasises the cognitive value of myth at the expense of other functions, namely the social, political, emotional and philosophical roles of myth – roles it shares in common with stories, as we saw above. A concentration on structure also causes myth to be detached from everyday life. More recent views on myth in anthropology try to redress the balance by focusing on the role of myth in everyday life, rather than as grand structures or overall systems of knowledge (Brady 1991, Bruner and Turner 1986). Myth is both situated within context and examined as performance. Similarly, other authors stress the complexity of myth, which can carry many different meanings at once (Douglas 1966). Myth in everyday life in C-Life had many important functions, including style, entertainment value and moral outlook. There is context and performance. So there are different levels of myth, including the structuralist view of myth at its unconscious level, and the conscious use of myth in everyday life. I argue that if myth did not have the latter, it would not survive as myth. Myth is now seen as an expression of how people see the world, and as an expression of meaning – in a moral sense – of the surrounding world. Because of this, they are easily used for political purposes. This is also helped by the fact that myths tend to be subscribed to fairly unthinkingly.

Indeed, employees often seemed to subscribe to company-promoted ideologies in a relatively unreflective way. They would, for example, exclaim in a *tatemae* manner that they were all one family, when drinking with people with whom they needed to cultivate good relations. They would reminisce emotionally: we are all Japanese in a group together; that can't be helped, when they were facing something unpleasant and helping each other out. This suggests that they subscribed to ideology in a fairly shallow way, a point we have already seen in considering the fixity of ideology. But at the same time, they would participate in analysing why the president might have pushed a 'family' ideology in a speech that morning, and take it apart and deconstruct it. They especially did this in response to my questions. In everyday life, there was no great need to deconstruct existing ideology, always present and taken for granted. It was only in cases of crisis, as I have argued, when employees had been jolted out of their everyday existence, that they needed to sit down and think through what the company said, and what, in fact, they themselves had believed. It was then that they had to separate the different strands that until then had been taken for granted as a woven pattern. In sum, I suggest that all of the employees danced in and out of consciousness of what socio-cultural structures they were operating within, and what ideologies were supporting them.

Nihonjinron*: a comment*

We encountered the *nihonjinron* literature in chapter 5. There, we saw briefly that it was characterised by a belief that the Japanese are culturally unique, and that this uniqueness was used to explain why they were so economically successful.

The *nihonjinron* literature was diverse, but it tended to present a decidedly idealised version of Japan. According to Gibney (1998), for example, Japan is a true meritocracy where one can progress through obedience and competence. Reischauer (1977) suggests that the emphasis on progress through examination in Japan means that opportunities are equally available to all. Christopher (1983) points out that there is no strong sense of class consciousness, and no group of ultra-rich in Japan, where wealth is more evenly distributed than in other countries. Ouchi (1981) pointed out the very close relationships between different members of Japanese groups, suggesting that these encourage honesty and openness between individuals. According to Reischauer (1977), employees take pride in their company, singing its songs and displaying its badges, creating an atmosphere of dedication, loyalty and self-sacrifice. Curtis (1969) described grass-roots level political campaigning, with a heavy emphasis on co-operation and little mention of conflict. And Nakane (1970) emphasised the differences between not only Japan and the West but Japan and other Asian countries as well.

The general image is a fairly idyllic one and, as we saw in chapter 5, it went down very well in Japan. However, with the collapse of the bubble, and even beforehand too, *nihonjinron* was criticised for its unrealistic approach. It was thought that it described a fantasy version of Japan, one that its proponents would have liked to believe in, but one that did not exist. And of course, with the collapse of the bubble and the realisation that the Japanese economy did not have some magic quality that protected it from the hardships undergone by other countries, this criticism was shown largely to be true.

This does not mean that the *nihonjinron* literature was wholly wrong, however. On the contrary, it remains highly useful if we think of it as somehow mythical in nature. Indeed, the nature of *nihonjinron* as myth has already been appreciated in the literature. Berque (1993: 101) writes:

> Western authors such as Peter Dale (1986) have more than once denounced the delusions of (*nihonjinron*) … its error of fact and methodological incoherence … Yet most of the critics fail to catch the mythological essence of the *nihonjinron*. Indeed, in a strict anthropological sense, the *nihonjinron* share two fundamental characters with myth: the abolition of time (history), and the abolition of the subject (the enunciating individual). Across the centuries, and across the personalities of their authors, the *nihonjinron* stubbornly tend to refer the Japanese to nature (or pre-history), that is, a set of characters untouched by socio-historical change; and these trajective patterns

> tend to reproduce themselves regularly, though this may be through some metaphorical transformations … On the one hand, as any social process, the vogue of the *nihonjinron* contributes to the construction of reality for the Japanese. Their trajective patterns partake in making this reality, a reality in between the realness of the thing in itself and the unrealness of representations. What must be seen, on the other hand, is that this logic has little to do with rational inference, or logic in the strict sense.

It has been said that nationalistic myths also arose in Japan in the past, during times of confusion (such as the Meiji revolution). But this wasn't true for C-Life during the economic confusion. It seems more likely that nationalistic myths arose during the Meiji revolution because Japan had a need to define and separate itself from the approaching West. During the bubble, myths of nationalism arose partly because of an expansive atmosphere of pride. In the recession, however, the C-Life employees had abandoned completely any notion of Japanese inherent economic superiority linked to cultural traits. As we have suggested, when the C-life men believed *nihonjinron*, they didn't look too closely at their belief, which was not very important to them. They freely admitted later that they were wrong. They didn't need to look too closely and they didn't want to. As long as it was fulfilling its purpose, it went unexamined.

The egos of the C-Life employees were inflated at the time of the bubble by the stories in the newspapers flattering the life insurers and calling them 'The Lifers' (*Za Seiho*!). During the bubble period, what had some basis in fact quickly became distorted into myth. The more that people participated in telling those myths, the more they came to form the dominant ideology. The *nihonjinron* literature that came from the West and was quickly translated into Japanese served to reinforce that myth. No longer was it only a Japanese opinion: it was boosted from abroad. The American reaction to the rise of Japan's economy served further to inflate the self-image of Japanese employees. In retrospect, C-Life employees called it the age of 'Japan as Number One', enormously impressed that an American like Vogel (1979) could have written a book with such a title.

The C-Life employees all told me, and I can testify to it myself, that being part of that period was a heady experience. There was no need to question the ideology seriously. It was only as their livelihood became threatened – first as a company and then, as the recession wore on, as individuals – that they were forced to define more clearly what was going on. It was when change struck that the C-Life men felt they needed to examine the myths properly for perhaps the first time. As Malinowski (1948) argued, myth is not about an explanation of the past – the rationality of it is beside the point. It has psychological and social value, and is extremely valuable as we will see later in my discussion of particular ideologies in C-Life. Thus, the *nihonjinron* literature was itself part of an ideology.

Burridge (1979) makes an important point in this regard: that the same people are individuals (who defy the order) and persons (who embody the traditional categories) in different respects at different times. This, in other words, is *honne* and *tatemae*. Persons inherit socio-cultural assumptions, whereas individuals exist in spite of them and create new ones. But each person has both and can switch between them. This is in line with my understanding that in order to account for *honne* and *tatemae* there must be a private and public self.

This appreciation of *honne* and *tatemae* is essential to a proper understanding of the *nihonjinron* literature and its function. Although the literature since the bubble abounds with both praise and criticism of *nihonjinron*, I found it impossible to find agreement over which works actually constitute *nihonjinron* literature. Whereas some authors have considered it to be works with a flagrantly nationalistic agenda, or works with blatant factual errors, others have regarded almost all of the 'cultural' literature on Japan as *nihonjinron*. This is rather unfair as many of these works were sound ethnographies in themselves but have been discredited by association with less careful writers, who have cited them as evidence for Japan's economic success. Some of the literature is interesting and sound – if one reads it as an 'ideal' version of Japan or the Japanese company – what I have called ideal ideology, or group ideology (company ideology). As such, it is of interest if one does not try to read it as 'reality'. In other words, I believe it to be important to understand the professed beliefs, thoughts and ideologies of individuals, not just the 'reality' as the anthropologist observes it. I disagree with those anthropologists who focus on the latter to the exclusion of the former. Such an approach results in an account that is just as one-sided as the *nihonjinron* literature was. Van Wolferen (1989), for example, one of the most vocal proponents of portraying the 'reality' of the Japanese company at the expense of ideology, cannot reconcile the dual *tatemae*/*honne* that he finds in the companies that he studies. He is forced to conclude that his informants are lying when they spout a *tatemae* view of affairs in the company. This is at best an extremely naïve view.

New work in the anthropology of organisations has sought to combine the insights of both the *nihonjinron* literature and the backlash against it. It has centred on incorporating the Japanese management 'ideal' as ideology, and, at the same time, described the practice of what they saw in everyday life in the workplaces they studied. By doing this, anthropologists have taken a major step towards reconciling the earlier ethnographies on Japan, which described a very *tatemae* view of Japanese society, with later works.

It seems, then, that the *nihonjinron* literature of the pre-bubble period was a narrative that the Japanese told about themselves, establishing who they were in the world; and it allowed them to sort the world into categories and find their own place within it. In other words, it had a self-defining role. It is in this sense that we can think of it as myth. And our discussion has helped to broaden our view of ideology in general, and *nihonjinron* in particular, by showing how ideology functions in these ways.

Narrative and interpretation

These points bring to the fore an issue that we have seen appearing throughout the chapters of this book, particularly the last two chapters. Different individuals interpret events in different ways; they follow different strategies and agendas; and, in Japan at least, they use *honne* and *tatemae* a great deal. How can we tell when people are saying what they mean? How can we tell what interpretation of a situation or a narrative is the true one? And how can we tell that our interpretations are not just in our own minds?

Earlier objections to collecting material that was seen to be non-factual, or that represented conflicting accounts, have been somewhat allayed by the realisation that it can provide a valuable insight into the thinking of our subjects. When a story is repeated enough, and embellished and re-embellished we see that it has value for them. The challenge, from the anthropologist's point of view, is not only to discern and dissect these different values, but to report and analyse them as accurately as possible without changing them in the process. That is, it is necessary to recognise that anthropologists themselves have their own reactions and individual meanings that they attach to the events being studied and reported, and that they must be careful not to allow such beliefs to inform their understanding of their subjects' points of view. A certain reluctance to acknowledge the possibility of doing this lies, in part, behind the old reluctance to admit non-factual or inconsistently interpreted material. As Geertz (1988: 140) puts it,

> the resistance to the notion that ethnographic writing requires the employment of stories, pictures, symbols and metaphors is due to the confusion between the imagined and the imaginary, the fictive and the false, 'making things out' and 'making them up.'

I have argued in this work that although it takes some care to 'make things out' without slipping into 'making them up', it is not impossible to do this. This is what I have sought to do in my account of life at C-Life; and in the last chapter I have described some of the ways I went about it. As I suggested there, determining when someone is speaking *honne* and when they are talking *tatemae* is not an exact science, but that does not mean that it cannot be done at all – especially if we understand the ways in which *honne* and *tatemae* work, some of which I have described in chapter 7.

It is, at least in part, a matter of understanding how ideology works at its different levels, in the context of both the group and the individual. We have seen, over the past chapters, how the interaction of different ideologies, powered in part by individuals' own agendas and strategies for achieving those agendas, is an essential and pervasive element of life in a society such as C-Life. To understand that society properly it is therefore essential to take account of this mesh of meaning and to try to portray it as accurately as possible. It is for this reason that, as I have suggested above, it is wrong simply to dismiss the *nihonjinron* literature because it portrayed an unrealistic image of Japan: that image, however false, was an important element of life in Japan at the time.

It is important to recognise, in other words, that value is not simply a matter of factual accuracy. How our subjects engage with the events that they participate in, witness or hear about is just as important as what actually happens. And when we recognise this, we recognise too that to take account of it fully involves dealing with an intrinsically messy situation: a complex and contradictory array of different views and personal responses and reactions, including our own. Czarniawska (1999: 112) comments:

> Management and organization studies confront a world that is, and will remain, polyphonic and polysemic. The uneasy task of organization scholars is to render this state of affairs in our texts, which requires a skillful balance between centripetal and centrifugal textual moves.

Further reservations about collecting contradictory material have thus been allayed by the realisation that social facts are inherently contradictory. We are dealing in the meanings that are rendered from the facts, not only in the facts themselves. Berger and Luckmann (1995) describe modern society as an open market for meanings. Rather than deciding which of two opposing claims is true, we need to look at how these claims are understood in their context, and how they become the basis for collective action.

In doing this, it is paramount to take context into account. It is context that determines the different meaning that the same events will have for different participants, and the different narratives that they will create from the same material. We saw this in chapter 7, when considering the role of different levels of ideology in the way that *honne* and *tatemae* function; and this is what I have aimed to do here. Throughout this book I have tried to interrupt my narrative to examine the significance and meaning of what I am looking at, from the point of view of the actors themselves – recognising that they all brought their own different interpretations to events, none of which should be taken as definitive. My purpose has been to bring a clearer and more authentic sense of what C-Life was to my own narrative about it; as Lejeune (1989: 72, original emphasis) has said:

> Up to and including chronological order, it is *meaning* finally that organizes the narrative.

10 C-Life goes under

In October 2000, the gloomy predictions of analysts and the media were finally proved right. Just a few months after I completed my fieldwork at the company, C-Life finally went bankrupt. In this chapter I describe the circumstances surrounding its demise and return to some of the employees examined in the preceding chapters of this book. We see here how they are dealing with the bankruptcy of their company.

The demise of C-Life

C-Life finally filed for protection from creditors with 2.9 trillion yen (£18.7 billion, US$27 billion) in liabilities. C-Life – by that time the twelfth-largest life insurance company in the industry, with 1.7 million policy-holders – was the fifth insurance company to go bankrupt since the bubble burst, and the fourth in the 1997–2000 period. Its collapse came just two months after Taisho Life Insurance Co. was shut down by regulators. However, dwarfing Taisho's negative net worth of 36.5 billion yen, C-Life had a massive 311.9 billion yen negative net worth (as of March 2001). It was the largest life insurer to go under since World War II. The value of its bad loans and other assets that are unlikely to be recovered is estimated to be 487.5 billion yen.

The bankruptcy didn't come as a great surprise to either analysts or to the media, who had widely predicted the failure. As I have already commented, the negative reports of the media had been a key factor in large-scale flights from the insurance sector by policy-holders.

On C-Life's collapse, the *Financial Times* commented dryly:

> Callous though it may seem to rejoice over the collapse of a 96-year-old life insurance company with 1.7m shareholders, it is hard to shed many tears over C-Life's filing for bankruptcy. If it were done when 'tis done, then 'twere well it were done quickly – and in C-Life's case quickly should have meant at least two years ago.

The primary factor precipitating the collapse of C-Life was the fact that its main bank and one of its primary shareholders – Tokai Bank – failed to come to the ailing company's rescue. Tokai Bank intended to merge with Sanwa Bank and Toyo Trust in April 2001, and it is thought that the bank didn't feel it could afford to have this deal compromised by a messy situation with C-Life. Tokai Bank had made support for C-Life conditional on the company confirming a merger with a foreign partner. Although the bank announced this condition the week before the collapse, C-Life did not have enough time to confirm a partner. The very fact that a main bank failed to help in such a case will, of course, provide a precedent for future main banks to do the same, and is a further indication of the disintegration of the *keiretsu* system.

As I have outlined in earlier chapters, the long-term reasons for the collapse stemmed from the years of the bubble, which were characterised by a binge of risky lending to property companies and precarious stock investments. The company had battled with negative spreads throughout the 1990s, and this was exacerbated by the low interest rates during that period. At the time of its collapse, many of C-Life's liabilities were paying more than 6 per cent while interest rates were below 1 per cent: a clearly untenable situation. The company's solvency margin was dangerously low and nearing the 200 per cent level, which would have required the company to act to remedy it.

The procedure for bankruptcy is as follows. The company filed for court protection from creditors on 9 October 2000. The Tokyo District Court accepted the request and ordered its assets to be protected from creditors. C-Life was the first company to be protected from creditors under new fast-track legislation – introduced in June 2000 – aimed at making it easier for failed financial institutions to seek court protection. Customers are not able to cancel or change their policies while the firm is under court protection.

The company then had to devise a rehabilitation programme and present it to the court as per Japanese law. President Yoneyama and ten other board members submitted their resignations the same day to a court administrator and told the court that AIG had offered help to the company through the rehabilitation process managed by the court.

The policy-holders

The life insurance industry had a safety net in place, but it was not on the scale of that established for the banking sector. The banks had been protected by a 60,000 billion yen net since 1998, of which 25,000 billion yen is set aside to protect depositors in the event of a bank failure. The life insurance industry, in contrast, had only 400 billion yen – a wholly inadequate sum – and part of that had already been spent on failures which occurred before that of C-Life. Shortly afterwards, the government had supplemented the insurance industry safety net with another 400 billion yen. In total, at the time of C-Life's collapse, the policy-holders were protected by current reserves at C-Life (described below) and by 960 billion yen in the safety net scheme including the government's 400 billion yen. So despite the huge scale of C-Life's bankruptcy, the policy-holders did not bear the brunt of it.

AIG planning to take over C-Life

AIG (American International Group) had been cited as a potential buyer for C-Life since the time of the collapse. The company did, in fact, take over C-Life's operations in April 2001. This marked the latest show of interest of foreign companies in Japan's troubled insurance industry.

AIG is the largest of the foreign insurance companies that have been active in Japan. It is the leading US-based international insurance and financial services organisation. Under the plan submitted to the Tokyo District Court, AIG would make a capital contribution to C-Life of approximately 60 billion yen (approx. US$522 million).

AIG Chairman M R Greenberg told reporters that the rehabilitation of C-Life would allow AIG to expand its presence significantly in the traditional Japanese life insurance market and gain access to that market through a revitalised C-Life sales network. AIG says it intends to operate C-Life insurance separately from its existing operations in Japan under the American Life Insurance Company (ALICO).

Until recently foreign insurers were unable to penetrate the Japanese market, and they still make up less than 10 per cent of the market. But recently, as we saw in chapter 2, they have been flooding into the Japanese market, encouraged by opportunities opened up by the economic downturn and failing companies asking to be bought. Deregulation has also encouraged these companies to look at opportunities in the US$450 billion Japanese insurance market. Because of the very large size of the market, few foreign companies have been able to consider acquiring even small companies in Japan. The fact that the top five giants have constantly held more than 50 per cent of the market share is a dauntingly competitive proposition for new entries. In the long run, foreign companies wanting to establish a larger presence need to set up a distribution network of sales branches and sales people. Buying up the healthy assets of a failed Japanese insurer allows the company to access a ready-made distribution network. Thus, Prudential Insurance Co. has allied with Kyoei Life, GE Capital Corp. has acquired Toho Mutual Life and the French company Axa has acquired Nippon Dantai Life.

Once the foreign insurer acquires the assets of the failed company and works to improve efficiency and profitability, the companies have as good a chance in the market as any Japanese-owned competitors. One ING Barings analyst commented that apart from its negative spread and bad loans, C-Life's profitability in the normal insurance business was not that bad.

Responsibility

Bankruptcy still carries a huge stigma in Japan, although numbers of bankruptcies have increased sharply in recent years. The public do not make a clear distinction between, on the one hand, the assets and responsibility of the company, and, on the other, the personal wealth and responsibility of management. Managers of failed companies are pressured by creditors trying to recover money, and, in some cases, the yakuza – Japanese mafia – are involved in the attempt. A sense of personal responsibility is also likely to be behind the intense shame of managers of failed companies, which may help to explain the high suicide rates for these executives.

It is interesting to note that, in the case of C-Life, the former management were sued for inefficient management during their term of office. The finger of blame was pointed primarily at Yasutaro Kanzaki, who was president of the company for an unusually long fourteen years, from 1982 to 1996, when he finally retired age 75.

At the press conference following the collapse of C-Life, the then president, Reiji Yoneyama, while admitting to feeling 'deep responsibility as the manager' did not attempt to defray responsibility from Kanzaki. His following statement implies criticism: 'I understand there are criticisms (of Kanzaki). This will be dealt with by the trustee', he said. The trustee and lawyer, Hideo Sakai, added, 'Should any lack of transparency emerge, the court will be immediately informed. If necessary, civil or criminal action will be taken'.

Inside C-Life as it went under

Most of C-Life's employees learnt of their company's demise from fellow employees, their wives or from customers who saw the early morning news. The failure triggered mass panic among customers worried that their policies would be cancelled.

The following Yomiuri Shimbun article (11 October 2000) gives an idea of the atmosphere:

> One day after the abrupt announcement of C-Life's insolvency, the company's employees started arriving at its headquarters in Meguro Ward, Tokyo, at about 7 a.m. Tuesday. Asked by reporters how they felt about the timing of their company's move, some of the employees said, 'I don't know anything about it,' while some bowed their heads or covered their faces.
>
> At the headquarters reception desk, employees handed more than a dozen anxious policy-holders a notice headed 'To Customers'. Some policy-holders reacted angrily, banging the counter and shouting.
>
> 'I came here to redeem the insurance policy, but I was told it's impossible. I have to bear it. What can I do in the future,' said a 79-year-old unemployed man from Kawasaki.

> At C-Life's Ueno branch in Taito Ward, Tokyo, a policy-holder angrily complained, 'I rushed here because every time I telephoned the office the line was busy.'
>
> A 68-year-old housewife of the ward said: 'I had complete faith in the company, although I heard rumors of some concerns about its business condition, because it is a big company. I came here to hear an explanation. If I cannot get any insurance money back, it will be a disaster for an old person like me.'
>
> The Ueno branch manager, sounding exhausted, said, 'I didn't expect our company to go bankrupt since I thought Tokai Bank would extend us financial aid. I was surprised when I saw the television news (reports of the bankruptcy). Because a reconstruction plan is not in place, it is very difficult to explain to the customers. It is really frustrating.'

When I contacted the C-Life employees at this time, they were in various states of emotion ranging from glee of the 'I told you so' variety to severe shock. Most of them, however, were muted in their reactions, since, as I will elaborate further in this chapter, many had predicted that the company would go under.

Here I present the comments and attitudes of the employees in the immediate aftermath of the bankruptcy announcement in October 2000.

Former employees

The ex-employees had been following the news closely, but their contacts with people inside the company were rather limited. This was especially so following the collapse of C-Life. They said it would have been an extraordinarily delicate situation for an ex-employee sitting high and dry to contact former colleagues without it seeming like inappropriate curiosity at a time of misfortune. Therefore they generally stayed away rather than take that risk. However, N, an employee who had quit C-Life at about the same time as J, had been talking to quite a few people in the company.

N: The president made the decision virtually by himself. After the alliance with Tokai Bank didn't work out, the president could see from the mid-term balance sheet that the company was going to have excess liabilities of 3.4 trillion yen, and was doomed. So the decision was made then. So he would probably would have persuaded the other directors and made that decision.

N: There was a meeting at the company on Sunday night for some of the key employees – not all of them – and they were told. The directors only knew about it the day before, and Monday was a public holiday, so lots of people only found out from the papers that morning that they no longer had a job. Some people's wives told them – one I know was phoned by his sales staff at home.

The whole company is in a state of suspension.

N: There are lawyers in the company. Now that the directors have gone, the lawyers are disseminating information to the employees. All of the business has stopped – all investment and sales have stopped, and no-one can cancel policies any more. So there are customers arriving and not being allowed to cancel their policies. So the company is just waiting to see what AIG is going to do.

Given this situation, rumours are rife.

N: If AIG acquires C-Life, another 30 to 40 per cent of the personnel will probably be cut.

N: A big issue is how long it'll take to happen (the takeover). If it takes until March the company's assets will shrink to a third of what they are now. Many policies were cancelled shortly before the bankruptcy.

Some employees said that no-one knew where the directors were.

J: The directors had disappeared the day the announcement was made. They'll probably get their full retirement benefits, which are worth a lot.

N: Everyone is still going to the company as normal, but no one is doing their normal work. So all they're doing is maintenance work in the branch offices – if someone dies their family will still get their maintenance benefits. In the central office, people are there to answer AIG's questions. The employees are still turning up every day – no-one knows what to do because nothing is decided until the end of the month.

They explained that the incident that really brought about the bankruptcy happened on 4 October. C-Life had been asking Tokai Bank, a company in their business group, for additional loans. Members of the same business group in Japan normally help each other out, so they might have been expected to stand by one another; but because the recession had been so bad, and there are so many bad loans, banks have been distancing themselves from companies in their groups, and Tokai Bank refused. This refusal was the turning point for C-Life, as we have seen. One newspaper report (*Japan Times*, 11 November 2000) said that President Yoneyama had not looked into the possibility of filing at all until the three weeks preceding the company's action: 'We were absolutely sure of being rescued by the banking sector', he said.

J: Tokai is already merging with someone else, and they didn't want C-Life tainting it. When Tokai Bank refused permission, that was really significant, that the bank didn't trust C-Life to stay afloat. That was what basically did C-Life in. They had nowhere else to turn.

I, a former auditor at C-Life, seemed to know quite a bit about the situation, which was not surprising as he had been a director and presumably had knowledge sources that the others didn't. He said AIG would make the decision in March – which it eventually did – whereas everyone else believed it would happen by the end of October.

I: AIG are dealing with the lawyer who was appointed by the court. The directors are completely out of it. They probably won't get their pensions.

I: It's a great pity (*zannen*) about the company. Everyone has been saying that. I didn't really foresee it going under, although I've known it's been in a dangerous position for about five years.

Insiders

Insiders generally felt at a loss and overwhelmed by the necessity of dealing with a situation for which they were wholly unequipped. Not surprisingly, there was a lot of resentment expressed towards the directors and also about former management.

They were unsure who would come out of the situation well, since they were still evaluating the situation. This was so even for those who had predicted it, who ought to have been expecting it. When it actually happened they still seemed to be in a state of shock. The shock was exacerbated by the dramatic reactions of some of the customers and the unpleasantness of having to visit customers to apologise or to take phone calls from customers. Reassuring customers was especially difficult when they themselves didn't know what was going to happen.

I was told that some of the key members of the company – leadership candidates, especially those in the finance division – had known about the situation four or five days before it actually happened. This illustrates the actual inequality of information in the company. Those closest to the centre did have considerably more knowledge, more even than some of the directors.

Employees said that everyone was going to work as normal – that it was quite a normal atmosphere inside the company apart from the fact that there weren't many people left. They said there was no normal work going on – people were just providing information for AIG. Some did point out – often with an air of resentment – that many department heads had quit within the last six months or so, and they suspected that many of them must have been able to guess what was coming.

In practical terms, many of those inside the head office were also in sales positions, especially those in group insurance divisions. I found that most of these employees were still at the office even when I phoned them late at night, and they sounded exhausted and terribly stressed. They were spending all day dealing with customers and expected this to continue for quite some time.

The sales force

The sales force were in great distress when I spoke to them directly after the collapse. One employee said he was really riled about the situation (*sukkiri shinai desu ne*). 'Where is the responsibility?' he asked. He wanted the directors to take some of it. But they had disappeared and it was very hard on people like him who had been selling to the customers and now had to clean up the mess that was left. He was having a terrible time dealing with angry people all day and apologising to them. Some of them told him to 'Keep it up!' (*Gambarinasai*!) and offered encouragement. The customers knew from the newspapers that C-Life was still waiting for AIG's decision so some of them were quite sympathetic. They knew that the sales personnel would have been relatively unaware of the situation and that they had now lost their jobs. The salesman said he was very irritated (*iragachi*) by the situation. He couldn't respond to all the 15,000 clients at his branch office, but he was doing his best to deal with phone calls and send letters and visit some of the biggest clients personally.

The sales staff were still arriving at 9:30 and leaving at 4:00, but they don't get any basic pay – they only get commission. So why were they turning up to work for a bankrupt company that wouldn't pay them? The sales head commented that they were the ones who suffered the most psychologically, because the first people they sell insurance to are friends and family. So they were turning up out of a sense of responsibility. Even in the case of a company's collapse, human relations are first and foremost. The staff turn up because they are the personal face of the company and must provide a personalised apology.

In this situation, the remarks of S were particularly interesting. S was one employee whose expressed opinions had always been closest to company ideology, some of which were his own opinions. Strategising was natural to S; he was a true salesman, as shown by his continuous, half-tongue-in-cheek, half-serious efforts to sell insurance to my film crew! Now, he had changed his tune dramatically. He admitted that he had thought that the company was in significant danger even the previous year. He admitted that he'd thought the company might not survive when he was interviewed for the film – he was speaking only 'half-*honne*'. Yet at the same time he had only half-believed, and still seemed very surprised and shocked by what happened. He only learnt about the company's demise when he was called at home at 6:30 am by one of his staff members. He seemed shocked, not by the bankruptcy as such but by the way that the directors fled and left everyone else to deal with it.

Fundamentally, insurance is a business based on trust. On an everyday level that's how S deals with customers, by selling them trust – by appearing as trustworthy people to the customers. So if anything happens to affect that trust, business becomes impossible. It was as if he could sense that happening and had begun to lose faith in the company.

The wives

I talked to R the day after the collapse. The wife of one of the salesmen, she was living in the company dormitory with her three small children. The sense of panic was evident. As part of the company dormitory she was in a small society consisting wholly of several hundred C-Life families. She was very anxious about the whole thing – she said again and again that the company had told them absolutely nothing. The company had disseminated no information whatsoever – the directors were nowhere to be seen, so there was no-one to tell anyone anything. The company was now being run by the department heads. Unsurprisingly, under these conditions the gossip was incredible. R was living in a company dormitory with thirty or forty families. They had been told that they wouldn't be kicked out immediately, but they were still terribly anxious and uncertain of the future.

The subsidiaries

For D, work continued as normal, more or less, since his investment subsidiary was formally a separate company from C-Life. He continues to invest the money that has been entrusted to him by different companies and his company's performance has been good. He asked immediately who I'd talked to – he hadn't talked to anyone at all. This shows further the sense of hesitation shown by the people who are safe towards the people who are in the thick of it.

D reported that on Monday he got a call from the lawyers at C-Life, who were now looking after everything in the directors' absence, and they told him that the company had gone under. He had been thinking that the company was in serious trouble for about a month, during the time that Tokai Bank was making its decision. The fact that they were taking so long to do so was what told him it was the end. But the end came a lot sooner than he was anticipating; he didn't think it would finish in a single month.

The overseas offices

The overseas offices of C-Life were basically separate companies, owned by C-Life, with the principal aim of investing C-Life's money. The employees were still getting paid but as C-Life's funds were immediately frozen following the collapse of the company, they were unable to work and told me they were spending their time writing their resumes instead.

The attitude of the overseas employees was extremely dry. They said they were not at all surprised – they had been expecting it for two or three years. One employee said:

> If your premiums are going down and you have to have capital increases every year, and you look at the situation in Japan where lots of companies are merging with foreign businesses, then it's pretty obvious what's going to happen. Everybody else has been getting together, but we haven't, so obviously that's what we have to do. In the end they have to look after the clients.

These largely locally hired employees were quite unsympathetic to the employees in Japan who were surprised at the bankruptcy. One said, 'If you look at the balance sheet it's pretty obvious.' They believed that all the Japanese who had been in overseas offices had been quite aware of the general trend of what would happen for some time, perhaps because they're investment specialists whose job it is to analyse company performance.

The PR section

Shortly after I filmed my programme, the head of the PR department was given a rather unusual transfer (at his age) back into a sales position in the provinces. I wondered immediately if the programme had had anything to do with it but was assured that it had been due to other factors. The section chief who had been manipulating the information flow between himself and his boss during the filming suddenly quit in March or April. There was no-one left in charge of the PR section, so, with the collapse, the leader of my doki – Aoki – was sent to run the section. He had not been promoted to department head to match his new responsibilities, but, although still only a section chief, in practice he was running this important and high-profile department, acting as the key spokesman for the company and accompanying the top management to all their press dealings and press conferences. He was certainly living up to his promise – repeated throughout his interviews – that he would fight to protect the company no matter what happened.

The employees said that the PR section was terribly busy. They were spending the whole of every day responding to the media and to clients. All of the employees expressed pity for the people who had had to take on that job. But Aoki, the most loyal to the company of all the *doki*, must have been in his element.

The future

In the uncertain situation, how would the company fare? Most employees thought it would be a positive move for C-life to merge with AIG. They thought the company would remain in some form or other. They suspected that AIG's aim would be to acquire the sales offices of C-Life to give them an instant distribution network in Japan. In that case the sales people, already in a bad position as a result of the economic downturn, struggling to get sales and feeling in a precarious position because of their supposed lack of skills and inability to change jobs, might turn out to be in quite a strong position compared to the head office staff, who could still be the target of restructuring plans.

Much of employee speculation revolved around individual expectations: who would be safe; who would be in a good position; who was in danger from further restructuring plans. They suspected that anyone who spoke English fluently would be in a good position. Any international department people who are left should therefore be relatively well off, especially since lots of them had quit because the company was becoming more domestic. So those who did remain – and who must have been head-hunted or at least faced a difficult decision over several years whether to stay in the face of their colleagues deserting the sinking ship – should be in good positions since they can deal with the new foreign management.

Some of our key characters were in this fortunate position. A week after the collapse, V was, in practice, running the company. He was the most senior of the department heads, he spoke English and he had the financial knowledge that was crucial at a time when the main responsibility of C-Life was to make its books clear to AIG. This did not surprise the employees, as he was generally recognised to be a very able head.

The employees would have to live in uncertainty for months longer. The AIG people were inside C-Life analysing its state soon after its collapse, but it took time to agree on the terms on which they would become involved. Most C-Life employees and analysts thought that the government was working behind the scenes in negotiating the proposed merger or acquisition.

In fact, even while I was filming, some people inside C-Life had known that the company was negotiating with foreign companies. They even knew which ones (the name of Allianz was mentioned for example), a fact that did not become public until much later. The amount of information that some of the employees held was considerable.

11 Conclusion

In this book, we have looked at C-Life – just one of the many major, white-collar, traditional companies in Japan – as it succumbed to the continuous harsh economic climate of that country. The study differs from many others in that it has been based on fieldwork conducted over a fifteen-year period, enabling us to see some of the changes in the state of the company, and in the atmosphere, ideology and opinion of its employees. Moreover, through introducing a range of individual voices we have seen what the weak economy and continuing recession – which can be rather abstract and impersonal concepts – have meant on a very personal level to a group of ordinary employees. We have seen the careers and lives of these employees from their own perspectives.

A number of important issues came out of the ethnography. We saw the intricate nature of the economy and social structure in the organisation and how these affected each other. We saw issues centred around individuality versus the group, particularly the different levels of ideology that operate in these spheres. And we saw the importance of strategising: what happens in strategising, how it happens and what the stakes are. Taking these three areas one by one, I will sum up the main issues raised, beginning with the relation between the economy and culture inside C-Life.

We saw how economic difficulties forced the management of C-Life to implement various plans to try to save the company, culminating in the restructuring plan, and how this new era of uncertainty brought about social changes of its own. We saw that the employees were very heavily affected by the economic conditions and that many of the company's established cultural practices and organisational norms were swept aside in the economic climate. The economy was very powerful in determining – against the will of many of the company employees – what the company structure was to be, whether those in charge could retain former management practices, whether in fact they could retain their employees. However, other practices – especially ones that were not part of the official ideology about how the company should be, such as strategising behind the scenes – continued unabated through the company's demise.

Company culture was, at many points, strong enough to override immediate economic factors. For example, the principle that stronger employees should be pushed out to protect weaker employees, or that the whole organisation should suffer together, remained firmly in place throughout the restructuring period, although the company did go under in the end, perhaps in part as a result of its rigidity in staving off change. The company did in fact survive – not as an economic organisation called C-Life, but as a group of people who are still working together in a company with a different name. For some of the employees who managed to ride out the storm successfully and make it into the new company, life will go on much the same – or rather better, since they are now over the worst, in a more stable environment and protected by a new influx of capital.

This brings us to the main issue examined in this book – strategising. Strategising in different ways to maintain, advance or prevent social positions from declining was the everyday work of these individual employees. We saw how they weighed up the risks and rewards of their actions in the turbulent economic times before making moves. We recognised, however, that this strategising was not solely based on economic goods, but was very much a social activity, involving the search for, in particular, greater status among the society to which they belonged. We saw that they seized upon company ideology as a tool and used this to help themselves in their strategic efforts. Thus, sometimes they believed company values, but at other times clearly they used them to further their own ends. Much of the social action in C-Life lay somewhere between these two extremes. We saw that to be conscious of these two poles, and to be able to recognise when oneself and others are using *honne* and *tatemae*, is a basic social skill and a powerful tool in strategising.

These interrelated issues of the economy and culture, of economic circumstances and individual choices and strategies, of economic factors and individual life trajectories, are primary and important issues, which this account of one Japanese company has attempted to illustrate. It has done so through the lens of narrative: the narrative of the company, the narratives of its employees and the narrative of my interaction with them. It is in these narratives that the themes of economic context, the individual and the group, ideology and practice, and strategising come together and intermingle; and it is these narratives that give meaning to the themes examined here.

Bibliography

Althusser, L. 1971 *Lenin and philosophy, and other essays* London: New Left Books

Appadurai, A. 1991 'Global ethnoscapes' in Fox 1991

Bailey, F. 1971 *Gifts and poison* Oxford: Blackwell

Bakhtin, M. 1981 *The dialogic imagination* Austin, TX: University of Texas Press

Barth, F. 1959 *Political leadership among the Swat Pathans* London: Athlone

Barth, F. 1966 *Models of social organization* London: RAI Occasional Paper 23

Barthes, J. 1982 *A Barthes reader* ed. Sontag, S. London: Cape

Basso, K. and Selby, H. eds 1976 *Meaning in anthropology* Albuquerque, NM: University of New Mexico Press

Bateson, G., Jackson, D., Haley, J. and Weakland, J. 1974 'Towards a theory of schizophrenia' in Jackson 1974

Baumann, R. and Sherzer, J. eds 1974 *Explorations in the ethnography of speaking* Cambridge: Cambridge University Press

Berger, P. and Luckmann, T. 1966 *Invitation to sociology: a humanist perspective* Harmondsworth: Penguin

Berger, P. and Luckmann, T. 1969 'Sociology of religion and sociology of knowledge' in Robertson 1969

Berger, P. and Luckmann, T. 1995 *Modernity, pluralism and the crisis of meaning* Guetersloh: Bertelsmann Foundation Publishers

Berque, A. 1993 *Japan: cities and social bonds* Yelvertoft Manor: Pilkington

Blau, P. 1967 *Exchange and power in a social life* New York: Wiley

Bohannon, L. 1952 'A genealogical charter' in *Africa* 22

Boland, R. and Tankasi, R. eds 1991 'Perspective making and perspective taking in communities of knowing' in *Organization Science* 6/3

Bourdieu, P. 1977 *Outline of a theory of practice* Cambridge: Cambridge University Press

Bourdieu, P. 1984 *Distinction: a social critique of the judgement of taste* Cambridge, MA: Harvard University Press

Brady, I. ed. 1991 *Anthropological poetics* Savage, MD: Rowman & Littlefield

Bruner, E. ed. 1983 *Text, play and story* Washington, DC: American Ethnological Society

Bruner, E. and Turner, V. eds 1986 *The anthropology of experience* Urbana, IL: University of Illinois Press

Bruner, J. 1990 *Acts of meaning* Cambridge, MA: Harvard University Press

Burrell, G. and Morgan, G. 1979 *Sociological paradigms and organizational analysis* Aldershot: Gower

Burridge, K. 1979 *Someone, no one* Princeton, NJ: Princeton University Press
Christopher, R. 1983 *The Japanese mind: the Goliath explained* New York: Linden Press
Clifford, J. and Marcus, G. eds 1986 *Writing culture: the poetics and politics of ethnography* Berkeley, CA: University of California Press
Cohen, A. 1985 *The symbolic construction of community* London: Routledge
Cohen, A. and Rapport, N. eds 1995 *Questions of consciousness* London: Routledge
Curtis, G. 1969 *Election campaigning, Japanese style* New York: Columbia University Press
Czarniawska, B. 1997 *Narrating the organization: dramas of institutional identity* Chicago, IL: Chicago University Press
Czarniawska, B. 1999 *Writing management: organisation theory and literary genre*, Oxford: Oxford University Press
Dale, P. 1986 *The myth of Japanese uniqueness* London and Sydney: Croom Helm
Davies, B. and Harré, R. 1991 'Positioning: the discursive production of selves' in *Journal for the Theory of Social Behaviour* 20, 1
Devereux, G. 1978 *Ethnopsychoanalysis* Berkeley, CA: University of California Press
Douglas, M. 1966 *Purity and danger* London: Routledge & Kegan Paul
Dumont, L. 1986 *Essays on individualism* Chicago, IL: University of Chicago Press
Evans-Pritchard, E. 1976 *Witchcraft, oracles, and magic among the Azande* Oxford: Clarendon Press
Fernandez, J. 1995 'Amazing grace' in Cohen and Rapport 1995
Fox, R. ed. 1991 *Recapturing anthropology* Santa Fe: School of American Research Press
Frankenberg, R. 1966 *Communities in Britain* Harmondsworth: Penguin
Gabriel, Y. 1995 'The unmanaged organization: stories, fantasies and subjectivity' in *Organization Studies* 16/3
Gabriel, Y. 2000 *Storytelling in organisations: facts, fictions, and fantasies* Oxford: Oxford University Press
Garfinkel, H. 1972 'Remarks on ethno methodology' in Gumperz and Hymes 1972
Geertz, C. 1973 *The interpretation of cultures* New York: Basic Books
Geertz, C. 1988 *Works and lives: the anthropologist as author* Stanford, CA: Stanford University Press
Gibney, F. 1998 *Unlocking the bureaucrat's kingdom: deregulation and the Japanese economy* Washinton, DC: Brookings Institution Press
Giddens, A. 1984 *The constitution of society: outline of the theory of structuration* Cambridge: Polity
Giglioni, P. ed. 1973 *Language and social context* Harmondsworth: Penguin
Goodman, N. 1978 *Ways of worldmaking* Hassocks: Harvester
Graham, F. 2003 *Inside the Japanese Company* New York and London: RoutledgeCurzon
Gumperz, J. and Hymes, D. eds 1972 *Directions in sociolinguistics* New York: Holt, Rinehart & Winston
Harker, R., Mahar, C. and Wilkes, C. 1990 *An introduction to the world of Pierre Bourdieu* Basingstoke: Macmillan
Hymes, D. 1973 'Towards ethnographies of communication' in Giglioni 1973

Ingold, T. 1986 *The appropriation of nature* Manchester: Manchester University Press

Jackson, D. ed. 1974 *Communication, family and marriage* Palo Alto, CA: Science and Behaviour Books

Katz, R. 1998 *Japan: The system that soured: the rise and fall of the Japanese economic miracle* Armonk, NY and London: M. E. Sharpe

Kerby, A. 1991 *Narrative and the self* Bloomington, IN: Indiana University Press

Lejeune, P. 1989 *On autobiography* Minneapolis: University of Minnesota Press

MacIntyre, A. 1981 *After Virtue* London: Duckworth

Malinowski, B. 1948 *Magic, science and religion, and other essays* Glencoe, IL: Free Press

McCloskey, D. 1986 *The Rhetoric of Economics* Wisconsin, MD: University of Wisconsin

Mintzberg, H., Ahlstrand, B. and Lampel, J. eds 1998 *Strategy safari* Harlow: Pearson

Moerman, M. 1988 *Talking culture: ethnography and conversational analysis* Philadelphia, PA: University of Pennsylvania Press

Nakane, C. 1970 *Japanese society* Berkeley, CA: University of California Press

Ogasawara, Y. 1998 *Office ladies and salaried men: power, gender, and work in Japanese companies* Berkeley, CA: University of California Press

Ouchi, W. 1981 *Theory Z: how American business can meet the Japanese challenge* Reading, MA: Addison-Wesley

Rapport, N. 1993 *Diverse world-views in an English village* Edinburgh: Edinburgh University Press

Rapport, N. and Overing, J. 2000 *Social and cultural anthropology: the key concepts* London; New York: Routledge

Reischauer, E. 1977 *The Japanese* Cambridge MA: Belknap Press of Harvard University Press

Ricoeur, P. 1981 *Hermeneutics and the human sciences* Cambridge: Cambridge University Press

Robertson, R. 1969 *Sociology of religion* Harmondsworth: Penguin

Rosenberger, N. 1992 *The Japanese sense of self* Cambridge: Cambridge University Press

Sapir, E. 1956 *Culture, language and personality* Berkeley, CA: University of California Press

Schneider, D. 1976 'Notes toward a theory of culture' in Basso and Selby 1976

Simmel, G. 1971 (1908) *On individuality and social forms* ed. Levine, D. Chicago, IL: University of Chicago Press

Street, B. 1984 *Literacy in theory and practice* Cambridge: Cambridge University Press

Toren, C. 1993 'Making history: the significance of childhood cognition for a comparative anthropology of mind' in *Man* 28

Van Wolferen, K. 1989 *The enigma of Japanese power* New York: Alfred A. Knopf

Vogel, E. 1979 *Japan as Number One* Cambridge, MA: Harvard University Press

Wallace, A. 1964 *Culture and personality* New York: Random House

Weick, K. 1979 *The social psychology of organizing* Reading, MA: Addison-Wesley

Weiner, J. 1991 *The empty place* Bloomington, IN: Indiana University Press

Wong, H. 1999 *Japanese bosses, Chinese workers* Richmond: Curzon

Wood, C. 1992 *The bubble economy: the Japanese economic collapse* London: Sidgwick & Jackson

Yanow, D. 1996 *How does a policy mean?* Washington, DC: Georgetown University Press

Index